CONTEMPORARY
INDUSTRIAL REL

DATE DUE			
0 1 NOV 2004			
GAYLORD No. 2333			PRINTED IN U.S.A.

Also by Sid Kessler

CONFLICT AT WORK (*with B. Weekes*)

Also by Fred Bayliss

BRITISH WAGES COUNCILS

CONTEMPORARY BRITISH INDUSTRIAL RELATIONS

Sid Kessler

and

Fred Bayliss

MACMILLAN

First published 1992 by
THE MACMILLAN PRESS LTD
Houndmills, Basingstoke, Hampshire RG21 2XS
and London
Companies and representatives
throughout the world

ISBN 0–333–56745–5 hardcover
ISBN 0–333–56815–X paperback

A catalogue record for this book is available
from the British Library.

Copy-edited and typeset by Povey–Edmondson
Okehampton and Rochdale, England

Printed in Hong Kong

Reprinted 1993

To the memory of Allan Flanders

Contents

x   *Contents*

Tables

List of abbreviations

ABS	Association of Broadcasting Staff
ACAS	Arbitration, Conciliation and Advisory Service
AEU	Amalgamated Engineering Union (previously the AUEW)
AMMA	Assistant Masters and Mistresses Association
APEX	Association of Professional, Executive, Clerical and Computer Staff
APT&C	Administrative, Professional, Technical and Clerical grades in local government
ASLEF	Association of Locomotive Engineers and Firemen
ASTMS	Association of Scientific, Technical and Managerial Staff
AUEW	Amalgamated Union of Engineering Workers (later the AEU)
AUT	Association of University Teachers
BEC	Building Employers Confederation
BIFU	Banking, Insurance and Finance Union (formerly NUBE)
BMA	British Medical Association
BOAC	British Overseas Airways Corporation
BP	British Petroleum
BPIF	British Printing Industry Federation
BT	British Telecom
CAC	Central Arbitration Committee
CBI	Confederation of British Industry
CIR	Commission on Industrial Relations
COHSE	Confederation of Health Service Employees
CPSA	Civil and Public Services Association
DATA	Draughtsmen's and Allied Technicians' Association
DE	Department of Employment
EAT	Employment Appeal Tribunal
EC	European Community
ECSC	European Coal and Steel Community
EDAP	Education and Development Assistance Programme
EED	Electrical and Electronic Division of Ford Motor Company
EEF	Engineering Employers' Federation
EETPU	Electrical, Electronic, Telecommunication and Plumbing Union
EPA	Employment Protection Act 1975
ERM	Exchange Rate Mechanism

ETUC	European Trade Union Confederation
FWR	Fair Wages Resolution
FIET	International Federation of Commercial, Clerical, Professional and Technical Employees
GCHQ	Government Communications Headquarters
GKN	Guest, Keen and Nettlefold
GMB	General, Municipal and Boilermakers' Union
GNP	Gross National Product
GPMU	Graphical, Paper and Media Union
HRM	Human Resource Management
IBM	International Business Machines
ICFTU	International Confederation of Free Trade Unions
ICI	Imperial Chemical Industries
ILO	International Labour Organisation
IMF	International Monetary Fund
IPCS	Institution of Professional Civil Servants
IRSF	Inland Revenue Staff Federation
ISTC	Iron and Steel Trades Confederation
JIC	Joint Industrial Council
LA	Local Authorities
LFS	Labour Force Surveys
MSC	Manpower Services Commission
MSF	Management, Science and Finance Union
NALGO	National and Local Government Officers' Association
NAS/UWT	National Association of Schoolmasters/Union of Women Teachers
NATFHE	National Association of Teachers in Further and Higher Education
NBPI	National Board for Prices and Incomes
NCU	National Communications Union (formerly POEU)
NEDC	National Economic Development Council
NEDO	National Economic Development Office
NES	New Earnings Survey
NG	News Group
NGA	National Graphical Association
NHS	National Health Service
NIA	News International Advertising
NIC	National Incomes Commission
NID	News International Distribution
NIESR	National Institute of Economic and Social Research
NIRC	National Industrial Relations Court
NIS	News International Supplies
NJAC	National Joint Advisory Council to Ministers of Labour
NUBE	National Union of Bank Employees
NUCPS	National Union of Civil and Public Servants
NUJ	National Union of Journalists
NUM	National Union of Mineworkers
NUPE	National Union of Public Employees
NUR	National Union of Railwaymen
NUS	National Union of Seamen

NUT	National Union of Teachers
OECD	Organisation for Economic Cooperation and Development
OFTEL	Office of Telecommunications
OPEC	Organisation of Petroleum Exporting Countries
PAT	Professional Association of Teachers
PO	Post Office
POEU	Post Office Engineering Union
PRP	Performance Related Pay
RCN	Royal College of Nursing
RPI	Retail Prices Index
SERPS	State Earnings Related Pension Scheme
SIMA	Steel Industry Management Association
SOGAT	Society of Graphical and Allied Trades '82
SPA	Special Pay Additions in the civil service
SRB	Special Review Body of the TUC
TASS	Technical, Administrative and Supervisory Staffs of AUEW (previously DATA)
TECs	Training and Enterprise Councils
TEED	Training, Employment and Enterprise Division of the DE
TGWU	Transport and General Workers Union
TINALEA	'This is not a legally enforceable agreement'
TN	Times Newspapers
TUC	Trades Union Congress
TULRA	Trade Union and Labour Relations Acts 1974 and 1976
UCATT	Union of Construction, Allied Trades and Technicians
UCW	Union of Communication Workers
UMA	Union membership agreement
USDAW	Union of Shop, Distributive and Allied Workers
WIRS	Workplace Industrial Relations Surveys

Table of cases

Acknowledgements

We would first like to thank the Trustees of the Nuffield Foundation for giving us a grant under their Social Sciences Small Grants Scheme.

Next we would like to thank the forty or so industrial relations practitioners – mainly union general secretaries and personnel directors of major companies – who agreed to be interviewed by us. They are all eminent and busy people who willingly devoted their time and who answered our questions with great frankness.

When we were first considering and planning this book we received encouragement and constructive comments from Bill McCarthy, George Bain, Bill Daniel and Pat Lowry, to whom we are most grateful. We are also greatly indebted to Hugh Clegg, William Brown, Pat Lowry and Ian Kessler for reading our draft manuscript in its entirety and to Roy Lewis for reading the legal chapters. They all made invaluable and helpful suggestions.

We would also like to thank Anne Stewart, secretary of the HRM Division of the City University Business School, for her hard work, efficiency and good humour in undertaking the administrative and secretarial work involved in the preparation of this book.

Finally, we are both grateful for the support and encouragement of our wives, Irene and Mary.

Sid Kessler
Fred Bayliss

Note: The authors and publishers are grateful to the following for permission to reproduce tabular copyright material: The National Institute of Economic and Social Research for tables from its *Review*; The Controller of Her Majesty's Stationery Office for tables from *Economic Trends*; *The Financial Times* for an extract from its 'International Economics Indicators' table (June 1991); the editor of the *British Journal of Industrial Relations* for tables from its issue of March 1983; the editor of the *Australian Bulletin of Labour* for a table from its issue of June 1990. Every effort has been made to trace all the copyright-holders, but if any have been inadvertently overlooked the publishers will be pleased to make the necessary arrangement at the first opportunity.

Introduction

In the 1980s British industrial relations were affected by powerful forces of a kind previously unknown in the post-war period. Compared with the previous decades, the 1980s were years of new departures. These were the result of three major influences.

The first was political. During the whole decade there was a 'radical' Conservative government, which by a series of legislative steps, and in other ways, sought to limit the scope of trade union action, set new rules for trade union operations and enhance the role of management.

The second was economic. Unemployment rose to levels previously thought politically intolerable, reaching a peak of well over 3 million in 1987. Although unemployment fell in the latter part of the decade, prior to a new increase in 1990 and 1991, parts of the country continued to have unemployment rates of 10 per cent and more, while in parts of the south they came down to near full employment levels. The decline in manufacturing industry was a main reason for the high levels of unemployment but there were other significant changes taking place in the labour market. In particular, there was the continued growth of the private service sector and the increase in the proportion of the labour force which was female and part-time. In addition to labour market changes there were profound product market changes as a result of growing world competition, deregulation and the effects of new technology.

The third was change in management policies. As a result of product market competition and the swing in bargaining power, the initiative in the 1980s was firmly with management, who sought to achieve far greater cost effectiveness than they had in the past. It is against this background that the changes in industrial relations have to be considered.

Moreover, if the changes are to be fully understood, they must also be considered against the background of the traditional system of British industrial relations.

Accordingly, we commence in Chapters 1 and 2 with a description of industrial relations in the early post-war decades. At least until the 1970s industrial relations were conducted against a background of full employment

1

and steady economic growth, even if the latter was eventually seen as inadequate compared with that of our main industrial competitors. The post-war 'consensus' — shattered by Mrs Thatcher — included commitment by all political parties to the maintenance of full employment, the Welfare State and a mixed economy, that is to say an acceptance that the public sector as well as the private sector had a significant role to play. It was also accepted that trade unions had an important and legitimate role in industry and in society as a whole, even if there was a growing belief that the balance of power had swung too strongly in their favour.

In retrospect, industrial relations developments in the early post-war years appear to have been relatively unspectacular. But change was constantly taking place — above all in the growth in certain industries of the power of the shop floor. However, the 1970s saw dramatic events including the re-emergence of major national strikes, the imposition of incomes policies and a determined, but unsuccessful, attempt to change the law. All this took place against an economic background of rapidly rising inflation and a marked slowing down in economic growth — primarily the consequence of the quadrupling of oil prices by OPEC in 1973 and the economic reaction to that event by the leading industrial countries.

If industrial relations developments appeared dramatic in the 1970s, they palled almost into insignificance compared with the developments of the 1980s. We commence our analysis of the 1980s with the changing environment. In Chapter 3 we consider the economic background, in Chapter 4 government values and policies, and in Chapter 5 changes in the law. While we do not devote a separate chapter to technological change, we are conscious of its rapid development and application during the 1980s and reference is made to its important effects in a number of places in the text.

We then move on to consider the parties themselves. Thus Chapter 6 examines management strategies in the private sector, Chapter 7 examines the role of government as an employer and quasi-employer, while Chapter 8 looks at the trade unions, which have basically been at the receiving end of change and have had to struggle to adapt in adverse circumstances.

Having considered the changing political, economic and legal environment and the changes in employers and unions, we move on to examine the effects of these changes and their implications for the conduct of industrial relations in the future. Thus in Chapter 9 we consider the institutions of industrial relations, in Chapter 10 pay and productivity and in Chapter 11 strikes. Finally, in Chapter 12 we make an assessment of the changes which have taken place, their causes, and we look forward to what are likely to be the developments in the 1990s and beyond.

An important part of the preparation of this book was the holding of semi-structured interviews on a confidential basis with over forty key industrial relations practitioners. They consisted on the trade union side of general secretaries and senior officials of most of the major unions and the TUC. On the employers' side they included personnel directors of leading companies in both the manufacturing and services sectors, (including some non-unionised companies), public corporations and former public corporations, and major employers' associations including the CBI. We would in no way claim that this was a scientific sample. But we do believe that we have interviewed most of the key participants of the 1980s, the overwhelming majority of whom are still leading practitioners.

Our interviews were based on three simple, but major questions. What happened during the 1980s? Why did it happen? What are the implication for the future? The answers to these questions are woven into our assessment. The differences of judgement and emphasis in the responses are brought out as well as the areas of agreement. The book is a combination of academic description and analysis with the reporting of the opinions of those who have shaped the 1980s and will be in the driving seats in the 1990s.

CHAPTER 1

The early post-war decades, 1945–70

Introduction

Britain's post-war industrial relations system was determined in large part by the economic, political and social environment then prevailing. The immediate post-war economic environment was one of scarcity and shortages of most goods and raw materials. There was no need therefore to fear for full employment (particularly given Marshall Aid) or acute overseas competition, with most of Europe devastated by the war.

Politically, the scene had been set in many respects by the wartime coalition government and in particular by the White Papers on employment and on social insurance in 1944. The election of a Labour government in 1945 (see Appendix) ensured that the pledges made by the coalition government would be fulfilled. That government in a truly radical programme pursued, first, a policy of full employment; second, it nationalised certain basic industries, namely coal, gas, electricity, railways, air transport and water, a number of which required massive investment if they were to be modernised and made more efficient. Such investment, given the prevailing circumstances, was most unlikely to have been forthcoming from the private sector. Third, the Government introduced what became known as the Welfare State, the crown piece of which was the National Health Service, but which also included comprehensive social security covering unemployment benefit, old age pensions, sickness and industrial injuries benefit. Fourth, a massive housing programme was undertaken and, fifth, sweeping changes were made in the education system as a result of the Education Act 1944. All these changes had the support of the TUC. Socially they were in line with public opinion as evidenced by the overwhelming Labour victory in the general election of 1945 despite the personal popularity of Winston Churchill. There was a widespread determination that the nation's wartime sacrifices should not have been in vain and that a better Britain should be built in contrast to the inequities of inter-war Britain and its mass unemployment, poverty and many declining industries and regions.

In terms of the industrial relations system itself, the ground had again been laid during the War. Trade union membership had grown from 6.01 million in 1938 to 7.88 million in 1945. Recognition of unions had grown during the war, strongly encouraged by government, for example in the engineering industry and at the Ford Motor Company. In a sense, recognition and negotiating machinery were pushed forward as the complement to the direction of labour. The great expansion of union recognition was not so much built on unions steadily acquiring members, as on the fiat of the Ministry of Labour with Ernest Bevin, the general secretary of the TGWU, at its head. Moreover, during the war the TUC learnt about Whitehall and penetrated into its system of consultation, so that the National Joint Advisory Council (NJAC) to the Ministry of Labour was only the tip of the iceberg.

Unions had ceased to be 'the opposition' but had become almost partners both at governmental level and within industry – 'the Fourth Estate'. At national level, early in the war, the government considerably extended its control over labour matters, mainly through orders under the Defence Regulations. The most important of these was the Conditions of Employment and National Arbitration Order, 1940, familiarly known as Order 1305, which made strikes and lock-outs illegal and provided for binding arbitration. It lasted until 1951 when it was replaced by Order 1376, which ended the illegality of strikes but still provided for unilateral arbitration until 1959. Meanwhile, early in 1939, the NJAC had been established under the chairmanship of the Minister of Labour and National Service. It consisted of fifteen representatives each of the TUC and British Employers' Confederation and was intended to discuss matters of common interest and assist the Minister in formulating policy. It was largely superseded in wartime by a smaller constituent body known as the Joint Consultative Committee and this was important in getting cooperation for the main changes in working arrangements necessitated by the war. The NJAC was reconstituted in 1946, representatives of the newly nationalised industries were given seats on the Council in 1949, and it continued to function into the 1960s (ACAS, 1980a).

Union cooperation in the war effort had been readily forthcoming, helped when Ernest Bevin became Minister of Labour in the 1940 coalition government. In industry, the setting up of Joint Production Committees during the war enhanced the number and influence of shop stewards and greatly extended the practice of joint consultation. This was further enhanced in the immediate post-war years by imposing on the nationalised industries the duty to consult with and, indeed, to recognise representative unions and negotiate with them. The latter obligation considerably extended, in particular, the development of white-collar unionism. Despite the growth in the importance of shop stewards, collective bargaining in most sectors of the economy was firmly at industry or regional level and conducted primarily by full-time union officials and employers' associations. The procedures for collective bargaining had been left largely undisturbed during the war, with the exception of Order 1305, and they continued as such in the immediate post-war period.

Indeed, there was a considerable extension of collective bargaining machinery with the establishment of many new Joint Industrial Councils (JICs) and new Wages Councils — the machinery for legal minimum remuneration — for most of retailing and catering and for a number of smaller trades.

Account should also be taken of Bevin's successful plan to demobilise some 4–5 million servicemen between 1945 and 1947 without causing unemployment, which indeed stayed below 2 per cent between 1945 and 1948. While helped by the high level of demand, the relative ease of the transition from war to peace in the labour market was an important part of the compact between unions and both the wartime coalition government and the post-war Labour government.

Finally, it is worth noting that in the period 1948–50 Britain's first prices and incomes policy was introduced (*Personal Incomes, Costs and Prices*, 1948). It was introduced unilaterally by the Labour government and subsequently endorsed by the TUC. There was no doubt that the government — the political wing of the labour movement — was in charge and felt entitled to decide that there should be an incomes policy and that the unions — the industrial wing — must acquiesce. Arguably, this was to prove to be the most successful of British incomes policies until it was overwhelmed by inflation as a result of the Korean War and the subsequent upsurge of raw-material prices.

1951–64

1951 saw the electoral defeat of the Labour government and the Conservative Party won the two following elections as well (in 1955 and 1959), so that Conservative governments were in power from 1951 to 1964. However, the basic post-war consensus continued. There were no major changes in economic policy and full employment was maintained. Unemployment stayed well below 2 per cent throughout this period. There were no concerted attacks on the Welfare State nor on trade unions.

During the 1950s, national income continued to increase, as did productivity, at a fairly steady rate. Money earnings increased at a moderate rate, as did real earnings and inflation. However, inflationary warning signals emerged in the mid-1950s and became stronger in the early 1960s. In 1956 the Government published a White Paper (*The Economic Implications of Full Employment*, 1956) which called for wage and price restraint. In the following year, the Government established the Council on Prices, Productivity and Incomes which became known as 'the Three Wise Men'. Its task was to publish reports from time to time on the economy, which it was hoped would influence attitudes and ultimately behaviour. In total the Council published four reports during its four years of existence. The first report argued that wage and price increases were primarily caused by excess demand and that the Government should act to reduce demand. This report was attacked by the TUC and others. It was argued that the Council's task was to reconcile full employment with reasonable price stability, whereas the measures proposed meant the abandonment of full employment. In its fourth and final report, the Council changed its approach considerably (perhaps because of a change in the composition of 'the Three Wise Men'), and explored the possibilities of 'cost push' inflation as well as 'demand-induced' inflation and tentatively considered the question of prices and incomes policy.

Although increases in wages and prices continued at a moderate pace, compared with later periods, as did increases in economic growth and productivity, concern became increasingly expressed with regard to Britain's economic performance compared with that of her competitors. Thus while Britain's economic growth and productivity growth were high compared with her own historical record, they were seen as inadequate compared with those of her competitors. France and Germany, for example, as well as Japan, had recovered from wartime destruction and were all showing much faster rates of growth and increased productivity than Britain. International competition was increasing and Britain's share of world export markets was decreasing. Inflation was rising faster than that of our main competitors. There was also concern at what became known as 'stop–go', whereby periods of economic growth led to balance of payments crises which led government to restrict demand and hence slow down growth.

The Macmillan government's response to these problems was twofold; first it introduced a prices and incomes policy (*Incomes Policy: The Next Step*, 1962), and secondly it sought to increase economic growth and productivity. Its incomes policy started with a pay pause in 1961 and was followed by a pay norm or 'guiding light', as it was then called. This was originally set at 2.5 per cent – the estimated growth in national output – the argument being that if income increases were kept to the increase in national output and overall productivity such increases would be non-inflationary. The 'guiding light' was subsequently increased to 3.5 per cent as the 1964 general election approached. Furthermore, the government established the National Incomes Commission (NIC) in 1962, which was chaired by an eminent barrister and consisted of other independent figures rather than direct representatives of unions and employers. Its terms of reference were very limited and it depended on issues being referred to it by the government. In its two or so years of existence it issued only five reports. The one report which had a significant and practical effect was that on university teachers' pay and resulted in a significant pay increase. NIC tended to adopt an inquisitorial approach through public hearings; it relied primarily on the evidence of the parties, rather than on building up its own staff and carry out its own enquiries; and it took a year or so to publish reports. Its real importance was that it was the first body to be created which examined the pay of specific groups.

The second creation was the National Economic Development Council (NEDC) in 1962. This was a tripartite body, consisting of members drawn from the TUC, employers' organisations, government and independents, and having its own quite considerable staff. Its task was to examine and report on factors which would encourage faster economic growth. Its model was to a considerable extent the French Commissariat du Plan, for the success of French economic planning in achieving rapid growth was much admired at the time.

In terms of industrial relations there were no apparent major changes. Trade union membership grew slowly – from 9.54 million in 1951 to 10.08 million in 1964. However, this growth was virtually no more than proportionate to that of employment, so that union density did not increase significantly over the period (see Table 1.1).

Industry-wide bargaining continued to be the norm, helped by strong central union leadership in the 1940s and 1950s, although towards the end of the period there was increased awareness of the growth in the number and importance of shop stewards and the negotiations in which they engaged with plant managers. This appeared to be mainly in the engineering industry and above all in the motor car industry. The officially recorded number of disputes and the working days lost through disputes continued to be low (see Table 1.2), so much so that some academics were writing of the 'withering away' of the strike (Ross and Hartman, 1960). For most of the period the coal-mining industry accounted for well over half the total number of disputes. These disputes characteristically were unofficial and unconstitutional, involved few men and were of very short duration. Consequently, although they accounted for over half the total number of disputes, they accounted for only 5 or 6 per cent of days lost in most years. They were overwhelmingly the result of the piecework system then prevailing in the industry. Outside mining the average number of disputes rose significantly in the 1960s. However, again towards the end of the period, public awareness of small-scale unofficial strikes grew, and much publicity was given to some of these, particularly in the docks, in shipbuilding and in the motor car industry, where a stoppage by relatively few people could have major repercussions. Irrespective of the statistics, such unofficial, wildcat strikes had a major impact on public opinion.

Public concern about industrial relations thus grew at this time, partly through the rising number of disputes (many of which were given extra publicity through public enquiries) (Scamp, 1968), and partly as a result of the case of *Rookes* v. *Barnard* case (1964) and, to a lesser extent, *Stratford* v. *Lindley* (1965). The former concerned the dismissal of Rookes by BOAC because Rookes had left his union and a closed-shop agreement was in existence. The union – DATA (the forerunner of TASS and now the MSF) – threatened industrial action and BOAC thereupon dismissed Rookes. Rookes brought the

TABLE 1.1 **Union membership and density, 1945–69 – UK**

	Union membership	Potential union membership	Union density
1945	7 875	20 400	38.6
1948	9 363	20 732	45.2
1949	9 318	20 782	44.8
1950	9 289	21 055	44.1
1951	9 530	21 177	45.0
1952	9 588	21 252	45.1
1953	9 527	21 352	44.6
1954	9 566	21 658	44.2
1955	9 741	21 913	44.5
1956	9 778	22 180	44.1
1957	9 829	22 334	44.0
1958	9 639	22 290	43.2
1959	9 623	21 866	44.0
1960	9 835	22 229	44.2
1961	9 916	22 527	44.0
1962	10 014	22 879	43.8
1963	10 067	23 021	43.7
1964	10 218	23 166	44.1
1965	10 325	23 385	44.2
1966	10 259	23 545	43.6
1967	10 194	23 347	43.7
1968	10 200	23 203	44.0
1969	10 479	23 153	45.3

Source: Price, R. and Bain, G.S. 'Union Growth in Britain: Retrospect and Prospect', *British Journal of Industrial Relations*, March, 1983, Table 1.

Potential union membership = employees in employment (seasonally unadjusted figures for June), plus the number of unemployed in June.

case against the union officials involved for causing his dismissal and he was ultimately successful in the House of Lords, with damages awarded against the union officials. This was considered a disastrous judgement by the trade union movement which, together with most labour law experts, had considered that trade union officials were protected from such an action, as were trade unions themselves, by the Trade Disputes Act 1906. The trade union movement believed that unless the new legal position was rectified through legislation, union officials would not be able to carry out their essential functions.

Industrial relations thus became an issue between the major political parties in the 1964 election. The apparent difference between them was not, however,

TABLE 1.2   Industrial disputes, 1945–68 – UK

	Number of stoppages beginning in year		Number of workers involved in stoppages beginning in year		Aggregate number of working days lost in stoppages in progress in year	
	All industries and services	Outside mining	All industries and services	Outside mining	All industries and services	Outside mining
1945	2293	987	447	204	2835	2194
1946	2205	876	405	188	2158	1736
1947	1721	668	489	181	2433	1321
1948	1759	643	324	135	1944	1480
1949	1426	552	313	65	1807	1053
1950	1339	459	269	127	1389	958
1951	1719	661	336	201	1694	1344
1952	1714	493	303	29	1792	1132
1953	1746	439	1329	1161	2184	1791
1954	1989	525	402	198	2457	2008
1955	2419	636	599	235	3781	2669
1956	2648	572	464	223	2083	2031
1957	2859	635	1275	1010	8412	7898
1958	2629	666	450	201	3462	3012
1959	2093	786	522	331	5270	4907
1960	2832	1166	698	461	3024	2530
1961	2686	1228	673	424	3046	2309
1962	2449	1244	4297	4143	6798	6490
1963	2068	1081	455	303	1755	1429
1964	2524	1466	700	528	2277	1975
1965	2354	1614	673	555	2925	2513
1966	1937	1384	414	364	2398	2280
1967	2116	1722	551	510	2787	2682
1968	2378	2157	2073	2043	4690	4636

Source: Ministry of Labour Gazette and Department of Employment and Productivity *Gazette* (various).

great although Conservative Party pressure groups were arguing for greater legal constraints on unions (Inns of Court Conservative and Unionist Society 1958). The Labour Party stated that if elected it would immediately pass legislation reversing the decision in *Rookes* v. *Barnard* and restore the position to what it was thought to have been under the Trades Dispute Act 1906. It did, however, pledge that it would set up a Royal Commission to investigate the state of industrial relations, thus acknowledging the growth of public concern. The Conservative Party also pledged itself to set up a Royal Commission, the only difference being that a Conservative government would not take action on the *Rookes* v. *Barnard* decision until the Royal Commission had reported and that *Rookes* v. *Barnard* would be part of the terms of reference for such a Royal Commission.

1964–1970

The 1964 Labour government had a tiny majority, which was converted to a substantial majority at the 1966 general election. A major theme of the Labour Party during the 1964 election campaign was that Britain had suffered from 'thirteen wasted years' under Conservative governments. However, living standards had increased substantially in those years, hence the Conservative Party's slogan – 'You've never had it so good'. The Labour Party's thrust, however, was that the country had suffered from repeated 'stop–go' economic policies and that Britain's growth had been far less than that of her major competitors, with adverse consequences for relative living standards and for the future efficiency of British industry. The Labour Party's electoral pro-gramme was therefore based on the need for faster economic growth which would be helped by economic planning and by more capital investment, particularly by the greater use of new technology. It was feared, however, that faster growth would lead to increased inflationary pressures, and so there was a need for a prices and incomes policy. Further, there was a need for improved industrial relations, specific measures for which would depend on the report of the proposed Royal Commission. In order to further its plans for faster economic growth, the Labour government created the Department of Economic Affairs, transferring to it a large part of the NEDC's functions and staff. The new Department was given the task of producing a plan for economic growth.

At the same time, the government sought agreement with the TUC and the CBI on a prices and incomes policy. This proceeded in three steps. First, in December 1964 the government, TUC and employers agreed the objectives of such a policy in a tripartite Declaration of Intent namely:

1. To ensure that the British economy is dynamic and that its prices are competitive
2. To raise productivity and efficiency so that real national output can increase and to keep increases in wages, salaries and other incomes in line with the increase
3. To keep the general level of prices stable.

Second, in February 1965 (*Machinery of Prices and Incomes Policy*, 1965), the three parties agreed on the mechanism for implementing the policy. NEDC would keep under review the general movement of prices and of money incomes of all kinds and a National Board for Prices and Incomes (NBPI) would be set up to examine particular cases in order to advise whether or not the behaviour of prices or of wages, salaries or other money incomes was in the national interest as defined by the government after consultation with management and unions.

Third, in April 1965 (*Prices and Incomes Policy*, 1965), the criteria were agreed, namely a 3.5 per cent norm and four possible exceptions:

1. Where the employees concerned, for example, by accepting more exacting work or a major change in working practices, had made a direct contribution towards increasing productivity;
2. Where it was essential in the national interest to secure a change in the distribution of manpower and a pay increase would be both necessary and effective for this purpose;
3. Where there was a general recognition that existing levels of remuneration were too low to maintain a reasonable standard of living;
4. Where there was widespread recognition that the pay of a certain group of workers had fallen seriously out of line with the level of remuneration for similar work and needed in the national interest to be improved.

Much was to depend upon how the NBPI interpreted these exceptions. In practice, the NBPI strongly favoured the productivity exception and was extremely restrictive in its interpretation of the other three. For example, even where the NBPI found that low pay existed, it sought to link improvements in pay to measures to increase productivity, as it did in its report on manual workers in local government, the NHS, gas and electricity (NBPI, 1967a), where it argued that the solution to low pay was to increase productivity and hence earnings, to which end it advocated the introduction of payment-by-results schemes.

Where the Board found labour shortages, as in the case of the London busmen (NBPI, 1966a), it sought ways of economising in the use of labour and raising labour productivity, e.g. one-man bus operation, rather than advocating a straightforward pay increase above the norm in order to attract labour from elsewhere. It made the valid point that in conditions of full employment when one organisation raised pay to attract labour from other organisations, this would only result in labour shortages elsewhere or in the other organisations raising wages in order to maintain their labour forces. As a main part of its approach, the NBPI actively promoted the concept of productivity agreements. Early on it sought, and obtained, from the Government, a general reference on productivity bargaining with specific reference to a number of well-known cases, for example Esso Fawley, Esso Milford Haven, Esso Distribution, British Oxygen, ICI and Alcan's Rogerstone Plant. From a study of these and other productivity agreements, the NBPI in its reports (NBPI, 1966a and 1967b), produced a set of guidelines which were embodied by the Government in its subsequent White Paper on the next stages of incomes policy.

The NBPI had a number of notable achievements to its credit (Fells, 1972; Mitchell, 1972). Although firms and industries were referred to the Board only if their proposed pay or price increases were not in accord with the policy, the Board invariably took the opportunity to examine the whole range of firms' operations on the grounds that these affected their prices and the wages they could afford to pay. One example was the Board's persistent recommendation of the tachograph in road haulage. Apart from references on specific firms and industries the Board received a number of general references, for example, on payment by results, job evaluation, hours of work, overtime and shiftworking (NBPI, 1968a, b, and 1969), which produced guidelines which were widely considered by industry. Moreover, the Board encouraged the widening of the agenda of collective bargaining through its championing of productivity bargaining.

The Board was never negative in its approach and considered that in addition to its function as interpreter of the guidelines of incomes policy it had an advisory and consultancy function to improve efficiency and to improve industrial relations in British industry. There was widespread agreement that credit should be given to the Board for adopting a creative and constructive approach rather than a purely negative and restrictive one. The Board consisted of senior representatives of unions, employers, and independent academics, as well as ex-Ministers of both political parties. Its chairman for most of its life, Aubrey Jones, and its first secretary, Alex Jarratt, set the tone for its positive role, and in the field of industrial relations in its early years it had the benefit of Hugh Clegg as a Board member and Allan Flanders as its adviser.

Apart from its substantive achievements, the Board pioneered new methods of inquiry. The NBPI built up a substantial staff with seconded civil servants forming the admininstrative basis and specialist teams, originally of economists, industrial relations experts, and statisticians, which were soon joined by accountants and management consultants. Each reference was headed by a Board member and working parties were formed, normally with a civil servant as chairman, another as secretary, and members of appropriate specialist groups. These working parties conducted their own research and inquiries as well as taking evidence from the parties. One notable feature of most pay references was the carrying out of earnings surveys to discover the composition and distribution of pay and hours of work, instead of relying on average earnings figures or basic rates of pay. Indeed, the NBPI by exposing the inadequacy of government statistics on pay and earnings was instrumental in the introduction of the annual New Earnings Survey in 1968.

However, incomes policy soon ran into difficulties, with pay increasing faster than the norm. In 1965 the government announced (*Prices and Incomes Policy: an Early Warning System*, 1965) its intention of introducing compulsory notification of pay and prices increases. In 1966, a severe sterling crisis led the Government to abandon its voluntary incomes policy, to introduce a 6-months freeze (*Prices and Incomes Standstill*, 1966) and to introduce a statutory basis for the policy, backed by legal sanctions (Prices and Incomes Act 1966). The 6-months freeze on incomes and prices was followed by a period of 'severe restraint' when there was a nil norm and a tightening of the original productivity exceptions (*Period of Severe Restraint*, 1966). Subsequently further easements were made (*Prices and Incomes Policy After 30 June 1967* and *Productivity, Prices and Incomes in 1968 and 1969*). Indeed, with a general election looming there was a considerable loosening of controls (*Productivity, Prices and Incomes Policy After 1969*). In January 1970, statutory controls were lifted, although negotiators were urged to restrict settlements to between 2.5 per cent and 4.5 per cent, with exceptions for productivity agreements and where settlements included moves towards equal pay.

Although the policy had a number of achievements to its credit, there was also a debit side. Too much had been expected and in too short a time: trade union cooperation, which had been readily given at the beginning of the policy, was eroded, partly as a result of the statutory interference with free collective bargaining and partly because the administration of the policy almost inevitably bred anomalies. Such anomalies were increased by the fact that pay settlements were vetted first by the Ministry of Labour and then from 1968 to 1970 by the Department of Employment and Productivity, not the NBPI. The parties learnt a lesson which was to lead to problems with all successive incomes policies — if the parties could find ways round the policy, the vetters were either too over-burdened to challenge them or were pleased to find that a confrontation could be avoided. The application of the policy became an extension of bargaining with managers and trade unionists going to the Department to explain how what they had agreed met one or other of the criteria for exceptional treatment. In such a bargaining atmosphere, the professional negotiators had a great advantage. The Department was indeed inadequately staffed for this task. Also, it had to take account of political realities and was more inclined to let powerful groups through the vetting process, greatly stretching the criteria in the process. In contrast, if a reference was made to the NBPI, it on the whole abided by the criteria, partly because they provided its *raison d'être* and partly because it had to publish a public report to justify its conclusions in the light of the criteria.

The relaxation of criteria by the government meant rising expectations on the part of unions and employees, while management was conscious of the need to deal with anomalies. Real pay had been curtailed as a consequence of incomes policy and as a result of the devaluation of sterling in 1967 and the severe budgets which followed in attempts to deal with balance of payments problems.

The Donovan Commission

Meanwhile the Royal Commission on Trade Unions and Employers' Associations (or 'The Donovan Commission', after its chairman, Lord Donovan, a judge) had been established in 1965 with the following terms of reference:

> To consider relations between managements and employees and the role of trade unions and employers' associations in promoting the interests of their members and in accelerating the social and economic advance of the nation with particular reference to the law affecting the activities of these bodies.

The Commission was noteworthy, not only for the contents of its Report (it was after all the first Royal Commission on industrial relations for 60 years), but for the research it commissioned and published in a series of papers. It was, like the NBPI, not content simply to hear the formal evidence of the interested parties, but sought its own information in a systematic and co-ordinated manner.

The Commission's Report ('the Donovan Report') was published in 1968 (Donovan, 1968). Among its central conclusions was that collective bargaining was the best and most democratic means of conducting industrial relations and that the role of the law in collective relations should be a very limited one. It rejected various proposals for legal restraints, for example, to ban closed shops, to make collective agreements legally enforceable, to restrict the right to strike, to interfere in union rule books, and to impose 'cooling-off' periods and ballots before industrial action. Donovan did not say that the law should never be introduced to industrial relations. It said that it would be inadvisable to do so on practical grounds and that voluntary reform, if it could be achieved, was preferable.

Central to the Donovan analysis was that Britain had 'two systems' of industrial relations. One was the 'formal system', embodied in the official institutions of collective bargaining at industry level. The other was the 'informal system', based on the actual behaviour of managers, shop stewards and work groups at the place of work. The two systems were often in conflict, with the informal system undermining the formal system. One symptom of this was the growing gap between actual earnings and industry-wide basic rates of pay, called the 'wage drift'. Domestic bargaining had also led to fragmented bargaining and fragmented pay structures. Moreover, the growth of workplace bargaining had put industry-wide disputes procedures under pressure at a time when plant and company level procedures were virtually non-existent.

The Donovan Report related to the growing importance of workplace representatives as a result of the needs of managers and trade union members to have negotiators at the point where disputes over pay, overtime, discipline and recruitment occurred. Its recommendations brought the shop stewards into the official fold. Trade unions had to come to terms with them and employers had to accept them 'officially' in settled procedures. Indeed, Donovan's remedy was not the use of law, but the reform and reconstruction of industrial relations procedures by voluntary means. It was neither desirable nor possible to suppress plant and company bargaining. Industry-level agreements should be confined to those matters which they could effectively determine, while plant and company bargaining should be recognised and formalised. The objective was the development of authoritative collective bargaining machinery and comprehensive procedural agreements at plant and company level. The responsibility for this should rest with the parties themselves, although the prime responsibility was with top management, because they had the final power. However, to help the process the Donovan Commission proposed that larger organisations should register their agreements with the Department of Employment and Productivity and that an independent Standing Commission should be established to facilitate the voluntary reform of collective bargaining.

The Donovan Commission's recommendations had a mixed reception. There were some academic attacks in a special edition of the *Brititsh Journal of Industrial Relations* (1968) entitled 'The Report of the Royal Commission on Trade Unions and Employers' Associations: A Symposium', for example by Crossley (1968) and Turner (1968), that the Commission had concentrated too much on procedural and not substantive matters and that the Commission had generalised too much from the situation in the engineering industry. Those who had wanted substantial legal changes, such as restrictions on unofficial strikes and the legal enforcement of collective agreements, were disappointed. Unions were not on the whole dissatisfied (particularly as restrictive legal measures had not been proposed), while employers' reactions were somewhat mixed.

The Government's response was contained in its White Paper *In Place of Strife* (1969). It accepted most of the analysis of the Commission and its conclusions, including the immediate establishment of a reforming Commission on Industrial Relations as a body to promote collective bargaining and good industrial relations, on a voluntary basis. However, it felt that this was not sufficient to deal with our industrial relations problems and put forward some legal changes which went well beyond what Donovan considered practicable. It proposed reserve powers for the Secretary of State to enforce a conciliation pause in unconstitutional strikes and other stoppages where adequate joint discussions had not taken place; compulsory ballots in certain severe strikes; and measures to deal with inter-union disputes.

The proposed legal changes aroused strong opposition from the TUC and led to prolonged and often bitter discussions between the TUC and the Government (Jenkins, 1970). These culminated in an agreement whereby the Government withdrew its proposed 'penal' clauses in exchange for the TUC's promise to alter its rules so that more control could be exercised by the TUC over unofficial strikes, inter-union disputes and disputes which affected workers outside the company or industry directly involved. Within the Parliamentary Labour Party, James Callaghan had successfully argued that the 'penal' clauses would wreck the interdependence of the unions and the party to the disadvantage of both – the unions would be weaker in collective bargaining and voters would be driven away from the party.

Although the TUC did amend its rules – to little practical effect – the dispute between government and the TUC did great harm to the standing of the government, which was perceived by the public to have backed down. Also, while it enhanced the power of the TUC, it added weight to the perception of those who already thought that the unions were over-powerful and needed to be curtailed.

The Commission on Industrial Relations (CIR)

Meanwhile, the Commission on Industrial Relations started work early in 1969 with the support of unions and employers. The Commission itself was headed by George Woodcock, who retired early from the general secretaryship of the TUC in order to become chairman. Other members with a trade union background were Will Paynter (full-time), recently retired general secretary of the National Union of Mineworkers, and Alf Allen (part-time), general secretary of the Union of Shop, Distributive and Allied workers: those with an employers' background were Leslie Blakeman (full-time), former industrial relations director of Ford, and J. R. Edwards (part-time), former managing director of the British Motor Corporation. The final full-time member was a noted industrial relations academic, Allan Flanders, whose publications and evidence had had a significant effect on the thinking and conclusions of the Donovan Commission. The staff was headed by the secretary of the Commission, a seconded senior civil servant, Norman Singleton, and consisted of a number of other civil servants, mainly in administrative roles, and operational staff who were recruited from industry, trade unions and academia.

In its first general report (CIR, 1970b), the CIR stated that its broad purpose, which was derived from the Donovan Commission, was:

> that collective bargaining was the best method of regulating questions of pay and conditions of employment and of providing a means for orderly and constructive change and of conducting industrial relations generally. The practice of collective bargaining was, however, held to be deficient in many respects. Over large areas of employment it did not exist at all and where it did exist, its scope and subject matter was often narrowly limited. In many, including some of the most important, industries, actual pay and conditions, which were nominally the subject of

industry-wide agreements, were often in practice effectively settled informally by local managements and workgroups. One of the principal measures of reform recommended by the Donovan Commission was the creation of an agency specifically devoted to developing and improving collective bargaining and the general conduct of industrial relations.

The report noted that *In Place of Strife* had elaborated on the functions of the CIR and that under the Royal Warrant which had established the CIR, its role was the examination and improvement of 'the institutions and procedures for the conduct of industrial relations'. Such examination was carried out on the basis of references made to it by the Secretary of State for Employment and Productivity. These references were of four main types. The first was general references, which were not restricted to a particular company or industry, but were of general industrial relations application. Early examples were *Facilities afforded to Shop Stewards* (CIR, 1971a) and *The Disclosure of Information* (CIR, 1972b). Secondly, there were references concerned with industrial relations questions throughout a whole industry. Early examples were the shipbuilding and ship repairing industry (CIR, 1971b) and the hotel and catering industry (CIR, 1971c). Thirdly, there were company procedural cases where the purpose was to examine the conduct of industrial relations within a particular company or within selected establishments, for example Birmid Qualcast (CIR, 1970a). Fourthly, and finally, there were recognition cases where one or more unions were seeking recognition which the employer had been unwilling to grant, early examples of which were the Associated Octel Company (CIR, 1969a) and the General Accident Fire and Life Assurance Corporation (CIR, 1969b).

The CIR defined its role as that of a third party, the prime responsibility for the conduct of industrial relations being with unions and managements. However, it sought to distinguish its role from that of traditional third-party intervention — conciliation, arbitration and inquiry — by stating that it was not a 'fire-fighting' organisation but rather a 'fire-prevention' agency, and that it was concerned not with attributing blame but with helping with problems and with trying to achieve practical solutions.

With regard to the CIR's methods of work (CIR, 1970b), there were close similarities between its approach and that of the NBPI. This was not altogether surprising, because a number of the key staff at the CIR, as well as one of the commissioners, had worked at the NBPI and had played a vital role in establishing its enquiry methods in its early days. When a CIR reference was received from the Secretary of State, it was normally assigned to a commissioner supported by a small group of staff. A difference here with the NBPI was that whereas the CIR's operational staff were all essentially industrial relations experts, the NBPI's staff had necessarily come from a variety of disciplines.

At an early stage there were discussions with the parties about the reference, the information that would be required, and the best method of obtaining such information. When the main enquiries had been completed, there were further discussions with the parties about the issues that had arisen and the CIR's ideas for dealing with them. A draft report was prepared and discussed with the parties and their agreement sought on a course of action before the final report was published. Indeed, the whole process sought to carry the parties along with the CIR from beginning to end, and to that extent, took the consultative process further than had the NBPI. This was explicable, apart from its inherent desirability, by the fact that the CIR at this stage in its history, had no compulsory powers and its success depended on persuasion and achieving a voluntary agreement with, and between, the parties. With an emphasis on ascertaining the facts for itself, the CIR made use not only of documentary records and evidence from the parties, but conducted attitude surveys and often earnings surveys of its own. To quote again from the CIR's first general report:

> Much crucial information is, however, concerned with attitudes and beliefs of which there is no record and about which there can be serious misconceptions. We are concerned with how things work in practice and with what people actually think, as distinct from what it is assumed that they think. (For this type of information we have found structured interviews and attitude surveys to be useful working methods.)

Conclusion

At the end of the 1960s, the trade unions had emerged from the Donovan Commission and from the battle over *In Place of Strife* relatively unscathed and in an apparent position of enhanced power. Legal constraints had been rejected by Donovan and the restrictive legislative proposals contained in *In Place of Strife* had been withdrawn. The CIR had been established and had commenced work with the remit of extending and improving collective bargaining and its institutions and procedures, but on a purely voluntary basis. Formal incomes policies had run their course and the unions' objective of the restoration of 'free' collective bargaining had been virtually achieved.

Employers, for their part, were more ready to accept union recognition – particularly for white-collar employees – and tended to regard the extension of collective bargaining as inevitable. Some employers were prepared to engage in reform, as witnessed by some of the productivity agreements. Unfortunately, the making of productivity agreements the major exception to incomes policy constraints, had led to the 'debasing of the currency', and much of the good in the early comprehensive productivity agreements became forgotten as a consequence of numerous 'phoney deals', but not entirely so. The educational effect of NBPI Reports was not completely wasted and, for example, its constant emphasis on the link between real pay improvements and efficiency, and its attempts to improve pay structures through job evaluation and the reappraisal of payments systems continued to have an effect long after the demise of NBPI. Similarly, the recommendations of the Donovan Report and the continuation of its themes through the work of the CIR stimulated some companies to rethink their industrial relations practices and to seek to improve their workplace arrangements, in particular to try to reduce fragmented bargaining, to introduce more rational and formalised procedures in order to deal with grievances and bargaining matters and to acknowledge and formalise the role of shop stewards.

In conclusion, during the whole span of the post-war period up to 1970 the consensus underlying industrial relations had proved remarkably durable. Employers and unions together with successive governments had jointly supported collective bargaining as the means for determining pay and settling disputes. But there were signs of strain and the fabric was wearing thin in several places. Two were paramount. First, full employment tended to make negotiated settlements and the working of the labour market generate pay increases which exceeded what was compatible with low inflation or inflation as low as that of our competitors. Incomes policies had become progressively more complicated and more draconian; the fiercer they were, the more difficult they were to relax without them running out of control.

Second, the paramountcy of the industry-wide agreement had been sapped by the spontaneous growth of negotiations in the place of work. This was of great significance for incomes policies, which had to strive to restrain pay wherever it was determined, and it was obviously far harder to affect multitudinous local bargains than a limited number of industry-wide agreements. But it had a profound, long-term significance for both employers and unions. Local negotiations meant that senior managers had to consider how local managers' bargaining decisions could be fitted into company objectives. In trade unions the balance of power between workshop organisation and representatives and the established apparatus of full-time officials, delegate conferences and executive committees was changing and required a new response.

That the old order of the established consensus, born out of the war and the achievements of the post-war Labour government, would be put under severe pressure in the following decades was already clear by the end of the 1960s.

Moreover, the economic background was not propitious for continuing to improve industrial relations along Donovan's lines. Economic growth in the late 1960s had been constricted by balance of payments difficulties, leading belatedly to the devaluation of sterling and to a restrictive fiscal policy which was followed in an attempt to restrain inflation and to ensure that the benefits of devaluation in the form of increased exports and reduced imports were achieved, as indeed they were. The rate of increase in real incomes was significantly reduced and this in turn led to trade unions taking more militant action in an attempt to gain real improvements.

CHAPTER 2

The 1970s

Introduction

The 1970s was a decade of considerable economic and political upheaval. In the political field, the 1970 general election resulted in the return of a Conservative government under Edward Heath. The Conservative Party had moved somewhat to the right while in opposition and its programme envisaged much greater emphasis on free market forces, the abolition of prices and incomes policy and a strong new industrial relations law. After a tumultuous 4 years, during which it had done a U-turn on prices and incomes policy, the government went to the electorate in the midst of a national mineworkers' strike in 1974 on the issue of 'Who governs Britain?' and was defeated. The new Labour government had only a very small majority and a second election in 1974 still did not provide a significant Labour majority in the House of Commons. The Government was ultimately dependent on the support of the Liberal and the Scottish and Welsh nationalist parties. It had been elected at least partly on the basis that it knew how to get on with the trade unions and this indeed appeared to be the case in its early days with the 'Social Contract' in force.

However, with startling price and wage inflation, the Social Contract came under severe pressures, although for 2 years a voluntary agreed incomes policy with the TUC was remarkably successful in bringing down the rate of wage and price inflation, through a reduction in real pay. Such a situation could not continue indefinitely, and after 2 years of trade union restraint pressure mounted, culminating eventually in the so-called 'Winter of Discontent' in 1978–9, which played a large part in the defeat of the Labour Party in the general election of 1979 and the return of a Conservative government under Margaret Thatcher.

The economic background to those political events was equally dramatic. In 1973 OPEC quadrupled the price of oil with devastating effect. The Western world reacted to what it feared would be a major inflationary force by restrictive economic and monetary policies. World economic growth slowed markedly and indeed in some countries there was actually recession and a fall in GNP. Unemployment increased and some economists considered this the period when the consistent and high economic growth of the industrialised Western world since the Second World War ended. Equally, it was considered by many to mark the end of the post-war era of full employment. The new phenomenon of rapidly rising prices combined with an absence of significant economic growth became known as 'stagflation'. Britain's record was among the worst and consequently in 1976 the sterling exchange rate came under great pressure, resulting in the need for drastic action and in the government having to apply for a major IMF loan. This was granted, but, as was normal practice, it was accompanied by a number of restrictive conditions, paramount among which was that public expenditure should be reduced and a strict monetary policy adopted. These measures killed what little hope there was of a successful continuation of the Social Contract. With very low economic growth and consequently low growth in real incomes, with cuts in public expenditure and rising unemployment, antagonism between unions and government grew, culminating in the 'Winter of Discontent'.

1970–4

Incomes policy

The Heath government ended incomes policy and abolished the NBPI (although a small number of staff were transferred to a new organisation called the Office of Manpower Economics, whose main task was to service the pay review bodies and to study any general matters referred to it by the Government). In place of incomes policy, there was 'free collective bargaining'. Collective bargaining does not, however, take place in a vacuum and the fact that the government did not have an overt incomes policy did not mean that it did not have a policy for pay. The Government indeed sought to bring down the level of wage settlements in the private sector by persuasion, by creating more competitive labour and product markets, by more restrictive economic policies, and by the example of what could be achieved in the public sector. In the public sector, the government sought to reduce progressively the level of settlements by a policy which was dubbed by the press as 'N − 1'. This policy provoked a national postmen's strike in 1970 as well as other disputes in certain parts of the public sector, e.g. local-authority manual workers, electricity and coal-mining. The postal strike lasted several weeks, but in the end was defeated. The policy indeed in its early days had some degree of success.

However, in the end it came to grief with the national coal-mining strike of 1972 (the first national coal strike since 1926). Miners' earnings during the 1960s had slipped markedly down the earnings ladder from the top position which they had held during the 1950s. The industrial action began with an overtime ban at the end of 1971 and escalated into an all-out strike early in 1972. Coal production ceased and successful picketing reduced the movement of fuel supplies, in particular to power stations. There were power cuts, as there were to be again during the 1974 miners' strike. Thus industrial relations reached right into people's homes – their lights went out – and that raised the significance of industrial action in pursuit of pay claims to a new political level. With the position becoming critical, the government set up a Court of Inquiry under Lord Wilberforce who reported with great speed, recommending a very substantial pay increase and improvements in other terms and conditions (*Wilberforce Report*, 1972). The National Union of Mineworkers (NUM) did not accept the Wilberforce Report immediately, although the government did. Further negotiations took place with the government, which resulted in a settlement in which the NUM won further concessions. The NUM's success meant the end of the government's $N - 1$ policy.

Other unions sought to emulate the NUM by seeking very substantial pay increases, while the government reversed its position by seeking to obtain an agreed incomes policy. Talks with the TUC and CBI took place in the second half of 1972 and continued for several months. The government offered the TUC a place in the formulation of economic policy, based on the NEDC, which went further than anything offered by any previous government, in exchange for active support of an incomes policy. In the end the TUC drew back and, on the failure of the talks, the government proceeded to implement a unilaterally determined statutory policy in November 1972 (the Counter Inflation Act). The policy was implemented in three stages. Stage 1 – up to April 1973 – consisted of a complete freeze on pay, prices, dividends and rents. Stage 2 – from April to November 1973 – permitted maximum pay increases of £1 a week plus 4 per cent up to a maximum of £250 per year for any individual worker (the only exception being equal pay). Stage 3 – from November 1983 – permitted maximum increases of 7 per cent on total pay-bills (the 'kitty' principle), or £2.25 a week up to a maximum of £350 per annum for an individual employee. An extra 1 per cent of the pay-bill was allowed for restructuring and exceptions existed for equal pay, proven 'efficiency' schemes, the working of 'unsocial hours' and to deal with major 'anomalies' which had arisen as a result of the freeze. Finally, there was provision for 'threshold' payments at a flat-rate payment of 40 pence for each 1 per cent point increase in the Index of Retail Prices, to be triggered if the Index increased by more than 7 per cent. The government's expectation was, of course, that the Index would not reach that level, but it had reckoned without the oil price increase and the escalation of other raw material prices.

The Counter Inflation Act 1973 established the machinery to operate the policy – a Pay Board and a Prices Commission – and there were detailed and precise codes for the regulation of pay and prices. Pay settlements covering over a thousand workers had to be approved by the Pay Board, while settlements involving smaller numbers had to be notified to the Board. The institutions and guidelines of the Heath government's attempt at an incomes policy thus differed from those of the Wilson government in 1964–70. The machinery set up somewhat earlier by the Nixon administration in the United States to run its pay and prices policy was consciously imitated, especially on the prices side. First, two bodies were established – one for pay and one for prices – instead of a single body to deal with both as with the NBPI. Secondly, detailed rules were established for pay and prices increases with the Pay Board and Prices Commission having little scope for interpretation, unlike in the 1960s when the exceptions to the norm were phrased in fairly general terms, leaving the NBPI wide scope for interpretation and for acting in a constructive manner. Thirdly, having established precise rules, vetting of pay increases was in the hands of the Pay Board and not as previously in those of the Department of Employment with the NBPI as a long stop. In some respects it might be argued that the new arrangements were an improvement on the old, because there was only one interpreter of the policy, but in other respects they were clearly less flexible and hence provided less scope for a constructive and reforming role, although there were some signs that the Pay Board would be used to give general guidance, for example, in its references on pay anomalies and on London weighting.

The policy appeared to be working reasonably well until a dispute over the annual pay negotiations developed in the coal-mining industry. The NUM had received an enormous boost from its successful strike in 1972 and its bargaining power was enhanced by OPEC's quadrupling of oil prices – a remarkable contrast with the decline in its power and status in the 1960s, when it had acquiesced in, and indeed peacefully co-operated with, a major reduction in the size of the coal industry (and hence in its membership), and a relative decline in miners' real earnings. The government believed that it could accommodate the miners' pay demands within its incomes policy guidelines through its provision for unsocial hours payments. This proved not to be the case and after an initial ban on overtime in November 1973 a national strike was called in February 1974. Coal shortages soon developed and in particular the electricity industry was badly affected. Flying pickets of miners were organised to prevent the movement of coal – in which Arthur Scargill first came to national notice – and at Saltley coke depot the police were unable to control the large number of pickets, an event which had important repercussions when the use of legislation against trade unions was being considered by the next Conservative government. The government introduced emergency measures, including a 3-day week for industry and restrictions on domestic supply. It also referred the miners' case to the Pay Board, but this did not lead the NUM to call off its industrial action. Eventually, after many talks, including attempted conciliation by the TUC, the Government decided to call a general election in February 1974 on the issue of 'Who runs the country?'

Industrial relations inevitably was a major feature of the election campaign. Indeed, Mr Heath attributed his defeat to two industrial relations matters: first, the statement during the campaign, attributed to the deputy chairman of the Pay Board, that the miners' earnings figures as officially recorded and used by the government were inaccurate or at least misleading to the miners' disadvantage when used for comparisons with earnings in other industries; second, the statement during the campaign by the then director general of the CBI that the government's 1971 Industrial Relations Act had been a disaster. When the Pay Board reported at the end of the general election it found in favour of the miners.

Industrial relations and the law

The Heath government had included in its election manifesto proposals for major changes in industrial relations law and these were embodied in the Industrial Relations Act 1971 (ACAS, 1980a, and Weekes *et al.*, 1975). The Act established a new industrial relations institution — the National Industrial Relations Court (NIRC); put the Commission on Industrial Relations (CIR) on a statutory basis; revised and extended the jurisdiction of industrial tribunals and that of the Industrial Court (renaming the latter the Industrial Arbitration Board); and replaced the Registrar of Friendly Societies with a Registrar of Trade Unions and Employers' Associations with whom independent trade unions and employers' associations could be registered if their rules and procedures, particularly those relating to the rights of the members and the holding of ballots, conformed to certain standards laid down in the Act.

NIRC was made part of the High Court and consisted of both judges and lay members with industrial relations expertise from both sides of industry. The Act removed from the jurisdiction of the ordinary courts most legal proceedings arising out of industrial disputes and partly replaced traditional common law by a new ground for legal proceedings — a complaint of 'unfair industrial practice'. The traditional immunities were in general limited to unions which registered under the Act. In addition, registered unions were given special facilities, notably over access to the NIRC, and one major new immunity over breach of commercial contracts. The CIR was given statutory powers to deal with union recognition disputes. However, the Act made post-entry 'closed-shop' agreements void and sought to make pre-entry closed-shop agreements unenforceable by giving workers the right to belong or not to belong to any union, and by making it an 'unfair industrial practice' to prevent anyone from exercising this choice. As an alternative, an 'agency shop' could be established under which employees had to join the union, or pay the union the equivalent of its subscription in lieu of membership, or pay the equivalent sum to charity (CIR, 1973a). The Act also allowed in exceptional circumstances for an 'approved' closed shop on application to the NIRC and after reference, inquiry and recommendation, by the CIR (CIR, 1972a and 1973b).

The Act contained a number of other provisions, for example, the Secretary of State was given the power to order a 'cooling-off period' of up to 60 days where an industrial dispute threatened the economy or public health or safety, and to restrain industrial action in certain circumstances while a compulsory ballot was conducted (CIR, 1973a). This power was used only once – in 1972 – and involved a major railway dispute. The unions obeyed the court order and suspended industrial action while the CIR conducted a ballot among the membership. The ballot resulted in an overwhelming majority for union action. Picketing at a person's home (unless it was also his place of work) was exempted from statutory immunity for 'peaceful picketing'. Written collective agreements were presumed to be legally enforceable contracts unless they expressly contained a disclaimer. A code of practice was issued giving guidance on good industrial relations practice, and while failure to observe the code did not render anyone liable to legal proceedings, it could be used in evidence before industrial tribunals or the NIRC. The Act also extended individual employee rights in a major way to include a right not to be unfairly dismissed.

As can be seen by this brief summary of the contents of the Act, it was an attempt to deal with everything at one fell swoop and much of it was based on American law. It sought to control by legislation the status of collective agreements, the rights of individuals *vis-à-vis* trade unions and the closed shop, picketing, industrial disputes in essential services, and the registration of unions eligible for immunity from legal action. Over-arching it all was the NIRC, to which all breaches of the Act's provisions would be directed. It was naive in its scope and its intention. Its originator and the master of its detail was Geoffrey Howe, the Solicitor General, who to all intents and purposes became a minister at the Department of Employment until the bill reached the statute book. It was the lawyers' solution to politically defined industrial relations problems. It marked the end of the Conservative Party's acceptance of the 1906 Act's definition of trade union immunities and of the Labour government's repeal in 1946 of the Trade Disputes Act 1927. From this point on, the use of law by all governments to bring about changes in industrial relations was permanently on the agenda.

Consequences of the 1971 Act

The Act was bitterly opposed by the trade union movement. Member unions were advised by the TUC to boycott it, not to co-operate with the CIR and the NIRC, not to enter into binding collective agreements and not to serve on industrial tribunals. The major plank of TUC opposition, however, was to advise and eventually to instruct, affiliated unions not to register with the new Registrar. The government sought to counter this policy by automatically transferring to the new register unions who were already registered with the Registrar of Friendly Societies. TUC unions therefore had to actively deregister, which caused special problems for some who were required to be registered under their rules. The overwhelming majority of unions including all of the largest, followed TUC policy and deregistered, even though they lost tax advantages in the process, as well as legal protection for most forms of industrial action. Some thirty unions did not deregister, including a few medium-sized unions such as the NGA and NUBE. They were all consequently expelled from the TUC (to be readmitted a few years later, after the repeal of the 1971 Act by the next Labour government).

Employers, whose bargaining power the legislation was intended to strengthen, generally did not seek to enforce the provisions of the Act. They readily accepted the insertion of a clause in collective agreements, initiated by the unions, that 'This is not a legally enforceable agreement' ('TINALEA') and most closed shops were undisturbed. Trouble did, however, develop with the dockers, whose employment opportunities were being threatened by containerisation, especially when the loading and unloading of containers was carried out at inland depots. The dockers demanded that this work should be carried out only by dockers and, in seeking to enforce this demand, depots were picketed and the movement of goods boycotted. One firm – Heatons – applied for, and was granted, an order from NIRC that the boycotting should stop. The TGWU refused to appear in court, in line with TUC policy, and was fined £5000 for contempt followed by a further fine of £50 000 and a warning that all its assets would be frozen. The TGWU thereupon appeared before the court, with TUC approval, in order to defend itself. Its defence was that the union could not be held responsible for the actions of its stewards. The NIRC rejected this defence, but at the Court of Appeal the decision was reversed, only to be restored by the House of Lords (*Heaton Transport Ltd* v. *TGWU* 1973).

In the meanwhile, before the first appeal, a number of dockers' shop stewards were on the point of being sent to prison by the NIRC for contempt, when they were rescued (rather against their will) by the appearance of the Official Solicitor who argued that the evidence was insufficient to prove that these particular stewards had been engaged in the action. Soon after, the NIRC ordered five stewards to prison at Pentonville for refusing to end their picketing of another depot. Sympathy strikes broke out and the TUC set a date for a one-day general strike. The situation was saved, however, by the House of Lords' decision making the union liable for the actions of its stewards and the 'Pentonville Five', as they had become known, were released, although the union was heavily fined.

The other major union significantly involved in the operation of the Act was the AUEW. Its first involvement was in 1972 when Mr Goad (*Goad* v. *AUEW* 1973) obtained an order from the NIRC instructing the union to accept him into membership despite the opposition of the local branch. The union was fined £5000 for refusing to comply and then a further £50 000 for still refusing, with assets sequestered in order to obtain payment. Its second involvement related to a closed-shop agreement at Chrysler where Mr Langston, who had resigned from the union, was dismissed by the employer. The NIRC had reaffirmed his right not to belong to the union, but faced with union opposition and the employer's unwillingness to re-engage Langston, the NIRC deemed that it would be impractical to order his reinstatement, and so the closed shop was preserved (*Langston* v. *AUEW* 1973).

The third and final case concerned a small engineering company, Con Mech (*Con Mech Ltd* v. *AUEW* 1972), where the AUEW was on strike in order to obtain recognition. Con Mec obtained an order from NIRC that the strike should be called off while the recognition issue was referred to the CIR. To take industrial action while there was such a reference was an 'unfair industrial practice'. The AUEW refused to obey the order and had some of its assets sequestered in order to pay a fine of £75 000. The CIR's report (CIR, 1973c) recommended recognition but this was ignored by the company and could not be enforced by the union because it was not a registered union. The strike at Con Mech continued and there were a series of one-day strikes in the engineering industry in support. NIRC awarded £47 000 in damages to Con Mech and when again the AUEW refused to pay its assets were sequestered. An indefinite national engineering strike was called in protest and there were sympathy strikes in other parts of industry, including the national newspaper industry. The dispute was ended by an anonymous group of businessmen offering to pay the AUEW's fine, an offer which the NIRC accepted.

The Act was largely a failure (Weekes *et al.*, 1975). It was ignored by most employers, used by only a few small ones, and the government itself invoked its cooling-off powers only once when the ballot in the railway industry, required under the law, showed a very large majority in favour of industrial action. The government conspicuously failed to use it in the major strike of the NUM in 1974. The Act was the cause of several major disputes and was almost certainly a factor in the failure of the Heath government to obtain an agreed incomes policy. To some degree, it had also brought the law into disrepute. Indeed, its failure led to a widespread belief that such laws could not succeed unless they had widespread acceptance among trade unionists. The campaign of demonstrations called by the TUC and the resistance by the unions to the application of the Act showed that there was widespread hostility to the government's policy among trade unionists.

1974–9

Incomes policy

The Labour government came to office in February 1974 with the miners' strike still in progress. The claim had been referred to the Heath government's Pay Board, whose report recommended very substantial increases. The report was readily accepted by the new government and the dispute settled. The scene was not, however, a happy one. Prices were rising rapidly owing primarily to the oil crisis, threshold clauses were being triggered by price increases and wage settlements were being concluded at very high levels, mainly to recompense for rapidly rising prices and to make good the restraints and anomalies of the Heath incomes policy, particularly in the public sector. Thus executive and administrative Civil Servants obtained increases ranging from 24 per cent to 36 per cent, the Houghton Committee recommended teachers average increases of 27 per cent and the Halsbury Committee recommended average increases of 30 per cent for nurses.

The government had already renounced the Conservative government's incomes policy, abolishing the Pay Board but retaining the Prices Commission. However, in order to control the situation, the government and TUC concluded a Social Contract whereby the TUC agreed that wage increases should be limited to compensation for the rise in the cost of living and should be restricted to annual claims, while the government agreed to restrain prices, increase public expenditure and take other measures to reduce unemployment.

With soaring inflation and wages, the agreement did nothing to halt their upward spiral (between July 1974 and July 1975 average earnings rose by 26 per cent and so did the cost of living). An initiative came in the form of a proposal from Jack Jones, general secretary of the TGWU, adopted by the TUC, and accepted by the government (*The Attack on Inflation*, 1975) with only minor amendments – the Social Contract Phase 1 – whereby for the 1975–6 wage round settlements would be limited to a £6 per week maximum flat rate increase with nothing for those earning over £8500 per annum. The limits were generally followed and in the period July 1975 to July 1976 the increase in average earnings was reduced to 14 per cent and the cost of living to an increase of 13 per cent. This was followed by a further agreement between the TUC and the government – Social Contract Phase 2 (*The Attack on Inflation: the*

Second Year, 1976) – whereby for the wage round 1976–7 limits were set for pay increases of 5 per cent of total earnings, with a minimum of £2.50 per week and a maximum of £4.00. As part of the agreement, the government introduced certain tax reductions. Phase 2 resulted in a further reduction in the rate of increase in earnings to 9 per cent between July 1976 and July 1977 although the cost of living rose by 17.6 per cent in the same period. In the third year – Phase 3 – the government failed to get TUC support for a further formal agreement, although it got 'reluctant acquiescence' for its unilaterally determined limit of 10 per cent plus self-financing productivity agreements (*The Attack on Inflation after 31 July 1977*). The result of this government policy was a substantial reduction in the increase in the cost of living to 7.8 per cent, although earnings rose by 14 per cent, thus making good some of the fall in real earnings which had taken place in the previous round.

For Phase 4 – the wage round 1978–9 – the government again failed to get TUC agreement and went ahead alone with a wage limit as low as 5 per cent (*The Attack on Inflation after 31 July 1978*), plus self-financing productivity agreements, in spite of being warned by the TUC that such a figure was impossibly low. The government knew from the previous year's experience that earnings were likely to increase by about half as much again as the 5 per cent norm, so it was an increase in earnings of 7.5 per cent which the TUC was warning against, despite the prospect of lower prices. But it was by no means certain that TUC agreement could have been secured for any level of wage norm. The government had no statutory powers to enforce its policy and there was no machinery, such as the NBPI, to deal with exceptions. There was however the Central Arbitration Committee (CAC) whose awards were exempt from pay policy limits. Consequently, unions made great use of the Fair Wages Resolution (FWR) and Schedule 11 of the Employment Protection Act 1975, which broadly extended the principles of the FWR to all of industry, as a means round pay policy. In this there was often a form of collusion with employers and indeed in some instances employers initiated the procedure. Thus the number of FWR references increased from 35 in 1976 to 414 in 1978 and the number of Schedule 11 references reached 742 in 1977 (CAC, 1976, 1977, 1978).

In the absence of powers the government sought to enforce its policy in the public sector through strict cash limits and in the private sector by threats in the form of the loss of export credit guarantees and the withdrawal of government contracts. One celebrated example of the latter sanction involved the Ford Motor Company, but the government's threatened sanction of withdrawing contracts was defeated by a vote in the House of Commons towards the end of 1978, which resulted in the end of such coercive measures.

Meanwhile resistance in both the public and private sectors to the 5 per cent limit was increasing and culminated in the 'Winter of Discontent' which was particularly marked by industrial action by local-authority manual workers and by ancillary workers in the National Health Service. Since the government was the paymaster it had to stand by its policy. But the strikes in such services were bound to hit ordinary citizens hard, and many of them were trade unionists. The conduct of the strikes gave the impression that local trade union representatives were more in control of services like refuse collection and hospitals than were the government and the managers of these services. The impact on the public of these strikes was to go beyond industrial relations and to have long-term political effects.

To try to deal with such discontent in the public sector the government belatedly established in March 1979 the Standing Commission on Pay Comparability, chaired by Professor Hugh Clegg. The Commission produced some notable reports, for example on the pay of nurses, teachers and local authority and NHS manual workers (Standing Commission on Pay Comparability, 1980), but it was overtaken by events and the general election of 1979. Even so, the new Conservative government allowed it to complete all the cases which had been referred to it before abolishing it early in 1981. The Clegg Commission might have provided a sound long-term solution to the problem of pay comparability between the public services and other employment, but it did not have a chance to do so.

Industrial relations and the law

The Labour government came to power with pledges to repeal the Industrial Relations Act 1971, to introduce certain new rights for unions and employees, and to introduce a measure of industrial democracy. The first pledge was fulfilled by the Trade Union and Labour Relations Acts (TULRA) 1974 and 1976. These repealed the 1971 Act and essentially restored trade union immunities to what they were believed to have been under the Trade Disputes Act 1906. In addition, the Acts abolished the CIR, the NIRC and the Registrar of Trade Unions and Employers' Associations, the latter being subsequently replaced by the Certification Officer. They retained the unfair dismissal provisions introduced in 1971 (although amended to remove restrictions on the closed shop). They redefined the law on the status and regulation of trade unions, employers' associations and collective agreements and on behaviour in disputes.

The second pledge was achieved by the Employment Protection Act (EPA) 1975. The provisions of the EPA 1975 divide into those relating to collective matters and those relating to individual rights. On collective matters the EPA had six provisions.

The Advisory Conciliation and Arbitration Service (ACAS) was established on a statutory basis, it having started work in 1974. ACAS was given the general duty of promoting the improvement of industrial relations, and in particular of encouraging the extension of collective bargaining and the development, and where necessary the reform, of collective bargaining machinery. Its main functions were as follows:

1. To provide facilities for conciliation, mediation, arbitration and inquiry.
2. To provide a free advisory service on industrial relations and personnel practice.
3. To examine and make recommendations on applications for trade union recognition under a statutory recognition procedure. If ACAS recommended recognition and the employer failed to comply, the union concerned could apply to the Central Arbitration Committee (CAC) to award by means of unilateral arbitration specified improvements in terms and conditions of employment.
4. To publish Codes of Practice.
5. To provide conciliation where individuals considered that their rights under employment legislation had been infringed, for example, by unfair dismissal, where ACAS had a duty to conciliate before a tribunal hearing.

ACAS was governed by a council consisting of a full-time chairman and nine other members appointed by the Secretary of State for Employment, three after consultation with the TUC, three after consultation with the CBI and three independents. The EPA stated that 'The service shall not be subject to directions of any kind from any Minister of the Crown as to the manner in which it is to exercise any of the functions under any enactment.' The rationale behind the setting up of an independent service, instead of as hitherto having it as part of the Department of Employment, was trade union fears that a Departmental service was not fully independent of ministerial interference as, for example, in the refusal of Mr Heath to refer the dustmen's strike of 1970 to the conciliation service because the employer's offer already exceeded the government's unofficial norm. ACAS has continued to function as the EPA specified with the exception of the statutory recognition procedure, which was abolished by the Employment Act 1980, albeit on the recommendation of ACAS itself. The hiving off of conciliation, arbitration and the advisory services from the Department has had strong support from both trade unions and employers' organisations and there has been no political reason for overriding that joint commitment.

The Central Arbitration Committee (CAC) was established by the EPA, replacing the Industrial Arbitration Board which had itself replaced the Industrial Court in 1971. The provision of a standing national arbitration body – the Industrial Court – dated back to the Industrial Courts Act 1919, and had been recommended by the Whitley Committee. The constitution and proceedings of the CAC were set out in Schedule 1 of the EPA. There was an independent chairman and deputy chairmen with two panels of side members consisting respectively of experienced representatives of employers and trade unions. The CAC had a number of functions under the EPA, some inherited from the old Industrial Court such as voluntary arbitration and the application of the Fair Wages Resolution which obliged government contractors (and in practice virtually all public sector contractors) to observe terms and conditions of employment not less than those laid down in union agreements for that trade or industry or with 'the general level', and some new functions relating for example to Schedule 11 of the EPA, disclosure of information, the Equal Pay Act, and unilateral arbitration under the recognition procedures of the EPA (CAC, 1976). These have all been abolished by the Conservative governments of the 1980s with the exception of voluntary arbitration and the disclosure of information.

The Certification Officer was established by the EPA in February 1976 in place of the Registrar, who in trade union eyes had been tainted by his association with the 1971 Act. The Certification Officer was made responsible for:

1. Maintaining lists of trade unions and employers' associations;
2. Determining the independence of trade unions;
3. Seeing that trade unions and employers' associations kept accounting records, had their accounts properly audited and submitted annual returns;
4. Ensuring the periodical examination of superannuation schemes;
5. Securing observance of the statutory procedures for transfers of engagements, amalgamations and changes of name;
6. Supervising the statutory requirements as to the setting up and operation of political funds and dealing with complaints by members about breaches of political fund rules. (Certification Officer, 1977)

This, too, was a sound long-term development and the Conservative governments of the 1980s have given additional responsibilities to the Certification Officer.

Disclosure of Information to recognised independent unions for purposes of collective bargaining is an obligation placed on employers. Any information, without which unions would be 'materially handicapped' in collective bargaining and which it would be in accordance with good industrial practice to disclose, must be given on request. The Act does, however, provide employers with certain defences against such requests: for example, if it is harmful to the employers' undertaking or to national security, if it would be in breach of an enactment or confidence, or if it relates to an individual without his consent. If an employer refuses, the union may bring a complaint to the CAC who, at an informal meeting, will try to conciliate, with the assistance of ACAS. If conciliation fails or appears hopeless then the CAC will proceed to a formal hearing where if it finds the complaint well-founded it will make a declaration to that effect and specify what information is to be disclosed and the date by which disclosure should take place. If the employer refuses to comply, the union may make a further complaint accompanied by or followed by a claim for improved terms and conditions, that is to say, a right to unilateral arbitration. Any award on such a claim is binding on the employer. These provisions continue in force.

Consultation on redundancies with an independent recognised union is required by section 99 of the EPA. Consultation must begin at least 90 days in advance of the dismissals if the employer is proposing that 100 or more employees are to be made redundant at one establishment, and at least 30 days in advance if 10–99 employees are to be dismissed at one establishment. The employer must give similar notice to the Secretary of State for Employment. The reasons for the proposals, the number and description of employees involved, the total number of such employees at the establishment in question, the proposed method of selection for redundancy and the proposed method of timing of the dismissals must be given to the union in writing. The employer must further consider any representations made by the union and reply, stating reasons, if rejecting them. These, too, continue to be in force.

Schedule 11 of the EPA replaced section 8 of the 1959 Terms and Conditions of Employment Act and indeed extended it, so that employers or independent trade unions, representing a substantial proportion of the employers or employees in the trade or industry, could bring a claim to the CAC that an employer was not observing the recognised terms and conditions of employment or was paying less than 'the general level' in the trade or industry where there were no recognised terms and conditions. The CAC was empowered to make an award that was legally binding on the employer. However, schedule 11 was abolished by the new Conservative government in its Employment Act 1980.

On individual rights, the EPA provided for maternity pay and for the right to return to work after maternity leave; for the right to guaranteed pay for employees who were put on short-time working or laid off by their employers, for reasonable time off work for industrial relations and trade union duties and for public duties. The various individual rights in the EPA and those contained in earlier legislation such as the Redundancy Payments Act 1965, the Contracts of Employment Act 1972 and the TULRA 1974 and 1976, were subsequently consolidated in the EP (Consolidated) Act 1978. Other rights and protections were provided by the Sex Discrimination Act 1975 and the Race Relations Act 1976.

Finally, there was the passing of the Health and Safety at Work Act in 1974, which established the Health and Safety Commission and the Health and Safety Executive. The Act extended the protection of the law to some 8 million workers who were not previously covered by health and safety legislation. It placed statutory general duties on employers, the self-employed and employees in achieving acceptable safety standards at work. Subsequent regulations provided for the appointment of safety representatives, with considerable rights and powers, by independent recognised trade unions. In addition, at the written request of any two union-appointed safety representatives, an employer was obliged to form a safety committee.

The third pledge was legislation to further industrial democracy. As a first step the government established a Committee of Inquiry under the chairmanship of Lord Bullock with terms of reference to report on how representation of trade unions on boards of directors could best be achieved. The Bullock Committee's Majority Report (Bullock, 1977) recommended that companies with more than 2000 employees should have worker directors provided that any recognised trade union which represented 20 per cent or more of a company's employees requested a secret ballot of all the company's employees to see if they supported the introduction of employee directors. If a majority, totalling at least a third of the electorate, agreed, then employee directors would be chosen through the trade unions and the Board would be constituted on a $2X + Y$ formula – employees and shareholders would have equal representation ($2X$) and there would be a small, uneven number of independents (Y) who would be jointly chosen. If employees chose to adopt worker directors, then all the unions in the company would establish a joint representation committee (JRC) to decide how to allocate employee directorships and to co-ordinate the employee side.

The three CBI representatives on the Committee did not accept the majority report and issued their own minority report, while the CBI itself engaged in an energetic campaign against the Bullock proposals. The TUC was divided in its views and although the majority view favoured worker directors, many unions, including large and important ones, like the NUGMW and the AUEW, feared that trade union independence and collective bargaining freedom might be adversely affected by their having representatives on company boards. In the event the government issued a White Paper (*Industrial Democracy*, 1978) which considerably watered down the Bullock proposals, but even this version did not reach the statute book before the 1979 election and the defeat of the Labour government.

In this period an experiment on 'worker directors' was carried out in the Post Office (Batstone *et al.*, 1983). It lasted for only 2 years from 1978 to 1980, because when the time came to consider whether it should be renewed there was not only an unsympathetic Conservative government but opposition from the Board of the Post Office, who considered that the experiment had been a failure.

The main legislation affecting industrial relations was presented at the height of the social contract when the trade unions were at the summit of their ability to influence the government. That being so, it is important to notice that certain matters were not interfered with by the Conservative government after 1979: ACAS, the Certification Officer, disclosure of information, consultation on redundancies, health and safety representatives and committees, and most of the individual rights have so far turned out to be permanent legal changes.

Trade unions and employers

This chapter has so far been primarily concerned with the economic and political environment of the 1970s, the impact at macro-economic level of incomes policy, and legal changes. What was happening within this context to the primary actors in our industrial relations system and to their joint procedures and relationships?

It could be argued that in the 1970s the trade unions reached the pinnacle of their power in terms of membership and influence. First, there was a large increase in total trade union membership from 10.5 million at the end of 1969 to 13.3 million at the end of 1979, and in union density from 45.3 to 54.8 per cent, while TUC membership over the same period increased from 10.0 million to 12.2 million.

Growth was particularly marked among white-collar employees and certain unions showed remarkable increases in numbers (see Table 8.2).

Second, trade union influence with government reached its peak with the Social Contract. The repeal of the Industrial Relations Act 1971 was rapidly

TABLE 2.1   Union membership and density, 1970–9 – UK

	Membership (000s)	Potential membership (000s)	Union density (%)
1969	10 479	23 153	45.3
1970	11 187	23 050	48.5
1971	11 135	22 884	48.7
1972	11 359	22 961	49.5
1973	11 456	23 224	49.3
1974	11 764	23 339	50.4
1975	12 026	23 587	51.0
1976	12 386	23 871	51.9
1977	12 846	24 069	53.4
1978	13 112	24 203	54.2
1979	13 289	24 264	54.8

Source: Price, R. and Bain, G. S., 'Union Growth in Britain: Retrospect and Prospect', *British Journal of Industrial Relations*, March 1983, Table I.

Potential union membership = employees in employment (seasonally unadjusted figures for June) plus the number of unemployed in June.

achieved and further legislation followed, giving support and additional rights to trade unions and individual employees. Third, at company level, union recognition became more widespread, not just horizontally but in many cases also vertically, so that recognition and collective bargaining were extended to many groups of white-collar workers, going beyond clerical workers to supervisory, technical and lower managerial levels as well. The number of shop stewards and office representatives increased, in particular the number of full-time shop stewards. There was greater formal recognition of their role and that role itself was expanded with the widening of the scope of collective bargaining. This growth in steward numbers and influence was partly the result of employer policy, but it was also the deliberate result of decisions taken by certain unions. Whereas the gradual extension in the post-war years of steward numbers and influence had been largely an informal process, unions such as the TGWU, NUPE and NALGO made it a deliberate part of their policy in the 1970s to decentralise power and to increase steward numbers and strengthen their role in the unions.

Union power could be over-stated, however. While its exercise, for example through strikes, is highly visible and much publicised in the media, the exercise of employer power is much less visible and less publicised. The employers' power to determine what products and services to provide is largely unquestioned, as are their decisions on capital expenditure, on location of production − whether at home or overseas − on technology, indeed their power to make all major strategic decisions. Attempts in the second half of the 1970s to affect some of these powers, through planning agreements for example, came to nought, as did attempts to achieve greater industrial democracy. Even *vis-à-vis* the Labour government, at the height of the Social Contract, unions were unable to prevent higher unemployment and restrictions on public expenditure: and while money incomes rose fast in the 1970s, real pay increases were markedly less than those achieved in the 1950s and 1960s. Again, the favourable legislation on union rights did little more than restore union rights to what they were before 1971, and the improvement in individual rights did no more than move towards a position that had been common practice in most of Western Europe for many years. Yet the trade unions had been in a position without parallel to influence the Labour government. The Social Contract was unique. But the incomes policy which was at its heart was the cause of its collapse. The trade unions had seemed to be part of the government − one public opinion poll showed that a majority considered Jack Jones, the general secretary of the TGWU, to be more powerful than the Prime Minister − but in the winter of 1978−9 the exercise of that power helped to bring down the Labour government (as the miners' strike had been instrumental in bringing down the Heath Conservative government). If the trade unions had got above themselves, they could not be said to have consolidated their position.

Employers in the 1970s, as has been seen, faced a difficult economic environment. The growth in international trade suffered from the oil crisis and the resultant restrictive economic responses of governments dampened world economic growth at the same time as it increased inflation. International competition increased and the relative decline in British manufacturing intensified. At home, there was increasing concentration in British industry, increasing intervention by government and the increased power of trade unions. Industrial relations assumed greater importance for most companies, partly as a result of the growth of trade unionism and its impact, particularly at workplace level, and partly because of greater government intervention, not just through incomes policies but through laws enhancing the individual rights of employees, in particular unfair dismissal, but also laws on equal pay and equal opportunities, and safety and health legislation. Traditionally, in many industries, companies had left industrial relations to be dealt with by their employers' associations, which had the alleged advantage from the employers' viewpoint of keeping trade unions out of the workplace. For historical reasons this had never been completely true in Britain and certainly was no longer a valid policy in the 1970s for the reasons mentioned above, and as shown by the Donovan Report.

Many employers indeed accepted the Donovan analysis and its core recommendations and proceeded to seek to reform their industrial relations policies and their internal procedures. Industrial relations and personnel management specialists grew in number and in importance. Many large companies enlarged their recognition of stewards, accepted joint shop steward committees and indeed encouraged a marked growth in the number of full-time stewards. The check-off became widely accepted and there was an expansion of the closed shop. There was also the development of disciplinary and grievance procedures, and of formalised negotiating and consultative committees at workplace and company level. This wider acceptance of, and greater role for, unions at workplace level was partly the acceptance of the inevitable, in the light of greater union power. But it was also a policy whereby management sought to bring greater order out of relative chaos – in Flanders's often-quoted statement 'Management ... can only regain control by sharing it.' (Flanders 1967) It was also a means of legitimising management's decision-making authority through the involvement of stewards, particularly senior ones. This process of establishing order and control was not confined to the procedural side of industrial relations, but embraced the substantive side, through, for example, the reform of payments systems, in particular a reduction in the incidence of individual payment by result schemes, the growth of measured day work and work study, the extension of job evaluation and the reform of pay structures. The success of such reforms at workplace level is difficult to evaluate, but it was not insignificant. However, in public perception, such reforms were lost against the dramatic general developments which have been described in this chapter.

Conclusion

If the 1960s ended on a note of strain in the consensus, the 1970s ended with the most ambitious exercise in the consensus lying in ruins. The decade had seen a Conservative government committed to working through market forces and using legislation to catch the union tiger by the tail. But the government did an about turn and offered the unions a partnership in economic policy in return for the delivery of an incomes policy. Failing to secure that, it embarked on the most detailed of all prices and incomes policies. The Labour government in the second half of the decade had swung from the intimacy of the Social Contract to the bitter disagreements of the 'Winter of Discontent'. Both political parties had practised consensus and both had become the object of union hostility.

The general election of 1979 is now seen as having turned on the votes of trade unionists. The experience of the 1970s caused more of them than ever before to vote Conservative. What happened in the 1980s to industrial relations was in large part the product of the 1970s. It was the trade unionists' reaction to the events of that decade that put the Conservative government of 1979 in power.

CHAPTER 3

The economic background

Introduction

It is not the purpose of this chapter to delve into a detailed analysis of the British economy during the 1980s. The intent is rather to record very briefly the main changes in the leading economic indicators in so far as they are relevant to industrial relations. The Conservative government that came to power in 1979 was wedded to a firm belief in monetarism and a free market economy. The Prime Minister held to these beliefs as articles of faith along with a conviction that Britain's problems in the post-war decades (whether under a Labour or a Conservative government) were the result of a departure from this faith. Thus any form of corporatism or tripartism was anathema to her, as was Keynesian economics and most forms of public enterprise and public expenditure.

The 1980s can be divided broadly into four periods. First, there was the severe recession of 1979–81; second, a period of slow recovery between 1982 to 1986; third, the boom period of 1987 to 1989; and fourth, the period of recession beginning in 1990.

The first Thatcher government inherited in 1979 an economy with unemployment at 1 million, which although high by post-war standards, had fallen somewhat in the previous two years. Inflation was at 10 per cent and had begun to move upwards as had wage settlements, accelerated by the 'Winter of Discontent', after the relative success of Stages 1 and 2 of the Labour government's Social Contract in greatly reducing the rise in wages and the cost of living. The inflationary spiral was soon to be given a further boost by another large increase in OPEC oil prices in 1979–80 and by the Thatcher government's first budget, which doubled the rate of VAT and thereby added

4 percentage points to the RPI. The current balance of payments had shown a surplus of £966m in 1978 but a deficit of £661m in 1979. However, Britain's North Sea oil was beginning to flow, providing during the 1980s substantial tax revenues and eliminating for the first time in the post-war decades balance of payments constraints on Britain's economic growth.

The early 1980s saw the worst economic recession of the post-war years. GDP at constant prices declined by over 3 per cent between 1979 and 1981 before beginning to grow again, while manufacturing output over the same period fell by 14 per cent. Unemployment increased from 1 million in 1979 to 2.1 million at the end of 1980, to 2.8 million at the end of 1981 and to 3.1 million at the end of 1982. Thereafter, unemployment increased more slowly but stayed at over 3 million until 1987. This was despite the numerous changes in the definition of unemployment made by the government since 1979. Thereupon it declined significantly to well under 2 million by 1989. However during 1990 the country entered into another recession and unemployment started to move up again.

The cause of Britain's recession in 1979–81 was partly the worldwide recession and partly the government's economic policy. The government in its battle against inflation, which it saw as the greatest economic evil, pursued a tight monetary policy, raised interest rates to a peak of 17 per cent, sought reductions in public expenditure and removed all exchange controls. The effect of high interest rates and an emerging balance of payments surplus as a result of North Sea oil boosted the exchange rate of the pound against the dollar to an unrealistic level for British exporters. The effect on British manufacturing industry was catastrophic, causing the 14 per cent fall in output between 1979 and 1981 and the consequent redundancies.

Once growth began again from the low point of 1981 it was fairly steady until 1986, averaging over 3 per cent per annum. Employment started to grow, although most of the increase was in female part-time employment, and there were marked differences between the North and the South. Full-time male employment did not increase. By 1987–8 labour shortages had emerged in certain parts of the country, particularly London, the South-East and East Anglia, and in certain occupations. The RPI, after a dramatic increase of over 20 per cent from 1979 to 1980 – an increase in the post-war years second only to that of 1974–5 – increased by a markedly smaller amount by 1983 and then stabilised at an annual rise of around 5 per cent until 1988. By the end of 1988 the annual rate of increase had, however, started to accelerate again. The increase in average earnings also rose dramatically in 1979–80 to its second highest post-war level of over 20 per cent. During the next 2 years the annual increase in earnings also fell significantly before levelling out at around 8 per cent per annum for several years. However, towards the end of the 1980s, the increase in earnings started to move up again, reaching over 10 per cent per annum. In every year the rise in average earnings exceeded the rise in the RPI.

Output and productivity

Britain's GDP fell between 1979 and 1981 by over 3 per cent: thereafter there was a gradual recovery, which accelerated markedly in the middle to late 1980s but declined again in 1989 and 1990 (Table 3.1). The decline in manufacturing output between 1979 and 1981 was much more drastic, with a fall of 14 per cent: thereafter there was a gradual recovery, although it was not until 1987 that the 1979 level of manufacturing output was exceeded. In 1987 and 1988 the rate of increase in manufacturing output speeded up considerably, but fell back in 1989 and 1990 as Britain entered into another recession.

TABLE 3.1 Output and productivity, 1979–90 – UK (per cent change on previous year)

	Whole economy		Manufacturing	
	Output	Output per person employed	Output	Output per person employed
1980	−2.8	−2.1	−9.1	−3.9
1981	−1.3	1.8	−5.9	3.4
1982	2.1	3.8	0.2	6.7
1983	3.4	4.4	2.9	8.6
1984	2.8	0.9	3.8	5.6
1985	3.5	2.5	2.7	3.2
1986	3.6	3.2	1.3	3.5
1987	4.6	2.8	5.2	6.1
1988	4.6	1.3	7.1	5.4
1989	2.5	−0.4	4.2	3.5
1990	1.1	0.3	−0.5	0.2
1990 level (1979 = 100)	125.7	120.0	112.1	150.8

Source: Adapted from National Institute Economic *Review*'s Statistical Appendix.

Output per person employed, both for the economy as a whole and for manufacturing industry, after an original fall in 1980, followed upward paths until towards the end of the decade, when the rate of increase fell markedly. However, the rate of increase in manufacturing was much greater than that of the economy as a whole, with an increase in 1979–90 of 50.8 per cent compared with 20 per cent. Nevertheless, manufacturing output in 1990 was only 12 per cent above its 1979 level. The overall growth in GDP of 25 per cent during 1979–90 was only slightly less than that of France and Germany, but compared with an increase of 30 per cent in the USA and 57 per cent in Japan (Table 3.2). However, none of the other countries experienced as sharp a recession in 1979–81 as did Britain, nor did they suffer the same decline in the rate of growth in 1989–90, or indeed Britain's absolute decline in 1990–91.

TABLE 3.2 Gross product 1979–90 – international comparisons (per cent increase on previous year)

	UK	USA	Japan	France	Germany	OECD
1980	− 2.0	− 0.2	3.5	1.6	1.5	1.1
1981	− 1.2	1.9	3.4	1.2	0.0	1.6
1982	1.7	− 2.6	3.6	2.6	− 1.0	− 0.3
1983	3.8	3.6	2.8	0.7	1.9	2.7
1984	2.1	6.8	4.2	1.3	3.3	4.7
1985	3.6	3.3	5.1	1.9	1.9	3.5
1986	3.8	2.9	2.8	2.3	2.4	2.8
1987	4.7	2.8	3.5	2.4	1.5	3.5
1988	4.2	4.4	6.3	4.3	3.7	4.4
1989	1.9	2.5	4.8	3.9	3.9	3.2
1990	0.6	0.9	5.5	2.7	4.6	—
1990 level (1979 = 100)	125.2	130.1	157.0	127.8	126.2	—

Source: Adapted from National Institute Economic *Review*'s Statistical Appendix.

Employment and unemployment

The deep recession of 1979–81 brought about a large increase in unemployment. It doubled between June 1979 and June 1981 from 1.14 million or 4.7 per cent of civil employment to 2.3 million or 9.4 per cent. Thereafter, unemployment continued to rise to over 3 million or 11.4 per cent of the labour force, reaching its peak in 1986: it then began to fall and there was a steady reduction in unemployment to nearly 1.5 million by the end of 1989. There were further small reductions in the early months of 1990, but during the second half of that year unemployment resumed its upward movement; by early 1991 it had exceeded 2 million and most forecasts estimated that it would increase to between 2.5 and 3 million before it began to fall. During the 1980s unemployment in the UK exceeded the OECD average in every single year (Table 3.3).

TABLE 3.3 **Unemployment, 1979–90 – international comparisons* (per cent of total labour force)**

	UK	USA	Japan	France	Germany	OECD
1979	5.0	5.8	2.1	5.9	3.2	5.0
1980	6.4	7.0	2.0	6.3	3.0	5.7
1981	9.8	7.5	2.2	7.4	4.4	6.6
1982	11.3	9.5	2.4	8.1	6.1	8.0
1983	12.5	9.5	2.6	8.3	8.0	8.5
1984	11.7	7.4	2.7	9.7	7.0	8.0
1985	11.2	7.1	2.6	10.2	7.2	7.8
1986	11.2	6.9	2.8	10.4	6.5	7.7
1987	10.3	6.1	2.8	10.5	6.2	7.3
1988	8.4	5.4	2.5	10.0	6.1	6.7
1989	6.9	5.2	2.2	9.4	5.6	6.2
1990	6.9	5.4	2.1	9.0	5.1	6.1

Source: OECD.

* Standardised according to international definitions by the OECD.

The number of employees in employment in all industries and services in June 1990 at 22.3 million was 0.4 million less than it had been in June 1979. Between 1979 and 1983 it declined by over 2 million, while during the rest of the decade it increased by nearly 2 million (Table 3.4). However, male employment declined by nearly 1.5 million while female employment grew by over 1 million. Well over half of the increased employment of women was in part-time employment.

Not only was the experience of men and women very different; so also was the experience of manufacturing industry on the one hand and the service sector on the other. Employment in manufacturing between 1979 and 1990 declined by 2 million or nearly 30 per cent, while employment in services rose by 2.2 million or 20 per cent. The decline in manufacturing took place almost entirely between 1979 and 1985 and thereafter it approximately stabilised. Employment in the service sector declined slightly between 1980 and 1982 and thereafter grew significantly. Self-employment during the decade also grew substantially from 1.8 million in 1979 to 3.2 million in 1990.

TABLE 3.4 Employment, 1979–90 – Great Britain

| June | Employees in employment | | | | | | Self-employed (000s) | HM Forces (000s) | Work-related govt. training programmes (000s) | Work-force in employment (000s) | Work-force (000s) |
	Male (000s)	Female All (000s)	Female (Part-time) (000s)	Total (000s)	Manu-facturing (000s)	Services (000s)					
1979	13 183	9 455	3 870	22 638	7 107	13 260	1 842	314	–	24 794	25 969
1980	13 018	9 440	3 941	22 458	6 801	13 384	1 950	323	–	24 731	26 176
1981	12 278	9 107	3 817	21 386	6 099	13 142	2 058	334	–	23 777	26 077
1982	11 930	8 985	3 783	20 916	5 751	13 117	2 109	324	–	23 348	26 012
1983	11 670	8 901	3 776	20 572	5 418	13 169	2 160	322	8	23 061	25 932
1984	11 619	9 123	3 889	20 741	5 302	13 503	2 435	326	168	23 671	26 582
1985	11 632	9 228	3 976	20 920	5 254	13 769	2 550	326	168	23 964	27 021
1986	11 477	9 409	4 081	20 886	5 122	13 954	2 567	322	218	23 992	27 095
1987	11 431	9 650	4 169	21 080	5 049	14 247	2 801	319	303	24 502	27 282
1988	11 702	10 057	4 232	21 760	5 089	14 860	2 926	316	335	25 336	27 561
1989	11 718	10 416	4 494	22 134	5 080	15 261	3 182	308	452	26 076	27 714
1990	11 776	10 550	4 604	22 326	5 046	15 497	3 222	303	412	26 263	27 723

Source: *Employment Gazette* and Historical Supplement No. 2.

Figures for June each year unadjusted for seasonal variation.

Inflation

The annual average RPI rose between 1979 and 1990 by 123 per cent. There was an increase of 18 per cent in 1979–80, 12 per cent in 1980–1 and nearly 9 per cent in 1981–2. Thereafter, there was much greater stability, with the annual inflation rate at about 5 per cent until towards the end of the decade when there was a rise of 8 per cent between 1988 and 1989 and of 9.5 per cent between 1989 and 1990 (Table 3.5). The increase in the RPI peaked in October 1990 at 10.9 per cent and thereafter there was a decline in the rate of increase.

In terms of international comparison, Britain's record has not been a good one. The increase in the UK's cost of living between 1979 and 1990 of 123 per cent compared with the OECD average of 97 per cent. France had an increase of 108 per cent but her record improved very markedly in the second half of the decade and was much better than that of the UK. The USA had an increase of 80 per cent, but also improved markedly in the second half of the decade; Japan and Germany had increases respectively of only 32 and 37 per cent.

Earnings

The movements in earnings are analysed in depth in Chapter 10. Here only a few brief points are made. Average earnings for men rose between April 1979 and April 1990 by 192 per cent and for women by 220 per cent (Table 10.1). This increase compared with an increase in the RPI of 130 per cent over the same period, so that there was an increase in real average earnings of 27 per cent for men and 39 per cent for women.

The rate of increase in average earnings was not spread evenly throughout the decade. In the first year of the Conservative government, 1979–80, the increase was over 20 per cent (Table 10.1). In the following 2 years the government was markedly successful in bringing down the rate of increase in earnings, although this was perhaps not surprising given the recession, mass unemployment and redundancies, falling profits and a falling rate of increase in the RPI. In the following 6 years the rate of increase was remarkably stable at between 7 and 8 per cent. However in 1989 there was a rise in the rate of increase.

Compared with the other main industrial countries, Britain's record in the 1980s was not good. Table 3.6 shows OECD figures for the movement in average earnings in a number of leading countries. Britain's increase was 179 per cent between 1979 and 1990. The only other country with an increase of a similar order of magnitude was France, with 136 per cent. Again, the crucial difference between the two was that whereas Britain's performance got worse

TABLE 3.5 Consumer prices, 1979–90 – international comparisons (per cent increase on previous year)

	UK	USA	Japan	France	Germany	OECD
1980	17.9	13.5	8.1	13.8	5.4	12.9
1981	12.0	10.3	4.9	13.1	6.3	10.5
1982	8.6	6.2	2.7	11.9	5.3	7.8
1983	4.6	3.2	1.9	9.5	3.3	5.2
1984	5.0	4.3	2.3	7.6	2.3	5.1
1985	6.1	3.6	2.0	5.8	2.2	4.6
1986	3.4	1.9	0.4	2.5	−0.7	2.5
1987	4.2	3.7	−0.2	3.3	0.8	3.3
1988	4.9	2.9	1.1	2.5	1.2	3.9
1989	7.8	4.8	2.3	3.7	2.8	6.2
1990	9.5	5.4	3.1	3.4	2.7	6.5
1990 level (1979 = 100)	222.6	180.1	132.1	208.1	136.6	197.0

Source: Adapted from National Institute Economic *Review*'s Statistical Appendix.
Figures are Annual Averages.

TABLE 3.6 Average earnings, 1979–89 – international comparisons (per cent increase on previous year)

	UK	USA	Japan	France	Germany
1980	19.6	9.1	7.9	15.9	7.4
1981	12.9	8.9	7.2	14.4	4.7
1982	8.9	6.0	4.3	14.2	3.7
1983	8.5	4.2	3.8	10.7	3.4
1984	5.9	5.3	4.7	8.0	3.2
1985	7.5	5.3	4.0	6.3	2.9
1986	8.2	3.7	4.0	4.3	3.9
1987	8.3	5.0	3.0	3.9	3.4
1988	8.4	5.7	4.4	4.3	4.6
1989	9.1	3.7	5.0	5.2	3.2
1990	11.1	4.7	5.5	3.0	4.7
1990 level (1979 = 100)	278.9	181.1	169.0	235.7	149.4

Source: Adapted from National Institute Economic *Review*'s Statistical Appendix.

towards the end of the decade, France's performance improved markedly. Among other main countries, the USA had an increase of 81 per cent, Japan 69 per cent and Germany 49 per cent.

Labour costs per unit

The movements in UK labour costs per unit and the reasons for them are discussed in Chapter 10. Here the record of the UK in comparison with that of other leading industrial countries is given (Table 3.7). Since 1965 the UK's record has been markedly worse than that of the main OECD countries. In the period 1965–73 the average increase in annual labour costs per unit over the previous period was 5.9 per cent in the UK and 4.9 per cent on average for the leading OECD countries. For the period 1973–9 the respective figures were 15.6 per cent and 9.4 per cent, and for 1979–87 they were 6.8 per cent and 4.9 per cent. The position worsened even further at the end of the decade, with 1990 showing an increase of 9 per cent in the UK compared with 0.1 per cent in the USA, 2.1 per cent in Japan and 1.9 per cent in Germany.

Monetary and fiscal policy

As stated in the introduction to this chapter, the Thatcher government which took office in 1979 was wedded to monetarism. In its extreme form this meant that if there was sufficient control over the money supply then all other economic variables would fall into place, in particular inflation would be solved and excess wage demands would cease or, if granted, would increase unemployment which would in turn drive down wages. However, the government also believed that for monetarism to work there first needed to be free labour, product and financial markets. Second, public expenditure had to be greatly reduced – certainly as a proportion of the GDP – and that budgets had at least to be balanced or else the public sector borrowing requirement (PSBR) would increase and that would add to the money supply. Third, the public sector also had to be greatly reduced, for by definition there was not a free market in the supply of public services.

Accordingly, in its early years the Thatcher government put great weight on seeking to reduce the money supply. In his 1979 Budget statement the Chancellor said that 'We are committed to the progressive reduction of the money supply'. The selected monetary target was 'M3'. The following year saw the introduction of the Medium Term Financial Strategy (MTFS). This set out the government's projections for both the money supply and the PSBR

TABLE 3.7 Unit labour costs in the business sector: international comparisons

(a) Average annual rate, per cent change from previous period

	1965–73	*1973–79*	*1979–87*
UK	5.9	15.6	6.8
USA	4.7	8.1	4.9
Japan	5.4	9.2	1.0
Germany	4.6	4.2	2.6
France	4.3	11.4	7.1
Total of above OECD countries	4.9	9.4	4.9

Source: *OECD Economic Outlook*, December 1990, Table 58, p. 130.

(b) Per cent increase on previous year

	UK	*USA*	*Japan*	*Germany*	*France*
1985	6.0	1.6	1.0	0.0	0.5
1986	4.5	−0.1	4.0	4.0	1.5
1987	1.3	−2.4	−2.9	2.9	2.3
1988	2.8	0.9	−5.0	0.0	0.5
1989	4.2	0.7	0.0	0.9	2.1
1990	9.0	0.1	2.1	1.9	n.a.
1990 level (1985 = 100)	123.7	99.2	98.0	110.0	n.a.

Source: *Financial Times*, 10, June 1991: International Economic Indicators.

Figures are seasonally adjusted, measured in domestic currencies: Germany – mining and manufacturing; other countries – manufacturing industry.

over the next 4 years. When the government failed to meet its targets for M3, it used other monetary measures which it thought would be easier to control (Robinson, 1986, p. 417). The government also put great emphasis on interest rates, the Chancellor stating that 'No government that is interested in controlling the quantity of money can be indifferent to its price.' The government accordingly raised the bank base rate in 1979 from 12 per cent to 14 per cent and then to 17 per cent and through most of 1980 it stayed between 16 and 17 per cent.

The first Thatcher Budget in 1979 introduced a cut in the standard rate of income tax from 33 per cent to 30 per cent and in the top rate from 83 per cent to 60 per cent. To pay for these cuts and to reduce the PSBR, VAT was doubled to a single rate of 15 per cent and there were big increases in the prices of nationalised industries. The 1981 Budget was also deflationary – in the midst of the severest recession since 1929–31.

Indeed, throughout the decade the Government sought to reduce public expenditure and the PSBR, but its efforts with regard to the former were thwarted for many years because of the greater cost of social security through the increase in the number of unemployed and in the number of old age pensioners, as well as increases in expenditure on defence and law and order. The government was successful however in reducing the PSBR and indeed for a short period the PSBR was negative thanks to the boost to government revenue from North Sea oil and the proceeds of privatisation.

Towards the end of the decade much less was heard of monetarism and the PSBR. Indeed a budget deficit re-emerged and was defended by the government as being reasonable in the midst of a recession.

In 1987 there had been the deregulation of financial markets and the 'Big Bang' on the Stock Exchange. There was also a massive 'give-away' budget which slashed the top rate of income tax to 40 per cent and further reduced the standard rate. What followed was an upsurge in consumer expenditure fuelled by the tax concessions and a credit boom which in turn led to falling unemployment, rising inflation, rising wages and a large balance of payments deficit. To control inflation, interest rates were raised drastically from 7.5 per cent in May 1988 to 15 per cent in October 1989 – the only weapon acceptable to the government. By late 1990 inflation had started to fall at the cost of a new recession and with unemployment rising again and manufacturing output and GDP falling.

Distribution of the national income

In the years 1979 to 1990 gross trading profits increased by 173 per cent, and if North Sea oil profits are excluded, the increase was 212 per cent; interest and dividends rose by 168 per cent, rent and self-employment income by 229 per cent and wages and salaries by 174 per cent. Total fixed investment in real terms increased by 39 per cent, but fixed investment in manufacturing industry increased by only 6 per cent and throughout the decade remained below the 1979 level until 1988.

Between 1980 and 1990, consumers' expenditure on durable goods rose by 75 per cent in real terms, and on non-durable goods in real terms by 36 per cent. In money terms, consumer credit during 1980–9 rose by 271 per cent, and building society mortgages 1980–90 rose by 364 per cent.

Balance of payments

Britain in 1979 had a current balance of payments deficit of £661 million which consisted of a deficit in visible trade of £3449m, largely offset by a surplus on invisible trade of £2788m. The next 6 years saw significant surpluses on the current balance and indeed in the first 3 of these years there was also a surplus on visible trade, largely the consequence of a relatively depressed demand for imports due to recession and the large boost to exports provided by North Sea oil. However, from 1983 onwards there was a steadily increasing deficit on visible trade, which reached £24bn in 1989. Indeed, in 1983 Britain for the first time since the Industrial Revolution imported more manufactured goods that she exported. By 1986, the invisible surplus was no longer sufficient to offset the deficit on visible trade, so that the current balance from 1986 onwards also showed steadily increasing deficits, reaching £20bn in 1989. Between 1979 and 1989 the volume of imports and services rose by 64 per cent while the volume of exports and services rose by 28 per cent. With the slowing down of growth and then recession in 1990–1 there was some improvement in the visible and current balances in 1990, but the former was still £17.9bn and the latter £12.8bn. Thus the 'era of North Sea oil' which it was originally thought would provide Britain with a lengthy period free of balance of payments difficulties, in fact did so for no more than 6 years.

Conclusion

The main significant features of the changing economic environment for industrial relations were, first, the drastic cut-backs in manufacturing industry in 1979–81, where unions had traditionally been strongly organised, and the resultant large-scale redundancies. Second, there was the near trebling of unemployment to well over 3 million between 1979 and 1987, which meant *inter alia* a more competitive labour market. Third, there was the changing structure of the economy and consequently of the labour force, in particular the decline of manufacturing; the growth of the service sector; the growth of female employment − much of it part-time − and the decline of male employment; the growth of white-collar employment and the decline of blue-collar employment; and the growth in self-employment. Fourth, there was the growth of international competition in product markets. International competition meant among other things attempts by employers to reduce labour costs, certainly in the first instance by the large-scale shedding of labour and the closure of plants and subsequently by the speeding up of technological change, organisational change, a fall in the average size of manufacturing units, increased take-over and merger activity, and very substantial investment abroad, including the transfer of manufacturing capacity.

One remarkable fact, in view of all the above features, was that throughout the 1980s average money earnings and indeed real earnings continued to increase significantly, albeit that the increase was very unevenly distributed. This is a fact to which we will return in subsequent chapters.

CHAPTER 4

Government values and policies

Introduction

At the general election of 1979 a Conservative government was returned with a majority of 43 seats over all other parties with the support of 44 per cent of those who voted. The manifesto on which the government was elected heralded major changes in industrial relations and, in particular, steps to curb the power of trade unions. The Conservatives were returned again in 1983 with a greatly increased overall majority in the House of Commons of 144 seats and with the support of 42 per cent of the electorate. They were returned a third time in 1987, with an overall majority this time of 100 seats, but with the proportion of votes unchanged at 42 percent.

Throughout the 1980s the government rarely felt under any threat at a general election. In 1983 the improvement in their popularity as a result of the Falklands War played an important part in their victory, and unemployment at over 3 million turned out not to be the political disadvantage it had widely been believed to be in the 1970s by many Conservatives, a belief which lingered on into the 1980s among those who were called 'wets'. But in both 1983 and 1987 the opposition was divided, with the Alliance taking 25 and 23 per cent of the votes compared with Labour's 28 and 31 percent. Moreover, many of the trade unionists who voted for Conservative candidates in 1979 continued to be loyal to them in 1983 and 1987.

As for many other areas of policy, the significance for industrial relations of the command of the Commons which the government possessed throughout the 1980s without effective electoral challenge was that a whole sequence of legislative steps could be confidently taken. There was a sharpening of the government's intervention later in the decade when the legislation, and plans for legislation, became more extreme than the first steps taken in the 1979 to

1983 Parliament. Contrary to the usual rhythm of politics, continued power was not associated with a tempering of the attack on trade unions, but with yet deeper interference.

Of course, industrial relations were part of a wider canvas in 1979 and more general objectives set the scene for the government's action in that field. There were two particular, related, general ideas which had profound implications for industrial relations and both marked departures from the assumptions which had underlain successive governments' policies for over 30 years.

These were a belief that the results of the freest possible play of economic forces were almost always to be preferred, and that consensus between the two sides of industry and the government was almost always malign. It followed that impediments to the operation of market forces were in the government's sights. The workings of the labour market are not easily left to unimpeded market pressures because those who labour are not tins of beans – they have votes and a capacity to organise and act collectively. But the activities of trade unions and the processes of collective bargaining, perhaps even their very existence, were plainly at odds with the free play of market forces. The consensus of the post-war period which had varied in intensity was erected on the widely held belief that the determination of pay was bound to be dominated by organised action resulting in collective agreements which were major modifications of market forces. The consensus had been that those agreements would need from time to time to be subjected to an overall framework of restraint put together with the parties on the initiative of governments. That could not be reconciled with a free market approach.

A concerted attempt to weaken the fabric of collective bargaining in order to allow market forces much greater impact on pay and conditions of employment was one of the radical changes which the government inaugurated and pursued throughout the decade.

Full employment

A commitment to the maintenance of full employment had been the centre-piece of the former consensus. It had two sources. Out of the Second World War had come a universal hostility to mass unemployment and a general assumption that no party could win a general election unless it was committed to full employment. The second source was Keynesian economics; the means were available for managing the economy in such a way that full employment was maintained.

A central question of economic policy up to the end of the 1970s was how to manage other elements than employment in the performance of the economy – consumption, investment, taxation, savings, incomes – so that full employment could be preserved. It became progressively more difficult to do so on two fronts. The putting together of an effective incomes policy (usually covering prices as well as incomes and unearned as well as earned income) ran into more and more snags and collapsed in the most thoroughgoing way in the 'Winter of Discontent' in 1978/9. But, more importantly, the policies which kept the demand for labour at the full-employment level came increasingly to be seen as standing in the way of the long-term adjustment of the British economy to its international position. So not only did governments find it increasingly difficult to prevent unemployment rising but productivity, unit labour costs, prices, investment and profitability were getting increasingly out of line with Britain's major competitors in Europe and the rising economies of the Far East. The oil and gas of the North Sea were a bonus but under the pressure of short-term political demands they ended up being used to protect the weaknesses of the economy instead of being the means of their reform. As early as 1976, soon after he became Prime Minister, James Callaghan bluntly told the Labour Party conference that full employment could not be guaranteed: 'It used to be thought that a nation could just spend its way out of recession and increase employment by cutting taxes and boosting government spending. I tell you in all candour that that option no longer exists' (Labour Party, 1976, p. 188).

The new Conservative government was divided on whether action should be taken to prevent unemployment rising but the Prime Minister and her supporters succeeded in adopting policies which left the level of employment to be determined by the competitiveness of producers with unemployment coming out as a residual. More jobs would be created, it was argued, by greater success in competitive product markets, not by macro-economic management by the government. It was on this issue that the term 'wets' was most accurately used to describe unreformed ministers. It was the rising level of unemployment and the acceptance of it by the government as an adjustment which should be allowed to run its course which caused such alarm among them. They saw political penalties ahead, but they were proved wrong by the result of the 1983 general election.

The dropping of the commitment to full employment and the swift rise of unemployment between 1979 and 1982 from 5 to over 11 per cent on the OECD definition pulled away a major assumption on which collective bargaining had been conducted for over 30 years. It was seen most clearly, not in pay, but on the employment front. Trade unions and employers were precipitated into major redundancies in manufacturing industry as the rising value of the pound made exports dearer and imports cheaper and the government stood back from the consequential reductions in employment. Employment in manufacturing had fallen by about 0.75 million in the 1970s but between 1979 and 1984 it fell by 1.8 million – over 25 percent. The negotiators had to deal with the direct effects of the inability of British manufacturers to cope with foreign competition. The shock was as great for managers as for trade unionists; as factories closed the government did not accept that it should act to moderate the increase in unemployment.

Inflation

The commitment which replaced full employment was the reduction and, if possible, the elimination of inflation. The implication was that if unemployment helped to reduce inflation, unemployment there would have to be; or, if measures to reduce unemployment would be inflationary, they would not be taken. They came together in the belief that if inflation could be removed, non-inflationary growth would occur and that would bring growing employment and falling unemployment.

Stemming inflation, which had risen to over 20 per cent in the spring of 1980, required monetary policies as opposed to demand management; the government would concentrate on controlling the money supply and using the rate of interest, thus making otiose the apparatus of incomes policies, regional grants, investment subsidies, and all the other forms of intervention which had been used in attempts to prevent low levels of unemployment causing inflation.

The effect was to push industrial relations to the periphery of political concern. It had previously been at its centre, with successive governments constructing policies, at varying levels of detail, in consultation with the CBI and TUC in order to retain a consensus. A monetarist attack on inflation treated collective bargaining as one of the mechanisms for settling prices, albeit shot through with imperfections. Instead of being co-opted members of the ruling circle, leading employers and trade unionists were no longer needed in the corridors of Whitehall. Negotiators in the private sector were left to get on with pay settlements against the background of the unemployment, interest rates and exchange rates which prevailed at the time. It was assumed that the levels of pay arrived at would be compatible with the government's objectives and even if they were not, the government would not presume to know better than employers what they should pay their employees.

Public expenditure and the welfare state

It had been a major theme of the 1979 general election that the Conservative Party favoured people paying less in taxation, keeping more of their incomes, and deciding for themselves how to spend them. It continued throughout the decade to be a politically attractive theme to many wage and salary earners and was a strong element in the government's popular appeal.

Reductions in direct taxes helped to reduce inflation. Trade unionists who were paying less in income tax (although they could well be paying more in National Insurance contributions as their incomes rose) could be more relaxed about the size of their pay claims. In the 1970s the level of personal taxation and increases in it had played an important part in stoking up pressure for pay claims, and when Denis Healey was Chancellor of the Exchequer in 1976 he made attempts to trade off tax reductions against the size of pay increases.

There was a drastic change in the approach to public expenditure; from being the engine of the economy, changing speed as required to maintain full employment, it was cast in the role of wrecker. The more it could be reduced the better the economy would perform. Although it was not reduced as a proportion of national income until the end of the decade, downward pressure was exerted from the time the government came into office. Activities which were financed or subsidised out of public funds were suspect either in principle (and ought to be privatised) or in terms of their assumed inefficiency. Cash limits were used to set ceilings on what could be spent. If wages and salaries were settled at levels which put up the pay-bill by more than the cash limit allowed there would usually be no more money. The excess expenditure on pay had to be met by increased efficiency or by a reduction in the scale and quality of the service, both of which would reduce the number of jobs.

The settlement of pay and the negotiations about working practices in all activities financed out of public funds were powerfully affected. Trade union membership was high in the public sector and the government's approach to public expenditure was a direct challenge to the unions, the managers being, in most cases, bound by the government's policy.

Deregulation

The freer play of all markets which the government favoured, required a direct attack on the accretions of rules, regulations, limits, customs and practices which had been tolerated in the belief that if people had their interests protected in this way they would be more amenable to government proposals that they should exert their bargaining power moderately. Lord Young entered the government in 1984 with the specific remit to deregulate the economy and he retained it when he became Secretary of State for Employment in 1985.

The approach touched many established interests including the obvious candidates in the industrial relations field. In industrial relations, practices like the closed shop and restrictive practices came under the heading of deregulation. It was not only the Monopolies and Mergers Commission which was brought to bear. In disputes, like those in the newspaper industry, the removal of the regulations controlling entry to employment fitted in closely with the government's objectives.

The role of the individual

Emphasis on the obligation of the individual citizen to look after his or her own interests, such as getting on your bike to find a job, as Norman Tebbit advised the Conservative Party conference in 1983, was complementary to a preference for market forces. But impediments to individual action prevented citizens from doing things for themselves and so reducing their dependence on the state. The government had, therefore, to be interventionist, in order not only to create space for individuals but also to create an environment in which individuals could be pressed by government to be more self-reliant.

This had a direct link with government action on industrial relations. On matters like the closed shop, picketing, and balloting before strikes, the key idea was that collective action and its restraints on individual choice should be made to give way to wider individual preferences on whether or not to join a trade union, or cross a picket line, or join a strike even if a majority had voted in favour of it. Legislative action of a detailed kind on these matters was based on the belief that if individuals could choose they would tend to reject collective action and the government's objective of reducing impediments to the working of the labour market would be served.

This emphasis on the individual got stronger as the decade passed and by the general election of 1987 the legislative commitments of the Conservative Party gave the leading place to the right of individual members to challenge their unions in the courts with the aid of the Trade Union Commissioner 'with the power to help individual trade unionists to enforce their fundamental rights' (Conservative Party manifesto, 1987). This shift from concern with the legal status of unions and their internal government to subsidised access to the courts for individual members had a number of sources, not least the unwillingness of many employers to resort to the law.

But it drew on a much broader change lying behind industrial relations and going much deeper than specific legislative changes. The government rode on a wave of 'acquisitive individualism (which) tended to supersede both social solidarity and social service' (Phelps Brown, 1990, p. 8) in a range of policy areas including industrial relations. The same change lay behind the substantial shift of manual worker voters from Labour to Conservative at the 1979 general election which was sustained in the elections of 1983 and 1987. Enabling individual union members to challenge their collective leaders fitted in with the belief that 'the loyalty that sprang from the individual worker's sense of common interest . . . had ebbed away' (Phelps Brown, 1990, p. 11).

Reducing the public sector

The public sector presents a major problem to those who believe in the efficiency of markets as allocators of goods and services, because a number of public services are either not capable of being sold at a price, like defence, or are kept in the public sector by a political decision, like the NHS. But others could be put into the private sector. The government's desire to inject the discipline of the market took several forms — privatisation of monopolies subject to controls and limited competition (e.g. British Telecom, Mercury and OFTEL), contracting out of services after competitive bids (e.g. local authority refuse collection and the cleaning of hospitals), and the creation of internal markets with pseudo-prices (e.g. general practitioners' use of hospital services and the opting-out of schools from local authority control).

These changes were seen as having as one of their chief benefits the weakening of trade union bargaining power. The unions were strongest in the public sector and because of the absence of a market test they had been handed bargaining power on a plate. After privatisation and contracting out, managers would be in situations similar to those of managers in the market sector where they had to resist union claims in order to survive.

The trade unions

It was of crucial importance to the confidence with which the government took steps to curb the power of trade unions that it had the support of trade unionists. Until the early 1970s trade union membership itself worked in favour of Labour. By 1979 it was no longer an independent determinant of voting preference, and by the 1983 general election more trade unionists than non-trade unionists voted Conservative (Himmelweit *et al.*, 1985, p. 208). This positive attraction which the Conservative Party had for trade unionists can be seen in the decline of Labour voting among the growing number of owner-occupiers who were trade unionists; in 1974, 45 per cent had voted Labour, but by 1983 the proportion was down to 28 per cent (Rose and McAllister, 1986, p. 97). The EETPU found in a survey after the general election of 1987 that 45 per cent of its members voted Conservative, compared with 42 per cent of all those who voted. It is widely recognised by trade union leaders that the defection of more of their members from Labour to Conservative in 1979, especially in the south of England, was a major reason, if not *the* major reason as some would aver, for the return of a Conservative government in 1979 and its victories in 1983 and 1987.

Polls showed that a significant proportion of trade unionists were not hostile to the Conservatives' intention to curb the unions while at the same time believing that their own unions did a good job for them. The resolution of this apparent paradox is explicable in terms of a lesson which trade unionists had learned in periods of incomes policy – if you agree with what is proposed, do not fall in with it until it is enforced on all trade unions. Following that line of thought, the promise to curb the unions had an appeal even to trade unionists who took part in strikes during the 'Winter of Discontent'.

The unions' power had five objectionable aspects for the government. First, unions were too powerful in the system of pay determination; they pushed up pay beyond what was compatible with effective performance in the international economy. They protected practices which prevented increases in productivity. They stood out against changes which managers proposed in the interests of efficiency. They usurped managerial authority where they could, especially in the public services. The unions' defence was that they were legitimate organisations which existed to bargain about pay, productivity and working practices. Their right to bargain was mirrored by the employers' right to bargain. If there were cases where they were strong enough to reap the rewards of strength, there were many other cases where the boot was on the other foot and managers were able to make their proposals prevail.

But the government's position was not only that the balance of power had swung too far towards the unions, which was probably what had electoral appeal, but also that their very existence was at odds with an efficient labour market. The same legislative and other actions were appropriate to both positions to a considerable extent, so that differences between them were not of political importance at the beginning of the decade. Even so, there was no doubt that the government believed that firms which did not recognise unions fitted in better with their approach than those which did; IBM was more popular with them than ICI. So the second basis for hostility to unions was that they existed, and it followed that the government wanted employers without unions to resist granting recognition, and managers of new plants to avoid unions or to limit the degree of recognition.

The question of derecognition was fraught with practical difficulties. After all, the government was the direct employer of about 600 000 civil servants, most of whom were in trade unions and who even had their union subscriptions deducted from their pay by their employer under a check-off agreement. But a government which saw trade unions as organisations seeking to develop their position as monopolists in a labour market which needed to be made freer was clearly on the side of any employers who wanted to derecognise unions. The banning of trade unions at GCHQ Cheltenham in 1984, though ostensibly brought about for other reasons, showed that the government was prepared to practise what it preached.

The third source of hostility to trade unions was their place in consensus politics and industrial relations. In the post-war period the consensus approach had been based on the belief that if trade unions were incorporated in the apparatus of government along with employers they would use their power and influence reasonably, meaning with restraint. If they were kept outside the circle of government they were sufficiently powerful to wreck any government's policies, especially any policy of full employment. So not only was there a succession of incomes policies of varying degrees of complexity and bite but the TUC, as the national body speaking to governments on behalf of trade unions, and embodied most strikingly in George Woodcock, assistant general secretary and general secretary of the TUC from 1947 to 1969, had a finger in every aspect of government affairs in the economic and social fields. There were formal bodies like the National Economic Development Council (1963) and the Manpower Services Commission (1974) to which the TUC had, in effect, powers of nomination. Almost every public board from the Bank of England to the BBC had at least one TUC nominee. In the Woodcock era the TUC regarded the list of organisations for which it was invited to submit nominations as proof of its position as the fourth estate of the realm.

Incomes policies in the 1960s and 1970s depended on specially close tripartite arrangements which tended to go deeper and be more far-reaching as time passed. In long and detailed discussions with ministers and employers trade unions were party to schemes which limited the use of their bargaining power. They were represented on the bodies set up to admininster prices and incomes policies. They entered into compacts with governments in which they traded restraint on pay for benefits in other areas of policy. Although it was a common feature of incomes policies that unions became less able to deliver their side of the bargain as the incomes policy progressed, the idea that the economy could be successful only if the unions were closely connected with policy had a powerful hold across the political spectrum.

The Conservative government of 1979 saw trade union involvement with governments in all these ways as giving them an unfair advantage and not as taming them. As part of the change in economic policy trade unions had to be expelled from the places where the decisions of government were discussed. Their area of activity had to be confined to that of bargaining with employers. If they could not negotiate agreed settlements, strikes should be faced with the intention of defeating them. Arbitration should be refused because it always split the difference and gave unions more than they would get if their threats of action were resisted. As things turned out in the early 1980s, the extensive redundancies in manufacturing provided a helpful context for this approach. The unions' bluff was to be called; they should get no more than they could extract by their bargaining power alone.

Fourth, with the emphasis on the role of the individual in economic affairs, the government was sharp to notice any sign that collective action was bought at the cost of undue subjugation of individual members. At the root of this source of the hostility to unions was the belief that sturdy individuals pursuing their own self-interest would not wish to join a union if they could avoid it. Since they plainly did join in large numbers, it must be either because they were misguided in believing it was in their interests to do so, or they were being coerced to some degree, perhaps even compelled, to join in order to keep their jobs. On this view the poll results showing that while there was support from trade unionists for curbing the unions, respondents thought their own unions were doing a good job, could be interpreted as indicating a widespread wish to escape from tyranny combined with a reluctance to admit that it existed.

The government held that trade unionists would come to see the advantages of not being members of trade unions when their unions' power was clipped and when employers treated them as valued individuals and not as undifferentiated parts of a trade union lump. The coercion to which they were subjected could be removed by putting an end to the closed shop, by limiting picketing and the extent of lawful strike action, and by the introduction of ballots which would enable individuals to assert themselves against the small groups of activists who dominated the affairs of unions.

The idea that union leaders had power independently of their members was a central feature of the belief that individual citizens would not readily support what trade unions did. The over-mighty trade union barons with immediate access to ministers, or the jumped-up hospital shop steward who thought he ran the hospital, were important figures in the doctrine that if only the unions were in the hands of their members they would not behave so badly. So 'handing the unions back to their members' became a companion expression to 'get on your bike'.

The fifth reason for hostility to the unions, arising out of the period of the Labour government from 1974 to 1979 and reinforcing the other four, was the legislative protection given in that period to certain union aspirations. The Conservative Party manifesto of 1979 had two themes on the unions – they had fallen into the hands of a minority of extremists, and the Labour government had 'heaped privileges without responsibility' on them. They came together in the key sentence, 'Labour enacted a "militants' charter" of trade union legislation.' These privileges, like the right to have claims for recognition looked at by ACAS, and unilateral arbitration, were the first candidates for legislative repeal.

Lying behind these five sources of hostility to trade unions was the memory of events in the early 1970s which reinforced the desire to cut the unions down to size. The Conservative government returned in 1970 had made the transformation of the role of the unions through legislation a major feature of its policies. Sir Geoffrey Howe, as Solicitor General, was given special charge of the Industrial Relations Bill on the basis of his long association with proposals to reduce the legal privileges of trade unions as set out in the Inns of Court Conservative and Unionist Society's influential pamphlet *A Giant's Strength* (1958). But the Industrial Relations Act of 1971 was for the most part a failure. It gave employers opportunities to take legal proceedings which would check union action but they failed to do so, mainly because they believed they would be more trouble than they were worth. To the extent that it was used, the National Industrial Relations Court, under the present Master of the Rolls, Lord Donaldson, and cases which went before it, led to confrontations or to legal fiascos (see Chapter 2). That Conservative government got it wrong, the new one was determined to get it right.

The Heath government reversed its policy on consensus. Having been elected to set the country free from the chains of corporatism, the government turned round in 1972 and offered the unions closer involvement in the management of the economy than any government ever had. When the unions, in a muddled series of talks, finally rejected what was offered, the government pressed on with a prices and incomes policy of great complexity which involved detailed scrutiny by a Pay Board and a Prices Commission of pay settlements and price increases.

In the end, the Heath government got the worst of both worlds; not only did its prices and incomes policy represent a major change of direction but it led to the 3-day week and to the government seeming to be brought down by a miners' strike at the general election of 1974, which was fought on the question, 'Who governs Britain?' The defeat of the Conservative Party was a low point in its fortunes to which the trade unions and notions of consensus government were believed to have been major contributors. The distinctive flavour of the Thatcher administration derived in part from the reaction of the Conservative Party to the events of 1970 to 1974. The 1979 administration was committed to never repeating what were seen as the mistakes of the earlier period. Phrases like 'there is no alternative' and 'this lady's not for turning' referred directly to the Heath government's volte-face; the resonance of these phrases was not lost on those leading Conservatives who, like the Prime Minister herself, had held office in Edward Heath's government. If the 1979 government were to be true to what it believed in, the prime task was to see off the unions.

The employers

Since the government wished to end consensus and unleash market forces, it was bound to be critical of many employers on some of the same grounds as it was critical of trade unions. A willingness to operate incomes policies and to discuss economic policy jointly with government and the unions was what prevented employers adopting the economic policies for which the Conservative Party stood in 1979.

The new government distanced itself from the CBI, preferring the Institute of Directors, and also from the major firms which for decades had helped to make the consensus work. The government's preferred employers tended to be companies which were independent and not large; the managers it appointed to turn state enterprises round and take them into the private sector were often 'outsiders' like Michael Edwardes, Ian MacGregor and Graham Day, who were untainted by consensus and who wanted to put industrial relations on the sort of new footing of which the government approved. The personnel directors of large companies were particularly suspect because of their close association with the old ways. Small firms with managers who were owners stood especially high in the government's estimation.

The manner of the Labour government's end clinched the Conservative Party's conviction that private employers had to be reformed and that public employers had to be brought firmly under the government's control. The 'Social Contract' was at one and the same time the closest collaboration ever instituted between a Labour government and the trade unions and, after some initial success, in the end the least effective. This was partly because of external forces like the oil price shock of 1973 and the IMF intervention of 1976, but it was also because, when it mattered, neither side could deliver what was most important to the other.

The problem of public sector pay, which was always the most acute problem under all incomes policies, had been hived off very late in the day in March 1979 to the Comparability Commission under Professor Hugh Clegg. The Conservative Party committed itself to honouring Clegg's awards when it came to power and the cost of doing so served to reinforce its hostility to a solution of that type. The public-sector strikes which led to the Commission being set up marked the end of the claim that a Labour government could deal successfully with the unions. The Conservative government adopted a pay policy towards public sector employees which was the opposite of that represented by the Commission. Public-sector pay was to be governed by cash limits, not by comparisons with the private sector. Disputes were to be settled by trials of strength which the government intended to win. There was to be the minimum of arbitration. Only those who repudiated strike action, like the nurses, were allowed to join the select band with review bodies — the armed forces, doctors, dentists, judges, and senior civil servants. Improvements in efficiency and reductions in numbers, whether in their own right or as a means of living within cash limits, were largely separated from pay settlements. There was, therefore, a clear and co-ordinated policy on pay for the public sector, and the government believed that as an employer it was a model which private employers would do well to imitate.

Yet the government's approach made it impossible for ministers to tell private employers within what limits they should settle, although from time to time Chancellors of the Exchequer in particular would warn that high pay settlements endangered competitive ability and threatened jobs. In a freer labour market it was for employers to settle pay without interference because they alone were the best judges of their own interests. Yet, as the government knew, many large employers after the redundancies of the early 1980s were not inclined to resist pay claims as robustly as the government's objectives indicated was desirable. Employers persistently settled for increases which kept earnings moving up faster than prices; between 1979 and 1990 average weekly earnings for the whole economy rose by 192 per cent for men and 220 per cent for women, while prices rose by 130 per cent. In manufacturing the fast increases in productivity – 51 per cent between 1979 and 1990 – covered increases in pay in excess of inflation to a considerable extent, but over the whole economy average productivity was much lower at 20 per cent, well behind the rate of increase of earnings. As a result labour costs per unit of output rose much faster over this period for the whole economy (130 per cent) than for manufacturing (89 per cent). Such increases in unit labour costs, particularly outside manufacturing, marked many private employers as 'wet'. There were few strikes over pay in the private sector, by contrast with the large strikes over pay in the public sector, where the government usually succeeded in defeating the unions.

A change in private sector employees' attitudes to the unions and to collective bargaining was an essential part of the government's strategy. Whatever changes may have occurred, they did not include a willingness to wield the hammer against the unions on pay with the verve which the government itself displayed as an employer.

Conclusion

The government took pride in its convictions; pragmatism, fudging and nudging were what it rejected. But industrial relations is about bargaining between organised groups. The successful achievement of compromises, where the parties at first take their stands some distance apart, is the hallmark of its quality; back-up systems of conciliation and arbitration, often provided by government, are there to make good the failures of negotiators, not to inject new standards. As a method of regulating divergent interests in the workplace, industrial relations were based on a principle – that compromise is superior to conflict – which was the opposite of that adopted by the government – the market rules. The government was bound, therefore, to attempt major reforms in industrial relations.

The trade unions found the environment in which they were operating becoming more unfavourable to them as unemployment rose and as economic policy generally strengthened the hands of employers. But the government was not going to leave the future of the unions in the hands of employers. It set out to make a direct impact on the unions through legislation affecting both their internal government and their bargaining options.

CHAPTER 5

The law and industrial relations

Introduction

Under common law employment rights and duties are based on the individual's contract of employment. This is supposedly a contract between equals and one which is freely entered into. In fact, the individual employee is almost invariably in a weaker position than the employer. Hence the need and right for individuals to be able to organise in free and effective trade unions and the need for legislation in some areas.

Legislation from the 1870s onwards, culminating in the Trade Disputes Act 1906, sought to protect workers and counteract the inequality of bargaining power inherent in the employment relationship. The 1906 Act enhanced the characteristic feature of British industrial relations – 'voluntarism' – by providing trade unions with immunity from liability for civil wrongs (torts) and individuals, including union officials, with immunity from certain torts, namely, conspiracy, inducing a breach of contract of employment, and interference with a person's freedom to use his capital or labour, as long as they were acting 'in contemplation or furtherance of a trade dispute'.

This remained broadly the position until the introduction of the Industrial Relations Act 1971. The repeal of this Act by the Trade Union and Labour Relations Act (TULRA) 1974 and 1976 (as described in Chapter 2), and the new provisions of TULRA, practically restored the position to what it had been under the 1906 Act.

The new Conservative government of 1979, however, had pledged itself to restrict what it considered to be excessive trade union power, and this it proceeded to do in a series of Acts: the Employment Acts 1980 and 1982, the Trade Union Act 1984 and the Employment Acts 1988 and 1990. Also relevant to industrial relations were the Wages Act 1986 and the Sex Discrimination Act 1986 and the Employment Act 1989. The Thatcher governments pursued a step-by-step approach, rather than one large all-embracing Act, such as the 1971 Industrial Relations Act. In this chapter we first outline the main provisions of the legislation and then proceed to consider the use made of the new laws and some of the leading cases.

Employment Act 1980

The provisions of the 1980 Act fell into three main categories:

1. Limitations of trade union immunities in industrial action, so that peaceful picketing was limited to the workers' own place of work (section 16(i)) and secondary action was made unlawful except in certain limited circumstances (s. 17). Thus, s. 13 of TULRA only provided protection for secondary action where the contract concerned was a contract of employment, and where:
   (a) the employer was a supplier or customer providing goods or services under contract to the employer in dispute;
   (b) the principal purpose was directly to prevent the supply of goods or services during the dispute between their employer and the employer in dispute;
   (c) the action was likely to achieve that purpose.
2. A strengthening of individual rights against trade unions by providing legal remedies for unreasonable exclusion or expulsion from a trade union (s. 4 and 5) and extending the grounds on which an individual could refuse to join a union where there was the practice of a union membership agreement (UMA) (closed shop). Thus instead of protection only on account of religious belief was substituted the employee's protection from unfair dismissal:
   (a) 'if he genuinely objects on grounds of conscience or other deeply held personal conviction to being a member of any trade union whatsoever or of a particular trade union'; or
   (b) if he was not a union member before the closed shop came into agreement.
   In addition, for any new closed-shop agreement, there had to be a ballot in which of those entitled to vote 80 per cent voted in favour (s. 7).
3. A weakening of individual employee protection; for example, the burden of proof that he had acted reasonably in unfair dismissal cases was removed from the employer. Above all, in a number of steps, the individual was prevented from bringing a case of unfair dismissal unless he or she had been employed for 2 years.

The Act also removed the limited legal channel whereby unions might be able to obtain recognition by abolishing the recognition procedures contained in the Employment Protection Act (EPA) 1975 (s. 11–16). Furthermore, it abolished Schedule 11 of the EPA 1975 whereby a case could be brought for unilateral arbitration to the Central Arbitration Committee (CAC) that a firm was paying less than the recognised terms and conditions, or if no such terms and conditions existed, less than the general level.

Employment Act 1982

The 1982 Act, first, continued the attack on the closed shop. Thus whereas the 1980 Act required a ballot for any new closed shop (with a majority of 80 per cent of those entitled to vote), the 1982 Act extended the ballot requirement to existing closed shops where there had not been a secret ballot in the preceding 5 years (although in such cases a majority of 85 per cent of those voting was required). If these requirements were not met then an individual could bring a claim for unfair dismissal against the employer and the union with new provisions for punitive damages. In addition, a further exemption was made to membership where a closed shop existed, namely where an employee was bound because of his qualifications to observe a written code of conduct (s. 3–8).

Second, the Act made void any term in a commercial contract which required a person to use only union labour (or only non-union labour) in fulfilling a contract. It also made it unlawful to exclude someone from a tender list or to fail to award a contract to him or to terminate a contract with him on the grounds that anyone employed or likely to be employed on work connected with the contract was or was not a union member (s. 12). Further, the Act made void any term in a commercial contract which required the contractor to recognise, negotiate or consult with trade unions or trade union officials. It also made it unlawful to exclude someone from a tender list or to fail to award him a contract or to terminate a contract with him on the grounds that he did not negotiate or consult with trade unions or trade union officials (s. 13). Finally, the Act removed immunity from trade unions and other persons who organised industrial action to put pressure on an employer to act contrary to the above. It also removed immunity from those who organised or threatened industrial action which interfered with the supply of goods or services on the grounds that:

1. work done in connection with the supply of goods or services had been or was likely to be done by non-union (or union) members;
2. the supplier of the goods or services in question did not recognise or consult with trade unions or trade unions officials (s. 14).

Thirdly, and of even greater significance, was the repeal of s. 14 of TULRA which had restored the immunity of trade unions from actions in tort (s. 15). The effect of this was to restrict their immunities to those given to persons by s. 13 of TULRA. It thus abolished the special and wider immunities for trade unions and brought them into line with those given to other persons, i. e. individuals and union officials. As a result, those who suffered a loss because of unlawful action (for example, action which was not in contemplation or furtherance of a trade dispute; unlawful secondary action; and secondary picketing), would be able to sue a union for damages and seek injunctions (s. 15). While it was true that s. 16 set upper limits to damages awarded against a union, ranging from £10 000 for a union with less than 5000 members to £250 000 for a union with 100 000 or more members, the real threat to a union's power and financial stability (as a number of subsequent cases showed) was not damages but injunctions, which if not obeyed could lead to unlimited fines for contempt of court and to sequestration of all the union's assets. Section 15 also set out the circumstances in which a union would be liable for unlawful action organised by its officials. The union was to be liable for unlawful action which was authorised or endorsed by its executive committee, its president, its general secretary, or any of its officials with authority to call industrial action under the union's own rules. It was also to be held liable for unlawful action authorised or endorsed by its employed officials or any committees to which they reported, except where the authorisation was overruled by the executive committee, president or general secretary, or where the union rules prohibited the official from calling industrial action. As we shall see later, the Courts have interpreted the 'vicarious liability' of unions very strictly indeed.

Finally, the Act substantially narrowed the definition of a trade dispute in s. 29 of TULRA in that:

1. in place of the words 'between employers and workers' it substituted 'between workers and their employer';
2. the words 'or between workers and workers' were omitted;
3. in place of the words 'is connected with' was substituted 'relates wholly or mainly to'.

The first part of s. 29 now reads a 'trade dispute means a dispute between workers and their employer which relates wholly to . . .' instead of 'a dispute between employers and workers, or between workers and workers which is connected with . . .'.

In addition, industrial action relating to matters overseas ceased to be protected unless the persons taking the industrial action in Great Britain were likely to be affected by the outcome of the dispute as regards their own employment (s. 18).

Trade Union Act 1984

The Trade Union Act 1984 had three stated purposes. The first was to provide for secret ballots for election to union executive committees. Thus all voting members of union executive committees had to be directly elected at least once every 5 years. The Act laid down requirements for such elections; for example: entitlement to vote had to be accorded equally to all members (with certain exceptions); voting had to be secret, without interference, and by the marking of a voting paper; and so far as reasonably practical, voting had to be by post, although a union was allowed to hold a workplace, rather than a postal, ballot where it was satisfied that there were no reasonable grounds for believing that a workplace ballot would not meet the necessary requirements. In addition, a duty was placed on unions to compile and maintain a register of names and addresses of its members. Finally, a member of a union could apply to the Certification Officer or the High Court for a declaration that the union had failed to comply with the necessary provisions for a ballot and for an enforcement order.

The second purpose was to provide for a secret ballot before a union organised industrial action. Section 10 removed immunity from legal action (as provided in s. 13 of TULRA) where unions did not hold a ballot before authorising or endorsing a call for a strike or any other form of industrial action which broke or interfered with the contracts of employment of those taking part in it. It also made it a condition of immunity that a majority of those voting had voted in favour of the action; that the ballot was held no more than 4 weeks before the industrial action began; and that the ballot satisfied certain requirements, as laid down in s. 11 of the Act. These requirements were that entitlement to vote had to be given to those, and only those, whom it was reasonable for the union to believe would be called upon to take or continue to take strike or other industrial action. Immunity would be lost if any member was called on to strike after being denied entitlement to vote. The question on the ballot papers had to invite a 'yes' or 'no' answer and specify whether the action involved a strike or other type of industrial action involving the voter in a breach of his contract of employment. So far as was reasonably practical, every person entitled to vote had:

1. to be supplied with a ballot paper or have one made available to him during his working hours (or immediately before or after his working hours) either at his place of work or at a place more convenient to him;
2. to be given a convenient opportunity to vote by post *or* an opportunity to vote during his working hours (or immediately before or after his working hours) at his workplace or at a place more convenient to him *or* a choice between these two methods of voting. Finally, the detailed results of the ballot had to be made known to those entitled to vote.

The third purpose was to provide secret ballots for union political funds. Trade unions which had in the past balloted their members under the Trade Union Act 1913 to enable them to have political funds in order to spend money on 'political objects' had to ballot their members at least every 10 years if they wished to continue to do so (s. 10). Any of these trade unions which had not held a ballot in the nine years before 31 March 1985 had to do so before 31 March 1986. Further, the Act updated the provisions of the 1913 Act and required the approval of the Certification Officer for political fund ballot rules. In particular, it provided that the Certification Officer had to satisfy himself that the rules provided for ballots either by post or at the workplace; ballots had to be secret; conducted by the marking of a voting paper; and there had to be equal entitlement to vote. It was also made clear that the Certification Officer had to approve the ballot rules before each ballot (s. 13). The Act also contained an updated definition of 'political objects' on which trade unions were allowed to spend money only if they had authority from their members to do so. Most of these related to the financing of a political party, but s. 17(f) also stated:

> on the production, publication or distribution of any literature, document, film, sound recording or advertisement, the main purpose of which is to persuade people to vote for a political party or candidate or to persuade them not to vote for a political party or candidate.

This particular provision so alarmed a number of unions, particularly in the public sector, for example NALGO, that although hitherto they had not had political funds, they balloted their members (successfully) to establish such funds (Leopold, 1988)

Finally, the Act placed a duty on employers, who had 'check-off' arrangements for deducting trade union subscriptions from their employees' pay, to vary the level of check-off deductions by the amount of the political levy if they were informed by a trade union member in writing that he was exempt from paying the levy or had put in a request to be exempt to his union.

Wages Act 1986

This Act was in three parts: the first, entitled 'Protection of Workers in Relation to the Payment of Wages', ss. 1–11, repealed the Truck Acts and associated legislation, thereby leaving the method of wage payment to the employer or if unions were recognised, to negotiations. As a result, manual workers no longer had a statutory right to insist on being paid in cash, although existing rights under their employment contracts were not affected. In addition, certain protection was given against unlawful deductions from wages, for example workers in retail distribution were given special protection against deductions from wages because of cash or stock shortages, these being limited to 10 per cent of the employee's pay.

Part II, ss. 12–16, related to Wages Councils, the main provisions being, first, that Wages Council Orders no longer applied to workers under 21 years of age: second, Wages Councils were limited to setting one basic hourly rate of pay and one premium rate: third, Councils must consider the impact on jobs of the minimum rate they set: and fourth, a simplified procedure for abolishing or changing the scope of Wages Councils was introduced, namely the power was given to the Secretary of State, who was required only 'to consult such persons or organisations as he considers appropriate'. Finally, in Part III, Redundancy Rebates, ss. 27–29, employers with 10 or more employees were no longer to get rebates (of 35 per cent) from government for any redundancy payments they had to make.

Sex Discrimination Act 1986

In s. 1 the Act removed the exemption for small firms with five or fewer employees, which had been given in the Sex Discrimination Act 1975, from complying with the latter's employment provisions: that is to say, small firms must not discriminate against employees or prospective employees on grounds of their sex or because they were married, in recruitment, treatment during their employment or in dismissing them. Section 2 brought within the scope of the 1975 Act any provision made by an employer in relation to retirement, dismissal, demotion, promotion, transfer or training. Discriminatory retirement ages in state authorities were already unlawful under European law, which was directly effective in the UK. Private employers were no longer able to have policies which set different compulsory retirement ages for men and women in comparable positions, nor were they able to refuse promotion or training. Section 2 also amended the Equal Pay Act 1970 in a similar way so that such discriminatory terms in a contract of employment were contrary to the Act. Finally, s. 3 amended the unfair dismissal provisions of the Employment Protection (Consolidation) Act 1978 to ensure that men and women in the same position had the right to complain to an industrial tribunal of unfair dismissal up to the same age. Where the employment had no non-discriminatory normal retirement age, employees whether men or women could complain up to the age of 65.

Employment Act 1988

This Act contained a number of miscellaneous provisions, the most important of which were as follows:

1. A member of a union who claimed that the union had, without the support of a ballot, taken industrial action, could apply to the High Court for an order (s. 1). Under the Trade Union Act 1984 it was effectively employers only who had been given the right to apply for an injunction. A union member, or ex-member, was also entitled to take the union to court on an issue, despite any provision in the union rules preventing such action, for example, by saying that the union's decision or arbitration was final (s. 2).
2. An individual had the right not to be unjustifiably disciplined by his union for failure to take part in industrial action, even where there had been a majority in favour in a secret ballot. He was also given the right not to be disciplined for encouraging others to do the same; for consulting the Trade Union Commissioner or the Certification Officer; or for asserting that the union or any official was contravening union rules on the law (s. 3).
3. It was made unlawful for the property of a trade union to be applied to indemnify any individual for any penalty imposed on him for any relevant offence or for contempt of court. An individual member could bring an action for the union to recover any such payment if the union itself failed to do so (s. 8). Also, any union member could bring an action where the trustees proposed to use the union's property unlawfully. The Court could order the trustees to recover any such property, could dismiss the trustees and could appoint a receiver (s. 9).
4. Protection from actions in tort was removed in respect of industrial action to enforce membership of a UMA (s. 10):
5. With regard to ballots, s. 1 of the Trade Union Act 1984 was amended so that:
   (a) non-voting members of union executive committees had to be elected;
   (b) presidents and general secretaries had to be elected (s. 12).
   In addition, ballots for political funds had to be postal (amending the 1913 Act), and ballots for the election of certain officials had to be postal (deleting s. 3. of the Trade Union Act 1984) (s. 14). Also, for elections and political fund ballots, there had to be appointed an independent scrutineer, who would be responsible for supervising the production and distribution of voting papers, be the person to whom ballot papers were returned and be responsible for reporting the result (s. 15). Any member was given the right to complain, with regard to political ballots, to the Certification Officer or the Court, that the necessary requirements had not been met (s. 16).

6. With regard to ballots on industrial action, certain conditions were specified which had to be satisfied if a union intended to organise industrial action as a result of an aggregated ballot covering different places of work. These conditions were that the union must reasonably believe that each union member, whose votes were to be aggregated, had a factor, relating to his terms and conditions of employment, or occupational description, in common with one or more of the other members entitled to vote. This factor must not be the one which those employed by the same employer had in common as a consequence of working at the same place. Where these conditions were not satisfied, a union had to conduct separate ballots for each place of work (s. 17).
7. A Commissioner for the Rights of Trade Union Members was established, with power to support individual union members (for example, by giving advice and by paying costs) in complaints against their union.

A number of the above provisions were opposed at the consultative stage by leading employer and professional organisations, for example, the CBI and the Institute of Personnel Management, particularly the provision preventing unions taking disciplinary action against members who failed to take part in industrial action, after a democratically conducted ballot. Their fear was that ballots would be brought into disrepute and also that social action by workmates against the transgressing member could be more disruptive than official union discipline. Some also queried the necessity for the establishment of a Trade Union Commissioner, particularly bearing in mind other areas of national life, where it could be argued that the need of the individual for help in securing his rights was far greater and far more important, for example, in the field of social security entitlements. Indeed, since the proposals for this Act were produced shortly before the 1987 general election, it is hard to believe that their purpose was other than to provide a further stick with which to beat the unions during the campaign, on the assumption that many voters, including trade union members, approved.

Employment Act 1989

The stated purposes of the Act were, first, to remove many restrictions on the employment of women and young people; second, to help employers create jobs and become more competitive by easing the burden of regulation on them; third, to take forward the government's training strategy for the 1990s.

With regard to the first objective, most legislation that still discriminated between women and men in employment and training matters was repealed or amended to remove the discrimination. This included the ban on women working underground in mines and some restrictions on their working with machinery in factories. Protection was retained however in some special cases such as work which through exposure to radiation or lead might endanger the health of an unborn child. Restrictions on the hours of young people were removed, including the prohibition of night work. Certain other restrictions on young people's employment were also removed, for example, on street trading. The Act did not remove restrictions on working with dangerous machinery, nor did it remove any restrictions on the employment of children under school-leaving age.

With regard to the second objective, burdens on employers were reduced by a number of deregulatory amendments to the Employment Protection (Consolidation) Act 1978. Thus, under s. 13, employers with fewer than 20 employees were exempted from the requirements to provide employees with a separate note of particulars of disciplinary rules which applied to them. Section 14 amended s. 27 of the 1978 Act to limit the duties in respect of which an employer was required to allow officials of a recognised trade union time off with pay to carry out duties which were concerned with matters in respect of which the employer recognised the union, or with the performance of functions for which the union was not recognised but which the employer had agreed the union might perform. It similarly limited the duty to allow such officials to take time off with pay to undertake training which was relevant to those duties. Section 15 amended s. 53 of the 1978 Act to increase from 6 months to 2 years the qualifying period of continuous employment after which employees were entitled to be given, on request, a written statement of the reasons for their dismissal.

With regard to the third objective, the Act dissolved the Training Commission and transferred its property rights and liabilities to the Secretary of State for Employment. Sections 23–25 amended the Industrial Training Act in order to facilitate the transition of the remaining Industrial Training Boards (ITBs) from a statutory to a non-statutory status. The amendments also made possible the creation of employer-led statutory bodies. In addition, the amendments meant that in future the Secretary of State needed to consult only employers' organisations before making an order affecting the operation or existence of an ITB, and that the Secretary of State needed to consult only employer representatives before appointments were made to an ITB. A majority of the members of an ITB had to be employer representatives.

There were a number of other provisions which did not fall under the three stated purposes of the Act but were nevertheless of considerable significance. One such was s. 16 which removed the difference whereby men might receive statutory redundancy payments up to age 65 and women up to only age 60. Where there was a 'normal retiring age' for the job in question which was below 65 and was non-discriminatory, the entitlement of both sexes was to be restricted to that age. In all other cases the women's entitlement was extended to the age of 65, in line with that of men. This provision was made necessary by the EEC's Directive on Equal Treatment (No. 76/207) and Article 119 of the Treaty of Rome. A second provision, contained in s. 17, abolished the scheme entitling employers with less than 10 employees to rebates on their statutory redundancy payments. Rebates to all other employers had been abolished in 1986. A third provision, contained in s. 20, provided for regulations to be made to give an industrial tribunal chairman sitting alone, or a full tribunal, discretion at the pre-hearing stage to require a deposit of up to £150 as a condition of proceeding further, if it was considered that his or her case had no reasonable prospect of success, or that pursuit of it would be frivolous, vexatious or otherwise unreasonable.

Employment Act 1990

The Act had three main objectives – the abolition of the pre-entry closed shop, the removal of immunity from virtually all forms of secondary action and the regulation of unofficial industrial action. In addition, it increased the powers of the Commissioner for the Rights of Trade Union Members, made minor amendments to the rules for industrial action ballots, and provided for the revision or revocation of Codes of Practice.

With regard to closed shops, the Employment Act 1988 had made post-entry closed shops wholly unenforceable, removed immunity from any industrial action taken to impose or enforce a closed shop and made dismissal or discrimination of an employee who refused to belong to a union automatically unfair. The 1990 Act made it unlawful to refuse employment to a person because he was or was not a member of a trade union or because he would not agree to become a member or because he ceased to be a member (s. 1).

With regard to the second objective, the right to take secondary action had been severely limited by the 1980 Act. Under the 1990 Act it was virtually outlawed. Indeed, outlawed secondary action now included action organised among those doing work or performing services under any contract, including contracts other than contracts of employment.

The third objective related to union liability for unofficial action. The provisions of the Act (ss. 6 and 7) substantially extended the potential liability of unions and imposed stringent conditions over the steps that had to be taken if a union was to repudiate industrial action. This was done by largely rewriting s. 15 of the 1982 Act, which first made trade unions themselves liable in actions in tort arising out of industrial action not covered by immunity.

A union was now responsible (and liable) for the organisation of industrial action by any of its officials, including shop stewards, any of its committees or any group whose purposes included organising or co-ordinating industrial action and to which any of its officials belonged. The section also modified and extended the requirements which had to be satisfied if a union was to avoid liability. Thus the action had to be repudiated as soon as was reasonably practical after coming to the knowledge of the executive committee or the president or general secretary. Written notice of the repudiation had to be given to the committee or official in question and the union had to do its best to give written notice to every member who had taken (or might take) industrial action and to every employer of any such member. The written notice of repudiation had to contain the following statement:

> Your union has repudiated the call (or calls) for industrial action to which this notice relates, and will give no support to unofficial action taken in response to it (or them). If you are dismissed while taking unofficial action, you will have no right to complain of unfair dismissal.

The union had also to respond to any requests for confirmation of the union's repudiation made within three months by a party to a commercial contract which had been or might be interfered with by the industrial action.

Section 9 permitted an employer to dismiss selectively employees who took part in unofficial action, and such employees had no right to complain to an industrial tribunal of unfair dismissal. Where an action became unofficial because of union repudiation, a full working day was allowed following the day of repudiation before the union's members taking unofficial action became liable to selective dismissal. Industrial action because of such selective dismissal was deprived of immunity.

Finally, the Act extended the power of the Commissioner to cover assistance to union members in proceedings arising out of an alleged breach or threatened breach of the union's rules, relating for example to the appointment or election of a person to, or the removal of a person from, any office, disciplinary proceedings by the union, the authorising or endorsing of industrial action, the balloting of members and the application of the union's funds or property (s. 10).

The use of law

The conventional wisdom, based to a large extent on the débâcle of the 1971 Act (Weekes *et al.*, 1975), was that legal constraints imposed on trade unions would not succeed. This proved not to be the case in the 1980s. On the contrary, the use of law proved highly successful in restraining trade union power and in contributing to the defeat of unions in a number of major disputes. Evans (1987) recorded 77 cases of injunctions actually sought between May 1984 and April 1987 of which 11 related to picketing, 16 to secondary action and 47 to pre-strike ballots. In 65 of these cases the plaintiff was the direct employer (or ex-employer) of the defendants or their union. For the majority of employers their single aim in seeking the injunction was to lift the industrial action. Injunctions were secured in 73 cases and refused in 4. In only 13 cases were the defendants members, workplace representatives or local full-time officials compared with 67 in which the unions were defendants. In 31 cases the industrial action complained of was lifted immediately or otherwise quickly rendered ineffective, for instance by the withdrawal of support by the union or other workers. In only 3 cases were damages sought against unions, so it remains clear that in the overwhelming majority of cases employers were only really interested in an immediate injunction to stop industrial action. The use of injunctions seemed to be most marked in three sectors – printing, public services and shipping.

The effects of the law are shown through cases in the courts on three main areas – secondary action, picketing, and balloting before the taking of industrial action – as well as a number of other miscellaneous areas.

Secondary action

It will be recalled that secondary action was made unlawful by the Employment Act 1980, with only certain very limited exceptions. Under the Employment Act 1990 even these exceptions were made unlawful. Among the leading cases dealing with this aspect of the law were the following.

Merkur Island Shipping Corporation v. *Laughton* (1983) arose where the International Transport Workers' Federation (ITWF) had called on tugmen and lockmen to refuse to provide services for a Liberian-registered ship with a Filipino crew which had docked at Tilbury. This call for action followed a complaint by a crew member of low wages, which the union had taken up and which the employer had refused to remedy. The shipowner applied for an injunction on the grounds of unlawful secondary action. The House of Lords held that it was indeed unlawful secondary action. The decision turned on whether or not there was an existing contract for services between the shipowner, who was the employer of the crew, and the port authorities. It was held that there was not, because the contract for services was with the charterers of the ship and not the owner.

Another leading case was *Dimbleby* v. *NUJ* (1984), where Dimbleby had transferred the printing of his newspapers, after a dispute with the NGA and the dismissal of his NGA workers, to the non-union firm of T. Bailey Forman

(TBF). Dimbleby threatened to dismiss journalists who refused to co-operate with the transfer. The NUJ then called a strike of its journalists. The NUJ had been in dispute with TBF since the 1978 newspaper strike when TBF had dismissed its 25 NUJ journalists and gone non-union. On the application of Dimbleby, the High Court issued an injunction against the strike, which was upheld by the Court of Appeal and the House of Lords The Court ruled that although the NUJ had a legitimate dispute with TBF, TBF did not print its own papers. This was done by a separate company — TBF Printers — and although the two companies had the same directors, the same address and the same telephone number, they were, in the eyes of the law, separate companies. The NUJ's action was therefore held to be unlawful secondary action because its dispute was with TBF and not with TBF Printers.

The *Messenger Newspapers* dispute (1984) was a *cause célèbre* in the early 1980s in that it was portrayed by most of the media as the 'small' man fighting for freedom against a powerful trade union; there were many scenes of violence on the picket lines, and it was the first case of sequestration of a union's assets under the Conservative's overall legislative framework. From the late 1970s Eddie Shah's Messenger Group published a range of free newspapers in the Manchester area. The actual dispute revolved around three printing and type-setting companies set up by Shah. The first was Fineword Ltd. , Stockport, established in 1979. Shah hired six NGA members, agreed that there should be a closed shop and negotiated an agreement on pay and hours with the NGA. The second was a type-setting plant at Bury which was established in 1982. A closed shop was agreed, but there was a failure to reach agreement on pay and hours, whereupon Shah cancelled the closed-shop agreement and engaged non-union labour. The third was a printing plant at Warrington which started to recruit labour while negotiations on the closed shop were still going on at Bury.

The NGA was concerned at the recruitment of non-union labour at Bury and Warrington. However, employees at these two plants voted against NGA representation. The use of non-union labour was a breach of the industry's closed shop agreement and also counter to the union's rule which prohibited members handling work from non-unionists. The six NGA members at the Stockport Plant consequently took strike action and the company dismissed them. The NGA then obtained NUJ support, with the NUJ instructing its members at Stockport not to supply copy. The High Court ordered the NUJ to instruct its members to supply copy: the NUJ refused, but the journalists concerned supplied the copy anyway. The Court also issued injunctions to stop the NGA from exerting pressure on advertisers and to prevent NGA members from boycotting origination work to the company on the grounds that these were both unlawful secondary actions. Another injunction was issued to stop secondary picketing at Bury and Warrington.

When the NGA intensified picketing at Warrington, the company sought sequestration of the NGA's assets for contempt of court. The Court at that stage turned down the request for sequestration but fined the NGA £50 000. The union refused to pay, but it then appeared that an agreement had been reached on union membership. However, the company refused to take back the six strikers and picketing was intensified. The Court then imposed a further fine of £100 000 and ordered the sequestration of the NGA's assets. In response to sequestration there was 'spontaneous' industrial action by NGA members on national newspapers, which stopped their publication for one day. Six of the national newspapers issued dismissal notices and all of them took out writs for damages, although none of these writs was ever followed up.

Meanwhile, mass picketing continued and the company took further action for contempt, but the case was adjourned when the NGA agreed to lift its picketing to enable talks to take place. However, the talks broke down, picketing resumed, and there was a further fine on the NGA of £525 000. Thereupon, the NGA called on all its members to strike for 24 hours and also sought support from the TUC. A General Council sub-comittee decided in favour of support for the NGA in the form of a 24-hour newspaper strike, but Len Murray, the then TUC general secretary, cancelled the decision by ruling that the sub-committee had no power to take such a decision. At a full meeting of the General Council the general secretary's action was upheld and TUC support for the NGA in what was clearly unlawful action was refused. This was a dramatic moment and a key turning point in the TUC's attitude towards the new laws.

Eventually, the NGA called off its action and decided to purge its contempt. The dismissed 'Stockport Six' were found employment elsewhere in the industry. Shah had successfully challenged the NGA's power and the closed shop with the help of the law.

Another major case concerned Rupert Murdoch and his News International Company, which had built a printing plant at Wapping, equipped with the latest technology, in order, allegedly, to produce a new evening paper — *The Post* — for which a separate company had been established — The London Post (Printers) Ltd. Negotiations with the print unions did not result in an agreement, despite unprecedented concessions by the unions including unilateral binding arbitration and the acceptance of the direct input of editorial and classified material. With the failure of negotiations, the NGA and SOGAT called strikes after ballots of their membership at the *Sun*, *The Times*, *The Sunday Times* and the *News of the World* had produced overwhelming majorities for such action. The grievance was a claim for security of employment and indexed wages and the strike commenced in January 1986. The claim had been made in an attempt to avoid a charge of secondary action which might have arisen if the strike had been about the London Post. The company then announced that it would print the papers at Wapping, where a new labour force had been engaged, mainly from outside London. Journalists were ordered to report for work at Wapping 'or face instant dismissal: if they did report, there were to be given a bonus of £2000 and free private medical insurance. The

NUJ National Executive Committee instructed its members at News International not to co-operate with any publications from Wapping and to continue to work only at their normal place of work. However, the NUJ chapels disregarded these instructions and voted to work at Wapping — although in the case of the *Sunday Times* chapel the margin was very small indeed. The company was thus able to produce its papers at Wapping. It had also arranged a new system of distribution — through a transport company, TNT, which it half-owned — so as to bypass as far as possible the traditional distribution channels, which were organised by SOGAT.

SOGAT and the NGA picketed Wapping and SOGAT called on its distribution workers not to handle News International titles. In February 1986 News International obtained an injunction which prohibited SOGAT from interfering with the distribution of its papers (*News Group Newspapers* v. *SOGAT* 1986). The company also immediately dismissed all its striking print workers — over 5000 people — on the grounds that they were in breach of their contract of employment. SOGAT refused to obey the injunction and were first fined £25 000 for contempt of court and soon afterwards had all their assets sequestered. The injunction had been based on the grounds that SOGAT had not held a ballot of its members in wholesale distribution. However, it might equally have been on the grounds of unlawful secondary action. News International published its papers through two separate companies — Times Newspapers (TN) and News Group (NG), while separate companies had been set up for distribution (NID), for supplies (NIS) and for advertising (NIA). Newspaper wholesalers' contracts were with NID, but the primary dispute was with TN and NG, so that the union's action against the wholesalers could not be lawful secondary action under the 1980 Act.

Other legal actions at this time by Murdoch companies included a court order against the NGA to stop their members at Typematters and Northampton Mercury Company boycotting material so as to prevent the publication of the *Times Literary Supplement* and the *Times Educational Supplement*; an injunction to stop SOGAT and the NGA from interfering with Northern editions of the News of the World which was printed under contract by Express Newspapers in Manchester; and an injunction against the Union of Communication Workers (UCW) on the grounds of unlawful secondary action by refusing to deliver *Sun* newspaper bingo cards.

The law against secondary action had played a major part in Murdoch's defeat of the print unions but also of great importance was the common law which enables employers to dismiss strikers for breach of their contracts of employment.

Yet another much publicised dispute was that between P&O and the National Union of Seamen (NUS). Towards the end of 1987, P&O European Ferries had proposed drastic reductions in manpower and changes in working practices in order to cut costs to meet the forthcoming challenge of the Channel Tunnel. At this time there was an NUS strike at the Isle of Man Steam

Packet Ferry Company (in which P&O had a 40 per cent stake) over proposed redundancies and changed working practices. Towards the end of January the Isle of Man Steam Packet Ferry Company dismissed the 160 striking NUS members. The NUS then called a national one-day strike over the sackings. P&O and Sealink, whose employees were also involved in the strike call, immediately obtained an injunction on grounds of unlawful secondary action. The NUS defied the court order and the strike went ahead. P&O and Sealink then sought sequestration of NUS assets. The court refused sequestration but fined the NUS £7500. Meanwhile the Isle of Man dispute was settled with the help of ACAS conciliation, but the P&O seamen at Dover voted to continue their strike against P&O's cost-cutting proposals. Subsequent talks, with the help of ACAS, failed to end the dispute, with P&O insisting that their proposals must be implemented within 1 year, whereas the NUS, now prepared to accept the changes, wanted them spread over 3 years. P&O then issued dismissal notices to the Dover seamen and the NUS countered that it would hold a national strike ballot. P&O then got from the court an unprecedented suspended order that the NUS should not hold a strike ballot because an affirmative vote would have led to unlawful secondary action. The NUS obeyed the order, calling off the ballot, and talks resumed only to break down again. The company then announced it would seek to resume services. It wrote individually to the striking seamen offering them jobs on the company's new terms and conditions and also advertised in the national press for workers. It also withdrew recognition from the NUS. At the beginning of May, two ships sailed and the NUS called for national industrial action throughout the ferry sector. A court hearing followed immediately and the NUS was fined £150 000 and had all its assets sequestered. Soon afterwards the NUS ordered the end of all secondary action and the strike eventually petered out.

Picketing

As a result of the Employment Act 1980 lawful picketing was limited to the workers' own place of work (s. 16(i)). In addition, the government produced a Code of Practice on Picketing which came into effect in December 1980. The Code, *inter alia*, stated that in general the number of pickets should not exceed six at any entrance to a workplace. It should be recalled that irrespective of the legal changes of the 1980s, the law has always required that picketing should be peaceful and that its purpose was peacefully to obtain or communicate information or to persuade a person not to work. Breaches of the law may give rise to civil liability, but there may also be breaches of criminal law, for example, by threatening violence, by being abusive, by obstructing the highway or by obstructing a police officer in the execution of his duty. The police indeed have very wide powers of discretion.

Turning to some of the leading cases, in the *Messenger Newspapers* dispute (1984) – an account of which has already been given – the company obtained injunctions to prevent the NGA's secondary picketing at its Bury and Warrington plants: not only was there secondary picketing, but there was 'mass' picketing. The NGA continued its picketing despite the court order and after being fined for contempt of court, its funds were finally sequestered.

At the beginning of the miners' strike in March 1984, the then National Coal Board was granted an injunction against the Yorkshire Area of the NUM to prevent secondary picketing of the still working Nottinghamshire pits, but the injunction was never enforced. According to Adeney and Lloyd (1986), the Secretary of State for Energy, Peter Walker, with the support of his colleagues, decided to stop the NCB's action because it would generate sympathy for the miners. Also, it might be noted that, during the year-long dispute, like the NCB, neither British Rail nor British Steel, both of whom were subject to secondary picketing, took legal action. However, cases on secondary picketing did occur, for example *Read Transport* v. *NUM South Wales Area (1985)*, where Reads, independent road hauliers, with contracts to transport coke from Port Talbot Steelworks to various destinations around the country, obtained an injunction to prevent the NUM picketing the works. Picketing continued and the NUM South Wales Area was fined £50 000 for contempt of court, and their funds were subsequently sequestered. In *Thomas* v. *NUM South Wales Area* (1985), the action was brought by working miners who claimed that they had been subjected to intimidation and abuse by pickets which interfered with their 'right to work'. The court found that there had been regular abuse and intimidation and therefore that a tort had been committed, namely interference with the right to use the highway: it also pointed out that the pickets had been highly intimidating and that intimidation itself could amount to a tort. In granting the injunction the Court also ruled, in line with the Code of Practice, that the number of pickets should be limited to six. In effect the Court seemed to be saying that mass picketing, by its very nature, was intimidatory, as was the shouting of abuse. The actual circumstances in this case were that six official pickets had been agreed with the police and allowed to stand at the colliery gates, but there were also mass demonstrators who were kept by the police some distance from the gates. This case also raised the issue of 'vicarious liability'. Based on the ruling in *Heatons* v. *TGWU* (1972), the union was found liable for acts of its officials unless actively disowned.

However, in the miners' strike the main method used to counter picketing was the criminal law. It was calculated that nearly 10 000 were arrested in England and Wales and nearly 1500 in Scotland, of whom 81 per cent and 67 per cent respectively were charged. Over 4000 were charged with breaking the peace, nearly 1700 were charged with obstructing the police, 1000 for criminal damage and over 600 for obstructing the highway. In many of these cases, a common condition of bail was that the miners should not return to the picket line. Such a condition was upheld in *R. v. Mansfield Justices ex parte Sharkey* (1985). There was also the celebrated case *Moss v. McLachan* (1985) where cars containing Kent miners were stopped at the Dartford Tunnel and turned back by the police on the grounds that they were travelling north to picket and that they might cause a breach of the peace. The Court upheld the police action on the grounds that it was reasonable to suspect a future breach of the peace.

In the Wapping dispute, News Group Newspapers in July 1986 sought injunctions to restrain picketing and demonstrations at Wapping. The company alleged that the torts of nuisance, intimidation, harassment and interference with the performance of commercial contracts had been committed. The court held that the events at Wapping had resulted in an unreasonable obstruction of the highway affecting the public at large. It went on to say that in order to bring a civil action for public nuisance, there was a need to show special damage and this was the case with regard to some of the plaintiffs, for example the cost of busing workers. The court also held there was private nuisance in that the owners of land adjoining the Wapping printworks had suffered damage. Further, the Court held that there had been intimidation, that is to say violence or threats of violence. On the alleged tort of harassment, the plaintiffs relied on *Thomas v. NUM*, where the High Court had ruled that working miners had a right to go to work without harassment and that they could bring an action against persons who interfered with that right. The unions argued that this was not a well-established tort but a 'new' one which did not come within any of the accepted torts. The judge said that he was inclined to agree but as he had already ruled on nuisance and intimidation it was unnecessary to take a final view on harassment. On the allegation of interference with commercial contracts by unlawful means, the judge thought it likely that this had occurred in the case of the contract between News Group International (NGI) and TNT Distributors, the unlawful means being intimidation and nuisance through the twice weekly marches that were being carried out. The Court granted injunctions, first, to prevent the defendants from organising pickets and demonstrations in the vicinity of the Wapping premises, apart from six pickets whose purpose was peacefully to obtain and communicate information, and to require any marches or rallies to be organised so as not to interfere with the plaintiff's rights; second, to limit the pickets at Gray's Inn Road and Bouverie Street to six and to require them not to act in an abusive, insulting, threatening or violent manner. On the question of whether the pickets had immunity it was pointed out, first, that the 'Golden Formula' which provided immunity for actions 'in contemplation or furtherance of a trade dispute' covered only 'economic' torts and not other torts such as nuisance and intimidation. In addition, picketing had to be peaceful and it had to be at the workers' place of work — which was Gray's Inn Road or Bouverie Street, not Wapping. Second, on the question of whether the unions were liable for the actions of the pickets it was held that they were, despite the fact that they had condemned violence and instructed that the picketing should be peaceful, because they had made no attempt to control or discipline those responsible.

Balloting

It will be recalled that the Trade Union Act 1984 required unions to provide for secret individual ballots to be held every 5 years for the election of voting members of executive committees, including general secretaries and presidents; for secret individual ballots every 10 years for union political funds; and for secret individual ballots before industrial action was taken. The first ballot requirement has not on the whole caused unions any major problems. Virtually all unions already elected their executive committees and, many of their top officials, although in the latter instance the election was often until retirement age was reached, for example the TGWU and the NUM. In only two instances — NATFHE and the NUJ — has the existing general secretary been defeated in a re-election ballot. Similarly, the requirement for a ballot on political funds did not, contrary to expectations, cause unions a major problem. Every union with a political fund secured a majority for the continuation of that fund and indeed a number of unions who did not have a political fund secured majorities to establish such a fund, for example CPSA.

Far more significant has been the requirement to hold a ballot before taking industrial action. Some employers have used this provision to prevent industrial action where a ballot had not been taken, while towards the end of the decade it was becoming evident that unions were turning this provision to their advantage. A ballot in favour of industrial action was a powerful bargaining tool for unions to obtain an improvement in the employer's last offer: it also provided a legitimacy to the proposed industrial action which did not necessarily exist when action was proposed without a secret ballot of the membership (see Chapter 11). Largely for these reasons the government issued a Code of Practice on balloting in 1991.

Among the early cases on balloting was *Austin Rover* v. *TGWU* (1984). In this case a strike had been called by the union side of the Joint Negotiating Committee, after a show of hands, and it was officially endorsed by the TGWU. The company obtained injunctions on the grounds that a secret ballot had not been held. The other unions officially disowned the strike and it collapsed after 2 weeks. The company nevertheless pursued its contempt action and the TGWU was fined £200 000. In *Solihull Council* v. *NUT* (1985), the council got an order against the NUT because disruptive action (no cover for absentee teachers and no supervision of school meals) had been taken without a ballot. The NUT denied that this was industrial action: rather it was the withdrawal of 'goodwill'. The NUT lost and obeyed the court order, temporarily stopping the action, until a ballot was held. Solihull Council also got an injunction against the NAS/UWT to prevent a proposed half-day strike on the grounds that there had been no ballot. The NAS/UWT also obeyed the order, calling off the strike until it arranged a ballot. In *Express and Star* v. *NGA* (1985) there was a dispute over the introduction of new technology and the Company obtained an injunction against the NGA as a secret ballot had not been held. The NGA then held a ballot which overwhelmingly supported the action.

More recent cases have included *British Rail* v. *NUR* (1989), where British Rail during the course of a dispute with the NUR sought an injunction to prevent a 24-hour strike on the grounds that 32 railwaymen had complained that they had not received ballot papers. Both the High Court and the Court of Appeal rejected the application on the grounds that the NUR had complied with the balloting law requirements in that it had done all that was 'reasonably practicable' to see that those entitled to vote had been given the opportunity to do so. In the same year there was *London Underground* v. *NUR* (1989) where during a similar dispute London Underground went to Court on a complaint concerning the wording of the ballot paper, which had listed four issues. The judge said that he was not satisfied that the NUR could show that all four issues were the subject of the trade dispute and he therefore issued an injunction. The NUR thereupon held a new ballot with different wording. Also in 1989 there was a major dispute in the docks following the government's decision to terminate the National Dock Labour scheme. The TGWU sought a national agreement with the port employers which would provide some of the protection hitherto provided by the Scheme. The employers refused to negotiate nationally, stating that they were only prepared to negotiate locally. The union then held a strike ballot which produced a three-to-one majority in favour of a strike. The employers however sought an injunction (*Associated British Ports and others* v. *TGWU* 1989) alleging that the ballot paper was inadequately worded. It was headed 'Trade Dispute with your employer (including all matters arising out of and in consequence of that dispute)'. It then asked the question: 'Are you prepared to strike?' The High Court refused the employer's application, but the Court of Appeal granted an injunction. On appeal, the employers had introduced a new argument, namely, that the Dock Labour Scheme imposed a statutory duty on dock workers to work and a strike would therefore be unlawful. The Court of Appeal held that this argument deserved further legal consideration at a full hearing. On the balance of advantage, it further held that the High Court judge had understated the damaging effect a dock strike might have on the public interest and it therefore granted an injunction. On appeal by the union, the House of Lords overturned the Court of Appeal and lifted the injunction. However, by then more than 4 weeks had elapsed since the original ballot and to remain within the law the union had to call a second ballot. The union thus won the case but the employers had succeeded in delaying the strike. The employers' potential exploitation of such delays has now been limited by the Employment Act 1990.

Other legal matters

Among other important legal cases during the 1980s were a series of cases brought by working miners against the NUM and certain areas of the NUM, for example *Taylor* v. *NUM Derbyshire Area* (1985) and *Taylor and Foulstone* v. *NUM Yorkshire Area* (1984). These were not, however, brought under the 1980s legislation but under the common law interpretation of the implied contract between a union and its members. They were nevertheless vitally important in relation to the outcome of the dispute, for it was these common law actions which resulted in the eventual sequestration of the NUM's funds. Also, the experience of litigation by the NUM dissidents was a major inspiration for Section 1 of the Employment Act 1988, which gave individual members the right to bring injunctions against their union in certain circumstances and established the Commissioner with power to support such actions.

One important legal change brought about by the legislation was the narrowing of the definition of a trade dispute. The number of cases arising from this have been limited, however. The leading case was *Mercury Ccommunications* v. *Scott-Garner* (1984), where the POEU had given instructions that its members should not connect Mercury to British Telecommunications' (BT) network. The POEU claimed that it was motivated by fears of job losses and therefore covered by the definition of 'a trade dispute'. The Court of Appeal, however, unlike the High Court, ruled that the dispute was not 'wholly and mainly' about feared job losses. The Court looked at the wider union campaign against privatisation and the fact there was a job security agreement between BT and the POEU and granted the injunction. The employers in *Associated British Ports and Others* v. *TGWU* (1989) also raised the issue of whether or not there was a genuine trade dispute.

Under the common law the issue of the statutory duty of some workers to continue to work was raised. This happened in the 1989 docks dispute, where, as mentioned earlier, it was turned down by the House of Lords. It had already been raised earlier in *Barretts and Baird (Wholesale) Ltd* v. *IPCS & Duckworth* (1987), where the dispute involved meat inspectors employed by the Meat and Livestock Commission (MLC), who had agreed to industrial action in the form of one-day lightning strikes. The plaintiffs, mainly meat wholesalers, sought injunctions on the grounds that the union was inducing the MLC to act in breach of its statutory duties. The inspectors were responsible for issuing certificates to enable those entitled to receive certain subsidies and to export meat. Their authorisation was necessary to implement the MLC's statutory duty to pay the subsidies. The court held that there was no breach of statutory duty as there was no evidence of a failure to pay, only a postponement. However, the court did not doubt that a breach of statutory duty could constitute 'unlawful means' and that it was a tort in itself. Potentially, this could have very serious consequences for, say, teachers and for others in the public service sector, and for those working in public utilities.

In another important dispute — Wapping — which has already been discussed, News International summarily dismissed all the strikers without compensation on the basis that they were in breach of their contracts of employment. This again was not on the basis of the 1980s legislation, but on common law grounds. It nevertheless was highly significant and raised the question of whether such a thing as 'the right to strike' really existed at all. Clearly, it exists in the sense that 'lawful' strikes do take place. But strikers taking part in such actions can be legally dismissed by their employer without compensation. This threat was used effectively by the port employers in 1989 and was a not insignificant factor in the defeat of the TGWU, particularly as the threat was contrasted with the existence of a generous government-backed voluntary redundancy scheme. There was, of course, nothing new in this. Strikers had almost always been breaking their contracts. It was still unusual for employers to dismiss them on these grounds. However, such employer action, or the threat of it, was arguably more effective in the economic and political climate of the 1980s.

Another important legal issue was the nature and consequences of industrial action, other than strike action. This question had been raised a number of years ago in a case under the now defunct Industrial Relations Act 1971 — *The Secretary of State for Employment* v. *ASLEF* (1972). Here ASLEF's industrial action took the form of 'working to rule' and a ban on overtime. The Court held that to construe the rules 'unreasonably', and to put that unreasonable construction into practice so that the railway system could grind to a halt, constituted a breach of the workers' contractual obligation to serve their employer in good faith. With regard to the ban on overtime the court held that this was a breach of contract of employment only if the overtime in question was obligatory under the contract: where the overtime was undertaken on a voluntary basis, a ban was not a breach of contract.

The issue of industrial action short of a strike has arisen in a number of more recent cases. One such case was *Wilusznski* v. *Tower Hamlets London Borough Council* (1989), where the plaintiff was employed as an estate officer in the housing department. The major part of his work consisted of dealing with the complaints and problems of council tenants, but he was also required to answer inquiries from councillors on estate matters and on average received one or two such inquiries a week. Owing to an industrial dispute, NALGO decided to boycott all councillors' inquiries and the plaintiff followed his union's instructions, while continuing to carry out his other duties. He was suspended and the council refused to pay him any salary, whereupon he sued for the payment of salary. The Court of Appeal held that if, as part of an industrial dispute, an employee refused to perform certain parts of his contract of employment, he was in breach of his contract. The employer was then entitled to require the employee not to perform any of his duties until he was prepared to work normally and to refuse to pay him at all for the period during which he was in breach of contract. In *Miles* v. *Wakefield Metropolitan District Council* (1987), Mr Miles, who was the Superintendent of Births, Deaths and Marriages, worked 37 hours a week. One of his functions was to conduct weddings on Saturday mornings from 9.00 a.m. to 12.00noon. As part of a campaign of industrial action, Mr Miles on instructions from his union, NALGO, though willing to work a 37-hour week and to work on Saturdays, refused to conduct weddings on Saturdays. The council thereupon treated him as working only a 34-hour week and paid him accordingly. He sued for the rest of his salary. The House of Lords in their judgement held that the council was correct in its action. In order to establish a right to wages, workers must prove that they were ready and willing to work in accordance with their duties. Mr Miles had not been willing to do so and his employers, as was their right, were not prepared to accept his incomplete performance.

Conclusion

The leading cases in the courts are only the tip of the iceberg. Their existence indicates that there are large numbers of occasions when both employers and unions consult their lawyers about the relevance of the law to the options they are considering. There is no doubt that these occasions are far more numerous than they were before the 1980s. Moreover, in their day-to-day working trade union officials in particular have to be aware of what the law says. Unions today can be easily put at risk by the actions of members which 10 years ago were not unlawful and which many would still regard as ordinary trade union behaviour. The risks involved can include the union's very existence through the sequestration of its funds and property. The law is now an important part of the daily practice of industrial relations.

Strikes and conduct connected with them like picketing and secondary action are heavily represented among the cases and among the practical issues on which the law bears. The injunction has become a handy weapon for some employers, although the number of cases where an injunction restraining unions might successfully be applied for is legion compared with the number which are taken. Many employers regard them as more trouble than they are worth, but they are always potentially available. An injunction is a holding action, it is not the full legal action. Yet the cases show that the penalties for contempt which may follow disobedience of the injunction can be greater than the punishment exacted for guilt of the crime itself. This would seem to indicate that the procedure for securing an injunction should give the union every opportunity to be heard. Yet the procedure is dominated by the need for speed and judges make decisions at unlikely times and in odd places. Since so much can hang on the decision the procedure should, at least, make certain that the union has the same opportunity to make its case as the employer who applies for the injunction.

This is a prime example of the limits of the legal system when it is called on to deal with a new crop of industrial relations cases. The subject matter has its own special characteristics and, while the legal system is general in its applications, its acceptance requires understanding of the environment in which people work. Now that the law on industrial relations is so extensive the legal system should display a greater willingness to understand the context of cases.

CHAPTER 6

Employer and management strategies in the private sector

Introduction

In this chapter we look at changing employer industrial relations attitudes and strategies in the 1980s. One of the major academic debates during the decade was whether or not there had been a major shift by employers towards policies of 'macho-management', unitarism and anti-trade unionism. There has also been an extensive debate about Human Resource Management (HRM) – what it means, how widely it has been adopted, and what its implications are for traditional industrial relations and personnel management. These debates are in a sense part of the still wider question as to whether a 'new industrial relations' has developed in the 1980s. These issues are addressed in this chapter, although a final assessment is not made until Chapter 12.

The economic and political environment has already been discussed in Chapters 3 and 4 and only two points need to be emphasised here. The first is that the election in 1979 of a Conservative government and its re-election in 1983 and 1987 meant above all that there was throughout the decade a government which was overtly pro-employer and anti-trade union. It was a government pledged to reducing trade union power and removing burdens on industry. It was also a government pledged to reducing public expenditure, redistributing income and the tax burden in favour of the better-off – all objectives which most employers readily supported. The second is that employers faced a far more competitive environment in the 1980s than they had previously, and that both business organisations and competition were becoming more and more globalised. Alongside government support for the small firm sector, multinationals were extending their market share and were playing an ever-increasing role in world trade.

British industry almost immediately in 1979–80 faced a major and unprecedented crisis. As outlined in Chapter 3, the country was plunged into the worst recession of the post-war period. The impact on profits was drastic, above all in manufacturing industry. Industry's immediate response was wholesale redundancies and the widespread closure of plants. It was this response which gave rise at the time to the term macho-management. The extensive closures and redundancies indeed would certainly appear to justify the term. However, employers were preoccupied with survival. They were in business to make profits and not to create 'good' industrial relations. Industrial relations policy was subsidiary to wider changes in business organisation, strategy and policy, which were considered necessary to deal with recession and ever-growing world competition. Within this wider framework employers' industrial relations objectives were to control the work process and improve cost effectiveness; to assert managerial authority; and to move towards a more unitary approach and away from the pluralistic approach which had developed in the earlier post-war decades. As part of this process there was a move towards a more 'individualistic' approach with regard to employees and away from a 'collective' one.

There is, of course, a great danger in generalising about employers' objectives. There are variations in objectives, as well as in managerial styles and perhaps above all in the circumstances of individual firms, which in turn affect objectives, policies and style. Thus the type of company, its stage of development, its products, the product markets, its labour markets, the degree of competition it faces, its technology, its traditions and philosophy, all play a major part in determining its industrial relations objectives and the policies it adopts to attain these objectives. Nevertheless, the above objectives will serve as a starting point for considering companies' industrial relations policies. These policies will be examined under the following headings:

1. human resource management and management style;
2. attitudes to unions;
3. attitudes to collective bargaining;
4. involvement, consultation and participation;
5. flexibility;
6. levels and methods of remuneration.

Human resource management and management style

Human resource management (HRM) became an 'in-phrase' in the 1980s, although its meaning is by no means clear. First, it can be used as just another term for personnel management with nothing else changed. Second, it can be used as another term for personnel management, but suggesting or providing much greater emphasis on certain aspects of personnel work, such as training, motivation and employee development, and a decreasing emphasis on some traditional areas, such as industrial relations. Third, it can be used as implying a completely new concept whereby labour is regarded not so much as a cost but as an asset or resource, which needs to be developed to its maximum ability, so that emphasis is on the individual employee and on his or her motivation, training and development. Often this approach is allied to the stated belief that HRM is primarily the responsibility of line managers and not personnel managers. HRM can thus simply be a form of public relations or a major change in corporate policy or another form of management style.

Guest (1987, 1989) suggests that HRM consists of a combination of policies designed to produce strategic integration, high commitment, high quality and flexibility among employees. As he argues, in its full meaning, HRM should properly denote a package embracing a strategic and integrated approach to 'people management': the integration of employees on the basis of commitment and not mere compliance with instructions and an organic and devolved business structure as against a bureaucratic and centralised one. HRM thus involves the use of a coherent approach, matching HRM activities and policies to business strategy, and seeing employees as a strategic resource for achieving competitive advantage. Guest (1989) concludes that the evidence of such an integrated approach in Britain is so far limited. However, he argues that the underlying values, reflected in HRM policies and practices would appear to be essentially unitarist and individualistic in contrast to the more pluralist and collective values of traditional industrial relations. The unitary approach views the organisation as a team, all owing allegiance to an organisation, and where all share the same objectives: the pluralist view sees the organisation as a coalition of groups whose interests in some respect may differ and need to be reconciled. HRM poses a threat to trade unions in three ways. First, in companies in which unions are recognised, HRM objectives are likely to be pursued through policies that tend to bypass the union. Second, by practising 'good' management, the employees' need for the union as a protective device against poor management is likely to be reduced. Third, in companies where unions are not recognised, HRM policies might obviate any felt need for a union. Certainly in the USA HRM has been used by many companies as an anti-union device. In our interviews with managers, none spontaneously mentioned HRM as being a major new development in their employee relations. Mainly they regarded HRM as 'good' personnel policy and practice.

Turning to management style, Purcell and Sisson (1983) have, following Fox (1974), identified four 'ideal' types of industrial relations management, as follows:

1. *Traditionalists.* These have unitary beliefs, and are anti-union with forceful management. An example of such a company was Grunwick, which became a *cause célèbre* in the 1970s (see Chapter 11).

2. *Sophisticated paternalists.* These are essentially unitary, but there is a crucial difference from the first type in that they do not take it for granted that their

employees accept the company's objectives or automatically legitimise management decision making; they spend considerable time and resources in ensuring that their employees have the right approach. Examples of such companies given by Purcell and Sisson (1983) are IBM and Marks and Spencer.

3. *Sophisticated moderns.* To quote Fox (1974),

> Management legitimises the union role in certain areas of joint decision-making because it sees this role as conducive to its own interests as measured by stability, promotion of consent, bureaucratic regulation, effective communication or the handling of change. It recognises that its discretion is being limited in certain areas of decision- making but it legitimises these limitations and therefore does not counter with low trust behaviour and attitudes. (p. 302)

Purcell and Sisson subdivide this category as follows:

(a) *The constitutionalists.* These include, for example, Ford, where the limits on collective bargaining are clearly codified in the collective agreement. In those areas of decision making where management is under challenge from the trade unions, or where it may be expedient to concede joint regulation (in return for concessions from the union elsewhere), the frontier of control may be moved back, but is then firmly entrenched in a specific codified agreement. Clegg (1979) has described this as 'the statute law' model of collective bargaining where 'the formal assumption ... is that management is free to take their own decisions on matters which are not the subject of collective agreements.' (p. 117)

(b) *The consultors.* These accept collective bargaining, but there is no desire to codify everything in a collective agreement. On the contrary, every effort is made to minimise the amount of joint regulation and great emphasis is placed on joint consultation, with 'problems' having to be solved rather than 'disputes' settled. Examples of such companies given by Purcell and Sisson are ICI, BP and Esso.

4. *Standard moderns (pragmatic or opportunist).* These are considered to be by far the largest group. Trade unions are recognised, but industrial relations are seen as primarily fire-fighting and assumed to be non-problematic unless events prove otherwise. Consequently, the significance of industrial relations' waxes and wanes in the light of changing circumstances. Unlike in the earlier groups, there does not appear to be a set of values or assumptions which are held in common. Examples given by Purcell and Sisson are GEC, GKN and Tube Investments.

Taken together, the categories form a spectrum in which the adjacent ones shade into each other. Looked at in this way the categories are useful because a number of managers do see their firms as having shifted their position in the spectrum towards a lower-numbered category. The 1980s have seen them, if they are consultors, among the sophisticated moderns, reducing the scope of collective agreements compared with the 1970s, and getting managers' solutions to problems accepted.

Purcell (1987) argues that Fox 'in distinguishing between pluralist and unitary frames of management provided a powerful impetus to the debate about management style, but the mutually exclusive nature of these categories had limited further development.' (p. 546) Moreover, wide variations can be found within the unitary approach and within the pluralist approach. He therefore suggests an alternative distinction of 'individualism' – policies related to the individual employee – and 'collectivism' – the extent to which groups of workers have an independent voice and participate in decision-making with managers. Companies can and do operate on both these dimensions of style. Policies are likely to vary according to the type of product and product markets, technology and skill level. Indeed, a firm may well have a number of different styles for different occupational groups. For example, the treatment and development of managers may well be very different from that of shopfloor workers, as may the treatment of core workers and peripheral workers. As Purcell (1987) concludes, 'Once we recognise that modern companies are capable of making strategic business choices we must allow for preferences to exist in the way employees are managed, albeit in constrained circumstances.' (p. 547)

The debates about the unitary v. pluralist approach, the individualistic v. collectivist approach and the categorisation of organisations are valuable frameworks for analysis, but their main purpose is not to provide a practical typology. Rather, they help the analysis and understanding of developments in organisations. In the 1970s the trend by management was towards a greater acceptance of pluralism and collectivism, and there was some movement towards the 'sophisticated modern' model. In the 1980s the movement was towards the unitary and individualistic approach and towards the 'sophisticated paternalistic' model. Indeed one leading personnel director stated that 'there had been an irreversible shift to the involvement of the individual in the workplace. There will be no return to the collective masses.' However, such a view was not that of all the managers we interviewed and indeed it was very much a minority view. Most managers believed that in the 1980s they had significantly increased efficiency and in this achievement unions had played a full, co-operative part. We return to this issue later in the chapter.

Attitudes to unions

The macho-management policies of many manufacturing companies in the early 1980s were interpreted by some commentators as an employers' counteroffensive against alleged union excesses in the 1970s. The survey carried out by Mackay and Torrington (1986) showed a harder management attitude towards trade unions.

Further evidence was based on widely quoted specific examples, such as the (then) British Leyland Company, which at the end of the 1970s and early 1980s drastically cut manpower, confronted and defeated union power and imposed changed methods of work and changed procedures (Willman, 1984), the P.&O., and the Wapping disputes (see Chapter 5), and subsequently certain other national and provincial newspapers. However, the widely based surveys such as Millward and Stevens (1986), Batstone (1984), Edwards (1987) and Marginson *et al.* (1988) have suggested that there was not a major frontal assault on unions. Recognition has not been withdrawn in the overwhelming majority of cases although of course it has occurred in a number of well-publicised instances and some not so well publicised. A study (Claydon, 1989) recorded 49 cases of derecognition in 1986/7.

Overwhelmingly, the survey evidence shows that recognition, where it already existed, has been maintained, as has the joint machinery for bargaining, consultation and the handling of grievances. Had they wished, senior managers could have ended the recognition of trade unions in many places. That they have not done so was largely because they did not regard established recognition as an issue. Where unions were recognised, in the vast majority of cases managers accepted them. As one employer representative told us, derecognition had not taken-off because it had not been necessary. He added that what mattered for managers was putting their policies into action and the presence of unions seldom stood in the way of that objective. Managers could take the initiative and succeed in taking the matters forward which were of concern to them. Some firms have taken a more sophisticated approach and in co-operation with the unions have endeavoured to ensure that the nature of the competitive threat is understood by their employees. That has meant putting across the details of the business and it has lead to seeking common solutions to problems. In those cases the unions have become positive partners rather than passive bystanders.

The maintenance of union recognition and of collective bargaining machinery does not, however, tell us much about the relative power and relations of the parties. Indeed, there can be little doubt that bargaining power during most of the 1980s had swung decisively in favour of management and the effect of this will be considered later, as will the argument that management rather than launching a frontal assault on unions and joint machinery had sought to bypass them and to seek ways of doing things which reduced union involvement.

If superficially there has been little in the way of drastic change as far as recognition is concerned, where unions were already recognised, this appears less true where unions have not got recognition (Beaumont, 1987). Unions have found it harder than ever to gain recognition in greenfield sites, in new companies and in companies and sectors where recognition has always been difficult to obtain, for example large parts of the private service sector where there has been considerable growth in employment. Indeed, it was apparent from our interviews that managers often hold a different attitiude to unions in existing plants from that held towards the recognition of unions in a new or unorganised workplace. If they can avoid recognition they will, and if they cannot they often have a strong preference for a single union. This indicates that managers have different strategies according to whether they have the choice. They may have a good working relationship with unions where unions are recognised, but nevertheless keep them out or only admit the one they select on greenfield sites. They want whatever arrangement gives them the greatest freedom to take successful initiatives.

Employers have indeed had more choice than at any time in the post-war period as to whether they recognise a union or not and as well as a choice of which union they want to recognise and the terms on which they would grant recognition, for example a single union and a no-strike agreement. ACAS in its annual report for 1987 stated that union success in gaining recognition through conciliation was limited; unions no longer have a legal method for obtaining recognition (as they do in many other countries and as they did briefly in this country between 1975 and 1980). The nature of the unorganised trades and the growth in part-time employment were major reasons for the lack of success in gaining membership and hence the likelihood of recognition.

Collective bargaining

Two major developments in collective bargaining took place in the 1980s; the first concerned the level and the second its scope. With regard to the level of bargaining, there was a continuation in the reduced importance of industry-wide bargaining arrangements. This was shown first in the abandonment of industry-wide bargaining in a number of cases in recent years, for example, in the road passenger transport industry, national and provincial newspapers as far as journalists are concerned, the London clearing banks, multiple retailing, the water industry, independent television, the cement industry and engineer-ing. Brown and Walsh (1991, p. 49) state that at least 16 major national bargaining groups covering a total of over a million employees have been terminated since 1986. Where industry-wide bargaining has been retained, as in construction and commercial printing, its substantive agreements are more and more safety nets and there is usually considerable freedom for companies to reach their own agreements on most matters, although in construction there are no company agreements.

It is above all in the public sector that industry-wide bargaining has been maintained, although even here measures have been taken towards decentralisation and pay flexibility. This is discussed in Chapter 7. In the former public corporations, privatisation had as one purpose putting activities on the same basis as other commercial firms with the expectation that decentralisation would occur. What has happened so far in practice has varied. For example, in gas there has been virtually no change, and the Royal Ordnance factories still have central agreements, as does British Telecom. However, in iron and steel and the water industry there has been major decentralisation.

In private industry there has been a continuing move from industry-wide bargaining to enterprise bargaining. Within enterprises there has been a further move towards decentralisation, that is to say from corporate level down to divisional, subsidiary company or plant levels. This trend, however, is by no means universal; for example in manufacturing Ford and ICI still maintain company-wide bargaining and this is perhaps more importantly true of much of the private service sector, for example most of the large banks, the insurance companies and the large multiple retail chains. Although, in some banks and large insurance companies, there has been a degree of decentralisation on a business basis, the effect of this has not been very significant. It is, of course, also true that for example the retail stores may pay different rates in different geographical areas, and not just London versus the rest, but these variations are determined centrally. Indeed, even where bargaining is at plant level, there is conclusive evidence from Marginson *et al.*'s study (1988) that guidelines and controls are often set down centrally and that freedom to plant bargainers may be only within very strict limits. The Marginson study also makes the important point that generally the decision to decentralise pay bargaining was not taken on industrial relations grounds, but because broader business strategy had decreed decentralisation and the establishment of decentralised cost or profit centres and it then followed, if managers were to accept financial responsibility at plant level, that they had to be allowed some responsibility for wage determination. An earlier view regarding bargaining levels put forward by Purcell and Sisson (1983) and by Kinnie (1987) was that management sought the bargaining level which best kept union influence away from the level where major company decision-making took place. Thus, for example, an insistence on plant-level bargaining kept shop stewards and union officials away from strategic decision-making at corporate level.

While the theme of decentralisation is general and powerful, it does not lead to a single pattern; the relations between establishment managers and those at the centre of a company vary widely. Moreover, there is change and movement going on continually in the balance between centre and periphery. For example, one major company, providing a service nationally, moderated the high degree of local autonomy to which it had moved, because it had subsequently realised that the devolved local units were not sufficiently self-contained to justify the change. The performance of the network and services to customers depended on all the local units working together. Devolved management had set them against each other, while interdependence in the production of the service required central control. A second major company argued that in a single product business there must be common terms and conditions across the activity because the work is identical wherever it is done, although there was some flexibility on the manual side through overtime and bonus systems and on the white-collar side through the grading system. Indeed, in the future, this personnel director stated, there would have to be more conformity to a company-wide system, with national standard job descriptions to ensure equity. 'Equal pay for equal work is a great pressure for company-wide conformity to common pay for the same work,' and 'The only protection against ratcheting is a national system of pay for large employers.'

A third large company argued that it was essential for it to preserve centralised bargaining. Its personnel director stated that he was 'terrified of the power which local union barons would exercise if negotiations were decentralised'. Another major company had decentralised its bargaining because all control was now exercised through budgets down to the local plant. The drive to decentralisation followed from the decision to put the responsibility for meeting profit targets on to plant managers and the main pressure for it came from the variations in profitability between plants: managers claimed that they did not have the requisite flexibility. It is interesting that the company did not take the decision to decentralise bargaining until very late in the 1980s because of fear of a domino effect, that is to say, what was settled in one plant would be the basis of claims and settlements in others. Managers were judged by the financial results they achieved, which were set out in monthly, quarterly and annual targets. A dispute was bound to make it unlikely that they would achieve the expected results and so they would be judged to have fallen short. In the view of the personnel director, there would be a strong tendency to buy off a strike in the interests of maintaining short-term profits. The next manager up the line was likely to take the same attitude because he too was judged by monthly figures. So the result could be that decentralisation would greatly increase the potential bargaining power of the unions. In another large firm with a varied pattern of decentralisation in its component companies, the possibility of some return to centralisation was being actively considered. Decentralisation may be a tide which eventually turns.

So from management's point of view the decentralisation of collective bargaining is not a simple story: some firms have gone further than others, some have yet to decentralise, some have drawn back, some have found that the appropriate level for decentralisation is not the same in all parts of the firm, and some have found that the nature of the product and the technology of its production are a determining influence. Even so, the general trend in management has been, and continues to be, a preference for more decentralised bargaining.

Turning to the scope of collective bargaining, the 1984 WIRS showed that there had been a considerable reduction in the range of subjects which was covered by collective bargaining. In particular, there was a reduction in overt bargaining over operational issues, and these were the issues where management had sought to reassert its authority and unilaterally determine such matters. This may be illustrated by an examination of a number of new-style procedural agreements many of which state, for example,

> that the Union recognises the right of the Company to plan, organise, manage and decide finally upon the operations of the Company.

The old *status quo* and mutuality agreements found throughout engineering, whereby certain changes could not be introduced without prior agreement or the exhaustion of procedure, have gone, or been turned on their head, so that if there is a *status quo* clause at all, it normally says that employees shall carry out changes in practices required by management, even if they object and put the matter into the disputes procedure.

This is not to say that bargaining over work practices has disappeared. Notable productivity bargains have taken place in many organisations where union power is still significant, for example British Telecom, the Post Office, and Ford, and an analysis of the CBI data bank showed that a considerable proportion of agreements contain productivity elements. A number of these, particularly in the early 1980s were, however, in the nature of the exercise of *force majeure* by management with the alternative to acceptance by unions being the closure of the plant or a managerially imposed condition for a pay increase. As one employer representative put it – these days managers talk confidently about making changes with few references to trade unions. They can make changes to increase productivity in ways which were unthinkable in the 1970s when they had begun by wondering how they could overcome union resistance, or elicit union co-operation. One personnel director stated that 'something for something' bargaining had become the norm. The increases in productivity which had been achieved had been on such a scale that despite considerable pay increases the company was still internationally competitive on labour costs. Two other personnel directors used the same expression – 'something for something' – to describe their bargaining in the 1980s.

In contrast to the considerable reassertion of managerial authority over operational matters, bargaining has continued over pay and other terms and conditions of employment. Even here, however, there have been examples on pay of 'take it or leave it offers', or the unilateral imposition by management of its pay offer, even where it has not been acceptable to the unions. However arrived at, the settlements have usually been above the rate of inflation, thus facilitating acceptance. Also, through the growth of performance-related pay schemes, which are discussed below, some managements have sought to negotiate the minimum general increase possible and reserve the maximum discretion for itself through 'merit' awards.

Involvement, consultation and participation

There is a long history of attempts by unions to increase worker participation in industry, although unions' prime concern has always been with collective bargaining. During the Second World War, and in the years immediately afterwards, participation primarily took the form at workplace level of the widespread establishment of joint consultative committees. Later some degree of disillusionment set in with joint consultation (McCarthy, 1966) and, with the growth in the number and power of shop stewards, there was a considerable expansion, in particular in engineering, in the scope of workplace collective bargaining albeit on a largely informal basis. The development of productivity bargaining in the 1960s added a degree of formality to this process. In the 1970s, spurred by Britain's membership of the EEC and the need to take a view of the EEC's draft Fifth Directive with its proposals for worker members on boards of directors, as well as by trade union realisation that the extended scope of collective bargaining did not touch the major strategic decisions taken by companies, there was the demand for employee representatives on boards of directors, a process culminating in the *Bullock Report* (1977) and the subsequent White Paper *Industrial Democracy* (1978) and with limited experiments in the iron and steel industry and the Post Office. The then Labour government's White Paper proposed that under certain circumstances there should be employee directors on company boards. However, legislation was not enacted before the 1979 general election and after the advent of Thatcher governments, and with the changed balance of power between employers and unions, any move in this direction came to an abrupt halt. The Conservative government's view has been that such matters should be left to industry and that it would be wrong to seek to impose any statutory requirements — a view it has pressed within the EC as well as at home, in order to prevent what it has called 'social engineering'. The only concession made was the inclusion in the Employment Act 1980 of a requirement for companies to say in their annual reports what they had done, if anything, in this area. The government view has been strongly supported by most employers and their organisations.

Employers have, however, not been against greater communication, involvement, consultation and participation. On the contrary, many employers have claimed to be pursuing these matters with great vigour. Their objectives, their methods and their interpretation of the terms have, however, been very different from those of the unions. After the managerial dominance of the early 1980s, it became fashionable for some companies to espouse the cause of better communications and greater involvement. According to Purcell and Sisson (1983), there was a growing realisation that management dominance was not enough to meet current and future competition and that what was required was a workforce committed to the company's objectives. To this end many companies have espoused a wide variety of measures to communicate with and involve their workforce on an individual basis. Such measures have included direct communication by letter to workers at their homes or in their pay-packets, briefing groups, attitude surveys and quality circles. On one interpretation, these are all means of bypassing union channels and the position and standing of shop stewards. What distinguishes all these methods is, first, that they are based on individualisation and not on a collective approach and, second, as a consequence, they are entirely unitary, as opposed to pluralistic, in their purpose. They are aimed at enlisting employee opinion and behaviour behind management's objectives and not at incorporating the influence of employees' organisations in negotiated decisions. This has sometimes been called the 'consensual' rather than the 'adversarial' approach. Its unitary and individualistic nature is very apparent from a CBI statement on employee involvement, published in 1988, which is reproduced in full below:

The CBI believes that employee involvement:

- is a range of processes designed to engage the support, understanding and optimum contribution of all employees in an organisation and their commitment to its objectives;
- assists an organisation to give the best possible service to customers and clients in the most cost-effective way;
- entails providing employees with the opportunity to influence and where appropriate take part in decision-making on matters which affect them;
- is an intrinsic part of good management practice and is therefore not confined to relationships with employee representatives;
- can only be developed voluntarily in ways suited to the activities, structure and history of an organisation. Employment involvement promotes business success by:
- fostering trust and a shared commitment to an organisation's objectives;
- demonstrating respect for individual employees and drawing on the full range of their abilities;
- enabling employees to derive the maximum possible job satisfaction.

It is the responsibility of management to generate effective employee involvement through the systems and techniques at their disposal. These may include:

- systematic two-way communication on all company matters (within the limits of commercial confidence);
- regular consultation;
- problem-solving groups;
- decision-making at the lowest practicable level of authority;
- training for key communicators;

- financial participation;
- harmonisation of terms and conditions of employment;
- seeking individual contributions aimed at achieving continuous improvement in the organisation.

As already stated, the approach is individualistic and unitary, and some employers would regard their involvement policies as having failed if employees still attached importance to collective action through trade unions.

Flexibility

The concept and model of the flexible firm which was first put forward by John Atkinson (1984) of the Institute of Manpower Studies (IMS) aroused considerable interest, although its relevance was as a framework of tendencies, rather than as a practical description of what was found frequently on the ground. The flexible firm was said to consist of three groups of workers: first, the core workers who conduct key activities; as the nature of operations of the firm changes, they have to accept changes in their jobs through functional flexibility; they have good pay and conditions and relative security, as long as they are flexible; the firm invests much in their training and development. Second, there are the peripheral workers, who have less critical activities and more routine functions to perform; they are hired on contracts which permit easy adjustment to their numbers as demand changes. Third, there are the external workers – who are not employees at all: they represent activities from which the firm has distanced itself through subcontracting – the provision of contracts of service instead of contracts of employment. The model of the flexible firm thus envisages these three groups of workers – core, peripheral and external. Flexibility takes the form of numerical flexibility, functional flexibility and distancing. A fourth flexibility – that of remuneration – may be added to the list, and is discussed later in the chapter.

Numerical flexibility, according to the IMS, takes four major forms: the use of more temporary workers, the use of more part-timers, the greater use of overtime and more flexibility in working time, for example annual hours contracts and a growth in shiftwork.

Functional flexibility, which was said to apply mainly in manufacturing industry, has taken three major forms. First, maintenance jobs are being expanded horizontally into related trades and give rise to so-called multi-skilled maintenance craftsmen. Second, process and operator jobs are being similarly expanded to provide greater mobility between jobs at similar skill levels. Third, there is vertical flexibility across group boundaries, for example operators engaging in quality control and in minor maintenance work.

'Distancing [according to Atkinson and Meager, 1986] is associated with a wish to concentrate corporate resources in areas of comparative advantage, to find cheaper ways of undertaking non-core activities, to shift the burden of risk and uncertainty elsewhere and to reduce (or contain) formal headcount and wage bill.'

The concept of 'the flexible firm' has been much discussed and would appear to have been widely accepted in many management circles as the way ahead in times of rapid economic and technological change. It has, however, been strongly attacked by Anna Pollert (1987), who argued that managerial concern for flexibility was not new; for example, it was a major element in productivity bargaining in the 1960s and had been extensively analysed in dual labour market theory. What *was* new was the model's transformation of segmentation as a process into a deliberate management strategy for large firms, and this was not supported by the evidence. In so far as there has been an expansion of insecure and irregular work, this can be explained by sectoral shifts in the structure of employment − in particular the growth of the service sector − and by cost-cutting measures. There was also little evidence of widespread development towards functional flexibility (Cross, 1988) or of employment security for a core labour force. Indeed, definitions of core and periphery employees were shifting and unsatisfactory. Pollert further argued that the model was a mixture of description, prescription and prediction − a picture of a radical break from the past was created and projected into the future as an inevitable trend. The model concentrated on labour flexibility as a panacea. 'The probability that changes in labour arrangements are the result of far wider concerns with production organisation, marketing and industrial relations was not considered. The preoccupation with decentralisation trivialises the problems of co-ordination and control.' Moreover, the model neglected possible counter-productive effects of flexibility, such as lack of commitment by the peripheral labour force, and diverted attention from the need for training.

Indeed, the model of the flexible firm has been questioned in further work by the IMS itself. Thus Atkinson and Meager (1986), in a major study for NEDO and the Department of Employment of 72 large firms chosen at random, in engineering, food and drink manufacturing, retail distribution and financial services, showed that while there had been widespread changes in work practice and greater flexibility, management interest, particularly in the service sector, was more marked in deploying cheap peripheral labour, rather than changing the employment culture at the core. 'The outcome was more likely to be marginal, *ad hoc*, and tentative, rather than a purposeful and strategic thrust to achieve flexibility; short-term cost saving, rather than long-term development, dominated management thinking, save where substantial new investment was involved.' Rather than a universal adoption, changed working practices broadly reflected the different business strategies which were emerging in the four sectors. Thus part-time working was mainly of significance in the service sector, temporary working and functional flexibility was more important in manufacturing, and flexible working was more an aspiration than a reality save among part-time workers. The two main factors underlying the growth of service sector part-time working were to match manning levels to changing consumer patterns and the reduction of labour costs. However, while the concept of the flexible firm may be highly questionable, there is no doubt that employers' search for greater flexibility in the use of labour has been one of the important features of the 1980s and that this will continue to be so in the 1990s.

Levels and methods of remuneration

The move in the level of pay determination from industry level to enterprise level, and within enterprises to lower levels such as divisions and establishments, has already been discussed. It is a move which has had government support on the philosophical grounds that the labour market needs to be more flexible in order to take advantage of different supply and demand situations in different parts of the country, and of different financial situations in different firms, and in order to reward individuals on grounds of performance (Clarke, 1987). As well as exhorting the private sector, government has sought to introduce greater flexibility in public sector payments.

Of the main developments in levels and methods of remuneration the first has been the greater linking of pay to performance or, if one prefers, the greater 'individualisation' of pay. There is of course nothing new in this as far as managers in the private sector are concerned. What is new is, first, it has spread to the public sector; for example, to civil servants, university lecturers, schoolteachers, NHS managers and British Rail managers. Second, in the private sector, it has spread downwards from managerial levels to other white-collar workers, including clerical and in some cases to blue-collar workers. In addition, the size of the 'merit' element in pay has been increasing: indeed, some companies have announced that there would be no general pay increases at all, (regardless of the rise in the RPI), and that all increases would be based only on merit, for example the Abbey National Building Society. On the other hand there are signs that companies which have a long record of paying for individual performance have moved on to rewarding groups and teams and even to company-wide bonuses. Despite the absolute justification often given for performance-related pay (PRP) when it is introduced, it is not a stable component in management's strategy for pay but one which waxes and wanes.

The second main development has been a growth of profit-sharing and employee share ownership schemes, stimulated in part by favourable tax legislation, but above all by a belief that such measures would raise commitment and in some cases increase incentive. Companies with long experience of profit-sharing do not exaggerate the incentive effects and play up the significance of profit-sharing for developing a sense of involvement. They also emphasise the importance of the sum involved being of an appreciable size every year, which means less profit for the shareholders.

Third, there have been widening pay differentials, as shown in Chapter 10. Numerous surveys also show that managerial pay has gone up much faster than that of other employees, while the pay of top executives (not to mention their share options) has gone up even faster.

Fourth, there have been changes in pay structures, apart from the widening of differentials. Thus there has been a continuing simplification of pay structures, in particular fewer grades in order to achieve greater flexibility and to reduce job demarcations. Along with the simplification of pay structures, there have been increasing doubts in some of the more sophisticated companies about traditional job evaluation. For one thing, it was felt that job descriptions could inhibit flexibility, and for another there was a trend towards paying people for what they could do and how they did it, rather than for what they did in a specific job at a specific point of time. Finally, there were a number of examples of integrated pay structures, that is to say of manual and white-collar jobs, for example in Midland Bank, Pilkington and a number of American and Japanese companies. The main reasons for this appeared to be a desire to encourage teamwork and a feeling that everyone should be treated on the same basis, and to acknowledge the increased blurring of boundaries between blue-collar and white-collar jobs with the development of new technology. An added advantage from management's viewpoint related to the avoidance of equal pay cases and this was certainly the major factor in Midland Bank's adoption of an integrated structure.

Finally, there has been a growth of regional allowances and other pay settlements to reflect local needs and skill shortages. In the late 1980s the London clearing banks startled everyone – not least the unions – with a massive increase in their London allowances – for Inner London from £1750 p.a. to £3000 p.a. – and with the introduction of a 'Roseland allowance' of £750 for the rest of South East England. It was, of course, a reflection of the shortage of labour in London and the South-East at that time. Needless to say, their action was soon followed by many other organisations, for example insurance companies and building societies.

Conclusion

During the 1980s, management operating in an environment of increased competition in product markets and greatly reduced bargaining power on the part of the unions has been able to take the initiative in industrial relations. It has sought greater control over the work process and has in many areas asserted managerial authority. It has also sought to be more cost-effective (Brewster and Connock, 1985). Three major developments are apparent. First, there is the adoption by management of in many cases a more individualist approach to its workforce and less of a collective approach, as shown for example by the growth of performance-related pay, new measures for increased direct communications with employees, and attempts to secure greater involvement. There have also been drives for greater flexibility, new forms of employment contract and moves towards human resource management. A number of personnel directors we interviewed put considerable stress on individualisation and believed that they were moving with the spirit of the times: it is not just that unions are weaker.

The second major development, stressed by all the managers and management representatives we interviewed, is management's greater freedom to launch initiatives and to succeed in carrying them through. It seemed to be irrelevant whether the company concerned was unionised or not. Thus one employers' association told us that throughout the 1980s there had been much more emphasis on productivity, starting with an industry-wide enabling agreement which became more specific so that each year there had been further developments. As the unions absorbed changes, so more were easier to make. There are now, it was claimed, comprehensive clauses in agreements which bear comparison with any other industry. This association had adopted an evolutionary or step-by-step approach together with the unions which was in contrast with that of another association in an allied industry which had successfully adopted a 'big-bang' approach through confrontation and by seeking to break the unions. The main point made by the first association was that in the 1980s management got where it wanted to in the end, virtually irrespective of the method chosen. Generally management believe that its success is due in no small part to a better understanding by employees and unions of the need to be competitive. The third development in some of the companies we interviewed is that industrial relations have been marginalised, as have those who specialise in fire-fighting, as well as many trade union officials. Industrial relations have ceased to be, if they ever were, a preoccupation of top management. It is one part of the implementation of corporate strategy and policy on products, pricing, investment and technology.

These developments and their implementation have not been achieved by large-scale derecognition of unions or by destroying existing collective bargaining machinery, although recognition in greenfield sites has become difficult and collective bargaining has become more decentralised and its scope more limited. Whether the changes amount to a permanent new form of industrial relations for the 1990s is as yet uncertain and is considered further in Chapter 12. While the initiative in the 1980s has been very much with management and managers have been able to get what they want in ways which would not have been possible in the 1970s, most of it has been done with the agreement or at least the acquiescence of the unions and employees. However, the fact that unions have been weaker is no reason for supposing they have been of no account. A number of major companies have told us that they could not have achieved what they have achieved without the agreement and cooperation of their unions.

Our evidence supports the positive contribution of the unions, who have secured considerable increases in pay in exchange for what they have agreed to. The balance of power has tipped towards the managers, but the unions are still an important part of the scene.

CHAPTER 7

Government as employer and quasi-employer

Introduction

The government is directly responsible for the pay of nearly 600 000 civil servants, some 300 000 members of HM Forces and over 1 million employees of the National Health Service. With the removal of negotiating rights of school teachers by the Remuneration of Teachers Act 1987, it is also directly responsible for the pay of nearly 500 000 teachers. In addition, the government had an indirect, but powerful, influence on the pay of some 2½ million other local authority employees through its control over a large part of local authority finance. Finally, it has influence over the pay of employees in the public corporations, again because of the large degree of government control over their finances. The size of the public sector, as Table 7.1 shows, is still considerable despite the government's cut-backs in the civil service, the pressure on the NHS and local authorities to contract out services and the privatisation of most of the public corporations.

The Thatcher governments' beliefs in market forces and private enterprise reflected an ideological hostility to the public sector. There was a conviction that the public sector was inherently more inefficient than the private sector and that the public sector should not be doing things which the private sector could do and, as an article of faith, could do better. Consequently, one of the first acts of the first Thatcher government was to seek a 10 per cent reduction in the size of the civil service and to impose a 3-month ban on recruitment. The whole of the public sector was to be squeezed − primarily by the use of financial controls. However, wholesale privatisation was not a feature of the first Thatcher government, nor indeed was it included in the 1979 Conservative Party's election manifesto. Subsequently, privatisation was to become a major feature of government policy.

TABLE 7.1   Public-sector employment, 1979–90

	Mid-year		Change	
	1979	1990	(000s)	per cent
Central government				
HM Forces	314	303	− 11	− 3.5
NHS	1 152	1 226	+ 74	+ 6.4
Other	921	768	− 153	− 16.6
Total	2 387	2 297	90	− 3.8
Local authorities				
Education	1 539	1 429	− 110	− 7.1
Health and social services	344	416	+ 72	+ 20.9
Construction	156	115	− 41	− 26.3
Police and civilians	176	199	+ 23	+ 13.1
Other	782	806	+ 24	+ 3.1
Total	2 997	2 965	− 32	− 1.1
Public Corporations				
Nationalised industries	1 849	663	− 1186	− 64.1
Other	216	115	− 101	− 46.8
Total	2 065	778	− 1287	− 62.3
Total Public Sector	7 449	6 040	− 1409	− 18.9
(of which civil servants)	738	580	− 158	− 21.4
Total workforce in employment	25 393	27 338		
Public sector as per cent of the workforce in employment	29%	22%		

Source: 'Employment in the Public and Private Sectors', *Economic Trends*, December 1990.

In considering the public sector it is important in the first instance to distinguish between the public service sector, in particular the civil service, the NHS and local authorities (LAs), where for the most part there is no competitive market for their services and hence no prices, and nationalised industries where there are commercial markets for their products and a price mechanism exists. Largely because of this, comparability has for long played a major part in determining public service sector pay (Kessler, 1983). In the case of the non-industrial civil service, as we shall see, the role of comparability was formalised and institutionalised, whereas in the NHS and LAs it was more informal but almost equally as important. In two cases the comparability link has been by means of indexation – the police, whose pay is linked to the average underlying increase in whole economy earnings as a result of the Edmund Davies Committee of Inquiry (1978), and the firemen, whose pay is linked to the upper quartile of male manual earnings as part of the settlement of their strike in the winter of 1977–8. Such indexation has led the police and fire service to obtain pay increases during the 1980s which were well in excess of the public service sector generally (see Chapter 10).

Another important exception is that certain groups have had their pay determined by pay review bodies, for example, the armed forces, doctors and dentists, senior civil servants, the judiciary and more recently nurses and professions allied to medicine and (in 1991) teachers. Among factors playing a major part in the review bodies' deliberations has been comparability, and as a consequence these groups have tended to fare better during the 1980s than have other public service sector employees.

One final difference within the public service that it is important to note is that whereas the civil service and the NHS depend entirely on government finance, LAs depend only in part (although a vital part) on central government and therefore they have had a somewhat greater degree of flexibility in determining pay.

The civil service

In 1979 employment in the civil service was over 700 000, of whom some 560 000 were non-industrial civil servants. The traditional view of government as an employer was that it should be a 'good' employer. This did not mean high pay, but pay determined by the principle of 'fair comparability'. This was judged by a Royal Commission (Priestley, 1955) as fair to the taxpayer and fair to civil servants. The Priestley Commission's recommendations were accepted and the system for determining fair comparability was institutionalised and improved by the establishment in 1956 of the Civil Service Pay Research Unit. The first Thatcher government speedily disclaimed the principle of fair comparability, arguing instead that pay should be determined by 'ability to pay', which it itself determined by setting its own cash limits.

For 1981 and for subsequent years up to 1986, the government announced a specific pay 'factor' or 'assumption' contained within the overall cash limits. In each of these years, pay increases exceeded the pay factor but not by very much and in effect the difference had to be made good by staff economies or declines in the quality of services. From 1986–7, however, the central pay assumption was replaced by decentralised departmental running cost budgets.

Access to arbitration was requested by the civil service unions in 1984–5 and 1985–6, but was refused by the government. Apart from strict control over pay levels, the government sought greater flexibility in pay. Thus, during 1985 a merit pay system was introduced for senior officials and there was the introduction of 'special pay additions' (SPA) which consisted of temporary cash additions for a specified period – usually two to three years – to meet acute recruitment and retention difficulties in respect of particular skills and/or localities.

The result was that the pay of civil servants experienced a prolonged relative decline through most of the 1980s. The government withstood lengthy, costly, industrial action in 1981 which the civil service unions took in response to a low pay offer and to the abolition of 'fair comparability'. The eventual settlement included the setting up of an independent committee to make recommendations on the principles of future pay determination (Megaw, 1982). The committee, although criticising comparability as it had operated in the past, argued that it could not be ignored and recommended a modified form of comparability, whereby bargaining would take place within the inter-quartile range of pay increases for comparable employees in the private sector. To ascertain the latter, an annual survey should be conducted into private sector increases, while every 4 years there should be a survey into the pay levels of comparable private sector employees. Within these limits civil service pay should be determined by the need 'to recruit, retain and motivate'. It was not until 1987 however that the first civil service agreement – with the then Institution of Professional Civil Servants (IPCS) – was concluded embodying the Megaw principles. Apart from pay levels, the agreement included features which reflected the government's desire to increase pay flexibility, in particular the introduction of 'merit' increments (Kessler, 1990). This agreement with the IPCS was soon followed by similar agreements with the other civil service unions, namely the Inland Revenue Staff Federation (IRSF), the Civil and Public Services Association (CPSA) and the National Union of Civil and Public Servants (NUCPS). So the wheel had turned almost full circle but in the meantime great damage had been done to the morale and to the relative pay of the civil service. The government seemed to recognise, mainly under the pressure of the Megaw Report and changes in the labour market, that comparability was inevitably the core of pay determination in the civil service, though in a form more suited to the 1980s and 1990s than that adopted after the Priestley Report 30 years earlier. The unions took some time to accept merit pay and local additions as part of the package until the IPCS broke the log jam. In negotiations the government accepted the restoration of comparability albeit augmented by individual and market payments. The agreements made in 1987 and 1988 appeared to indicate 'new realism' on the part of the government and the civil service unions. However, late in 1991 the government gave notice to terminate these agreements.

In the non-pay area the government sought without success to eliminate index-linked pensions (Scott, 1981). It adopted a more robust managerial style. Thus in 1979, Sir Derek (now Lord) Rayner, from Marks & Spencer, was appointed to advise the Prime Minister on efficiency and he established a small Efficiency Unit which was continued under his successor, Sir Robin Ibbs from ICI. According to one study (Blackwell and Lloyd, 1989) 'attention was particularly focussed on the specification and achievement of clear objectives by managers and the need for managers to give much greater weight to value for money and cost considerations . . .' (pp. 90–1). Further, 'this undoubtedly provided a major impetus to the development of the new managerialism, in particular by emphasising the role of line managers and demonstrating how responsibilities could be delegated and decentralised' (p. 91).

In addition, the government reduced the consultative role of the unions, reduced the time off allowed and other facilities for union lay representatives and terminated unilateral access to arbitration. Whereas the civil service staff handbook used to state that the government welcomed trade union membership, it no longer does so. But the check-off has been maintained and it is the means by which most civil servants pay their union contributions. It survived the major strike in 1981 but the government position is now that the check-off is likely to be withdrawn where there is industrial action, such as has been carried out in the case of the Prison Officers' Association.

The removal of the right to trade union membership at GCHQ Cheltenham in 1984 and the eventual dismissal of those who refused to renounce their membership was a *cause célèbre* of the 1980s and was perhaps symbolic of the government's basic attitude to unions. The government's argument was that in the interests of national security it could not afford to have its communications network subject to possible industrial action. The civil service unions in order to meet this argument and prevent derecognition and the banning of union membership offered a no-industrial action agreement which was accepted by Sir Robert Armstrong, the then head of the civil service. He was however overruled by the Prime Minister. GCHQ civil servants were offered £1000 each if they relinquished union membership and the government set up a staff association in lieu of unions. The staff association was given sole bargaining rights although the Certification Officer subsequently ruled that it was not an organisation independent of the employer.

In protest at the government's action there was a well-supported one-day strike called throughout the civil service. The unions also took the government through the courts, but the House of Lords eventually ruled that the government's action was protected because it was allegedly taken on grounds of national security. The unions also took the issue to various international bodies, including the International Labour Organisation (ILO) which condemned the government's action as incompatible with the ILO's convention on freedom of association, of which the UK government was a signatory. All to no avail. However, one leading union participant in these events believed that in some ways they represented a major victory of the union. 'It brought general opprobrium on the government, especially in international circles, and there was less possibility of the government's approach being extended to other civil servants.'

Finally, over the years the number of civil servants was substantially reduced. In 1980, the government announced that it would seek to reduce manpower by some 100 000 by April 1984. This target was in fact exceeded and a new target of a further reduction of 6 per cent by 1988 was announced. The reduction has mainly been in industrial civil servants and achieved largely by contracting out, (for example there used to be some 10 000 cleaners and now there are only a few hundred); and by privatisation, (for example, the sale of the Royal Ordnance factories).

Subsequently, the government following the Efficiency Unit Report (1988) decided to devolve a large number of civil service functions, and the staff who provided them, to semi-autonomous agencies. It was envisaged that these agencies would behave in a more business-like manner. Each would have a chief executive, and would be given more freedom to manage from day to day in the style of the private sector, although still responsible to ministers. Performance targets would be set and they would have a degree of freedom in determining their own establishments and in determining levels of pay and pay systems. By the summer of 1990, 33 agencies employing 80 000 people had been launched. These ranged in size from the Employment Service which employed 35 000 people at 2000 locations across the UK, to the Queen Elizabeth II Conference Centre which had 50 people working off Parliament Square, and included HMSO, the Meteorological Office, the Ordnance Survey, the Patent Office, the Royal Mint, the Central Office of Information and the Driver and Vehicle Licensing Agency. The target was to have agencies applied to at least half the Civil Service by the end of 1991. As well as the 33 agencies launched, there were 27 publicly announced candidates for agency status including Social Security Benefits with 72 000 staff, with more to come. On top of this, the Chancellor of the Exchequer announced plans to ensure that Customs and Excise with 27 000 staff and the Inland Revenue with 60 000 staff operate fully on agency lines in due course. (Kemp 1990).

The agencies are the government's form of decentralised management, and they raise the same questions as in the private sector. Although the central agreements with the civil service unions apply to them there will undoubtedly be moves to make agency agreements and that will cause the parent departments, and the Treasury in particular, to consider how much independence is compatible with overall control of expenditure. If devolution is pursued with agencies like the Employment Service, and perhaps the Inland Revenue, as is the intention, agency management will have to consider how much is compatible with the provision of a national service of uniform quality.

Local government

Local government employs nearly 3 million workers. Apart from the police, firefighters and nearly ½ a million teachers, there are about 1 million manual workers and some 600 000 white-collar workers – administrative, professional, technical and clerical (APTC) grades. Up to the late 1960s industrial relations in local government, like the rest of the public service sector, were peaceful and pay and conditions were determined nationally. A number of factors contributed to a changed climate of industrial relations, including the introduction of bonus schemes for manual workers following Report 29 of the National Board for Prices and Incomes (1967a); the effects of incomes policy; the growth of unionisation and the policy of some of the unions to encourage decentralisation and the increase in the number of shop stewards; and the increasing formalisation of industrial relations at local level.

Local authorities (LAs) account for over a third of total public expenditure. Given this level of expenditure, it was inevitable that a government committed to reducing public expenditure and to controlling inflation would seek to exert considerable pressure on, and control over, local government. This took three main forms (Kessler, 1989). First, there was an emphasis on reducing LA manpower. Second, there was an emphasis on the need for LA services to be 'efficient' and 'to provide value for money'. The pressure, and eventually the statutory obligation, to put out to tender many LA services were part of this process, as well as being ideologically in tune with the government's philosophy. Third, and most fundamentally, there were major changes in the financial framework within which LAs had to operate. Thus there was at first a significant shift from central government to LA financing of local services as sizeable reductions were made in the proportion of expenditure met by central government grant – from 61 per cent in 1979 to 39 per cent in 1990. In addition, central government exerted an increasingly tight control over LA expenditure by such means as cash limits, targets, penalties and charge capping.

This culminated in the introduction of the Poll Tax or Community Charge in 1990 in England and Wales, it having been introduced a year earlier in Scotland. As a result of the poll tax and the introduction of the uniform business rate, some three-quarters of LA income was put under the direct control of central government. With the 1991 Budget and its large subsidy to reduce the poll tax, paid for by an increase in VAT, the proportion controlled by central government became even greater. Indeed, with the power to charge-cap, it could be argued that central government has virtually complete control over LA income and expenditure.

Such financial control obviously gave central government major influence over LA pay and terms and conditions of service and indeed for most of the 1980s LA pay – both manual and white-collar – fell significantly behind that of the private sector (see Chapter 10). In 1978–9 LA manual workers' industrial action was a much-publicised feature of the so-called 'Winter of Discontent'. The pay of these workers was one of the first references to the Clegg Standing Commission on Pay Comparability, established in April 1979 to deal with the problem of public service sector pay. LA manuals got a significant, but not exceptional pay award — the award being nowhere near what the unions had claimed — but in subsequent pay rounds they slipped behind again. Approximately two-thirds of LA manual workers are part-time women, employed mainly in the two largest LA services — education and social services — as school meals workers and cleaners and as home helps and care assistants. The remainder are mainly full-time male workers employed in refuse collecting and disposal, roadworks, leisure, parks and housing. In 1986, the LAs and unions jointly undertook a major job evaluation exercise which resulted in 1987 in a new six-grade structure. Particular weight was given in this exercise to the question of equal pay for equal value, and it resulted in a substantial change in the rank order of jobs: in particular home helps and care assistants scored highly relative to, for example, the refuse collectors (Lodge, 1987). One other feature of LA manual bargaining in the 1980s was that the settlement date in November was at the beginning of the annual pay round and was therefore given a great deal of publicity. This was seen as a handicap by the parties and there was pressure and subsequently agreement to move the settlement date to September, which was seen by some as the end of the pay round.

White-collar APTC workers had well under a quarter of their number employed part-time and the range of occupations covered was widespread, ranging from clerical and secretarial staff to social workers and other professional workers such as surveyors, architects, accountants and lawyers. Six unified APTC scales plus senior officer and principal officer scales ranged across a 49-point 'spinal column'. While the national manual agreement allocated each occupational group to a grade, the white-collar agreement allowed LAs to adapt most job requirements to fit the salary scale they wished to pay. At the beginning of the 1980s, APTC grades benefited from an 'in-house' comparability exercise which they preferred to conduct for themselves rather than be referred to the Clegg Commission. In subsequent years, like their manual counterparts, their pay increases fell below those in the private sector.

Financial constraints by central government on local government in the 1980s have meant not only a fall in relative pay, but constant pressure for increased efficiency and reductions in the size of the labour force. Employers have in addition sought greater flexibility. While the employers achieved significant changes, on the whole peacefully, NALGO scored a major victory in 1989 when by selective industrial action it succeeded in raising the employers' pay offer from 6 per cent to 8.8 per cent and the complete removal of the conditions which had been attached to the pay offer, namely:

- provision for performance-related pay, including the ability to withhold increments if performance was not satisfactory;

- the deletion of some grades from the pay scale leaving them to individual authorities' discretion;
- grading decision appeals to terminate at local level, that is to say no appeal to regional or national level;
- authorities to be allowed to negotiate local variations from the national agreement on working time and weekend pay.

The APTC's settlement in 1989 was followed by a similar settlement of 8.8 per cent to 9.2 per cent for LA manuals.

Nevertheless, despite NALGO's victory, there seems little doubt that the employers will continue their search for greater flexibility. Thus the growing uncompetitiveness of LA salaries at the top end has led to greatly enhanced salaries and remuneration packages, often including the provision of a car and generous resettlement packages. In London and the South-East salaries are also proving uncompetitive at lower levels and enhancement and upgrading is becoming common. The biggest step to cope with this problem and the consequent shortage of labour was taken by Kent County Council in 1989 when it withdrew from the national APTC agreement in order to pay significantly higher salaries because of its recruitment and retention difficulties. However, to date only Kent and Buckinghamshire and a few district councils have withdrawn.

It was a constant feature of the decade that a considerable proportion of local authorities were under Labour control. In addition, many Conservative authorities were unenthusiastic, if not openly hostile, to the government's policy towards local government. As a consequence, the government had not been able to further its objectives through the employers' side in negotiations. This was a major reason why it relied heavily on direct control of local government income and expenditure.

Teachers

Teachers' pay in the 1980s had been subject to government constraints, as had most of the public sector, and dissatisfaction was evident for most of the period. Pay had fallen behind in the second half of the 1970s and teachers were one of the references to the Clegg Comparability Commission. The Clegg Report (1980) provided a substantial increase ranging from 17 to 24 per cent, although the teachers' unions were disappointed that the award did not completely restore the Houghton Committee (1974) relativities. The 1980 pay negotiations ended in a failure to agree and in a substantial arbitration award of nearly 14 per cent. In 1982 there was again a failure to agree and the unions 'withdrew goodwill' in order to force a reference to arbitration. (The previous agreement, whereby reference to arbitration could be made unilaterally by either side, had been changed to a reference only by the agreement of both sides.) In 1984 there was again a failure to agree, with the unions asking for arbitration and the employers refusing. In order to obtain arbitration selective industrial action followed, including withdrawal from lunchtime supervision and selective 1-day and then 3-day strikes by the NUT. Finally, the employers conceded a reference to arbitration, although the eventual award of 5.1 per cent was a great disappointment to the unions.

It was 1985 however that saw the most prolonged industrial action and the most bitter dispute. The unions' claim was for 12.5 per cent and a common pay scale: the original management offer was 4 per cent. There followed prolonged industrial action by the NUT, starting with the withdrawal of goodwill and accelerating to extensive selective 3-day strikes. The NUT's action was followed by the NAS/UWT and eventually even by the Assistant Masters' and Mistresses' Association (AMMA). Action continued throughout 1985 and into 1986 (Seifert, 1989), when ACAS eventually got the agreement of the unions and employers to the establishment of an independent panel, headed by Sir John Wood, chairman of the Central Arbitration Committee. The terms of reference were:

> To guide, advise and assist as a matter of urgency, the management and teachers to provisional agreements on the pay, structure and career progression of the teaching profession and any other related matters, e.g. conditions of service and procedures for negotiation, which either party may wish to bring forward for discussion and negotiation.

It was agreed to set up four working parties, each chaired by a member of the independent panel, covering pay and structure; duties; appraisal; and future negotiating machinery. Discussions were complex and lengthy but at a 4–day residential negotiating session at Coventry at the end of July 1986 a list of Terms of Agreement was signed by the employers and five of the six teaching unions, the exception being the NAS/UWT, who considered that the proposed top salary for the main professional grade was inadequate. Discussions continued through the working parties to try to resolve the many outstanding points of detail. A further residential negotiating session was planned for Nottingham early in November 1986 to resolve outstanding issues. Shortly before this took place – on 30 October 1986 – the Secretary of State announced government measures for ending the dispute – increased financial resources were to be made available, the government having previously insisted that no more money would be forthcoming. However, the government proposed a different salary structure from that agreed by the parties in outline at Coventry, and laid down other conditions. The government also announced its intention to introduce legislation to repeal the Remuneration of

Teachers Act 1965, thus abolishing the then existing negotiating machinery — the Burnham Committee — and giving the Secretary of State power to impose settlements, with the help of an advisory committee.

The negotiations at Nottingham took place against the background of this bombshell. However, after very extended negotiations, agreement was reached covering in detail pay levels, salary structure, duties and co-ordination of service between the employers and unions representing a majority of teachers. Efforts were made to keep the overall cost of the agreement within the limits set by the government, but the agreed pay structure was different from that proposed by the Secretary of State. He therefore indicated that he would not be prepared to provide the additional funding, and early in 1987 Parliament passed the Teachers' Pay and Conditions Act under which collective bargaining for teachers was abolished, at least up to 1990, and the agreed settlement reached by the parties under the auspices of ACAS was set aside and replaced by terms and conditions imposed by the Minister.

Pay was increased by an average of 16.4 per cent — to be achieved in two stages — January and October 1987. A basic nine-point incremental scale was introduced from £7900 to £12 700, with five additional above-scale allowances of £900, £1800, £2800, £3800 and £4800. On conditions of employment, teachers' contracts were unilaterally altered by an increase of working days in the year from 190 to 195, of which 190 were to be for teaching and other duties and the other 5, so-called 'Baker Days', were to be for training. Teachers also had to be available for 1265 hours a year, excluding time required for preparation, marking and so forth. Standing in for absent colleagues was also required for up to 3 days. Teachers, however, were no longer required to undertake midday supervision, unless employed under a separate contract to do so. Many of these conditions had also been included in the defunct negotiated settlement, but the unions had obtained certain *quid pro quos*, for example assurances on class size.

It needs to be recalled that the employers' side had had since 1965 an informal concordat with the government that it would only make offers and reach settlements with the Secretary of State's agreement. However, at the end of 1986 the employers' side had renounced that concordat. As we have seen, in the face of industrial action, they proceeded to make an agreement without the Secretary of State's approval. The government's response was to abolish the teachers' negotiating machinery and to take over direct control of teachers' pay aided by an Interim Advisory Committee under Lord Chilvers. Ministers were committed to the eventual restoration of negotiating machinery and in July 1990 the Secretary of State announced that a bill would be introduced in the next parliamentary session to establish new negotiating machinery which would not however become effective before the 1992–3 pay round. The government then had second thoughts and in April 1991 announced that teachers pay in future would be determined by a review body and passed legislation in the Summer of 1991 to put this into effect.

Teachers' pay and conditions had also been the subject of a prolonged dispute in Scotland, but with a different outcome. In December 1984 a campaign of selective industrial action began after a refusal by the Secretary of State for Scotland to agree to a request by the teachers' unions to the establishment of an independent salary review. The request for an independent review was supported by the Scottish local authority employers, but was not agreed to by the government until over a year later in March 1986, when a Committee of Inquiry was appointed, chaired by Sir Peter Main. The report of the Main Committee (1986), which *inter alia* proposed a restructuring of salary scales and changes in terms and conditions of employment provided a basis for the eventual peaceful settlement of the dispute, without the removal of the bargaining rights of the Scottish teachers.

The National Health Service

The National Health Service (NHS) employs over a million people, the main categories being doctors and dentists, nurses, paramedics, technicians, clerical and administrative workers, ancillary workers and ambulance workers.

The NHS is primarily funded by the government although the staff are not employed by the government but by the Regional and District Health Authorities who have responsibility for the day-to-day management; since April 1991 some have instead been employed by self-governing trusts.

NHS ancillary workers along with LA manual workers were in the forefront of the public's perception of the 1978–9 'Winter of Discontent'. Their immediate pay problem was solved through the establishment of the Clegg Comparability Commission, mentioned earlier. Not only were ancillary workers referred to the Clegg Commission but so also were ambulance staff, professions allied to medicine and nurses.

The Conservative government's view was that public-sector pay should be determined on the basis of ability to pay, not on comparability, and the NHS was no exception. This led to the pay dispute of 1982, when the government offered a pay increase of 4 per cent to ancillary and clerical staff and 6.4 per cent to nurses. Limited industrial action ensued, the unions' actions being co-ordinated by the TUC Health Services Committee. The dispute was lengthy. However, concern for patients prevented the calling of an all-out strike, and with the government standing firm the unions were defeated, although they did succeed in getting a small increase in the government's original offer. Throughout the dispute the Royal College of Nursing (RCN) also campaigned for a higher pay offer, but they refused to engage in industrial action. Indeed, the RCN held a ballot on whether to change their rule which prohibited industrial action, which resulted in a large vote against such a change. In

January 1983, following the dispute, the government established a Review Body for nurses and midwives and for the professions allied to medicine. This was largely a reward for the RCN not engaging in industrial action and for having pledged not to do so in the future. (However, a considerable number of nurses are members of unions, in particular NUPE and COHSE, which have not renounced the strike weapon; nor has the BMA.) As a consequence, from that date, more than half of the NHS staff had their pay determined through the mechanisms of the review bodies. The result has been that those whose pay was determined by the review bodies have done better than those determined by conventional negotiation through the traditional Whitley Committee machinery because comparability has been used.

A second major development in the NHS was the appointment of general managers as the chief executives of health authorities, which followed from the Griffiths Report (1983). Moreover, a system of merit pay was introduced for these general managers dependent on their performance. Such performance-related pay had by 1990 spread to other senior managers and to those in middle-management positions.

A third major development was the pursuit by the government of a policy of encouraging 'efficiency savings'. These were to accrue from the increasing drive to contract out ancillary services, from more efficient management, improved working methods and the reduction of staff costs. In addition, from 1980 onwards, the government refused to fund pay awards above the percentage norm for the public sector. This underfunding provided strong pressure on health authorities to effect savings. Moreover, in 1983 manpower targets were set for all staff and regional health authorities were asked to monitor staff numbers closely and achieve a reduction in overall staff numbers of between 0.75 and 1.0 percent. Each year regional health authorities reminded districts what was required of them and revised targets were set at the beginning of each financial year (Mailly *et al.*, 1989).

Of particular significance was the government's policy of ordering health authorities to put out to tender cleaning, catering and laundry services. In 1981 the Minister of State for Health wrote to regional health authorities suggesting that they considered contracting out their 'hotel' services. There was little response, and in 1983 a further circular was sent requiring the health authorities to seek bids for their cleaning, catering and laundry work. As the Fair Wages Resolution had been abolished in 1983, private contractors were no longer obliged to observe NHS terms for pay and conditions, although many authorities required that they should do so. However, in 1984 the Minister wrote again to the health authorities instructing them not to require private contractors to abide by Whitley pay rates and terms and conditions. The government's policy had a significant effect, not primarily because private sector tenders were always the lowest, but because in order to win the contract in-house, substantial economies in staffing often had to be made. As in central and local government, contracting-out was often applied at the expense of the lowest-paid workers. The services put out to tender were mostly performed by those on the lowest rates of NHS pay. The effect of the contracting-out was to lower the rates of pay and worsen the conditions offered for the same work by the private contractors. The same workers were often employed by the contractors, who in many cases expected them to do more work with less supervision. As with the limitation of Wages Council legal minimum rates to those over 21 and to a single level of pay and to one premium rate, those who were most in need of protection because of their weakness in the labour market had their position worsened. It was not the case that these changes challenged the position of strong unions with monopoly power protecting well-paid employees: they picked out the weak for penalties.

Finally, with effect from April 1991, certain NHS hospitals have been encouraged to set themselves up as self-managing trusts, with freedom to determine the pay of their own staff, with the exception of junior doctors. To what extent this freedom will be taken up remains to be seen. It is however in line with overall government policy to seek to break public-sector national agreements, as with civil service agencies and local authorities.

The nationalised industries

As stated earlier in this chapter, the Conservative government of the 1980s had an inherent dogmatic suspicion and distrust of public enterprise and public expenditure and an equally inherent and dogmatic belief in the superiority of private enterprise. However, the 1979 government did not include wholesale privatisation in its election manifesto and such a policy only emerged after the 1983 general election. Nevertheless, the extent of privatisation in the 1980s is impressive. In the first instance a number of publicly owned companies or parts of companies were sold off, for example, Cable & Wireless, Rolls-Royce, British Aerospace, British Leyland and Inmos. These had been taken into the public fold in an earlier period, in most cases to save them from bankruptcy. Then, as Table 7.2 shows, in 1982 National Freight and Britoil were sold and in 1983 Associated British Ports; in 1984 British Telecom (BT) was privatised and the process of selling off parts of British Shipbuilders commenced; in 1986 British Gas was privatised and the process of selling off the subsidiaries of the National Bus Company began. 1987 saw the sale of British Airways, the British Airports Authority, the Ministry of Defence dockyards and the Royal Ordnance factories, while in 1988 British Steel was sold and the privatisation of passenger transport executives began. In 1989 the British water industry was privatised, and in 1991 the electricity supply industry. Virtually all that was left in public ownership was the Post Office, British Coal, British Rail and

TABLE 7.2   Privatisation, 1982–91

	Year	Employees
National Freight Company	1982	28 000
Britoil	1982	14 000
Associated British Ports (formerly British Transport Docks Board)	1983	–
Enterprise Oil (separated from British Gas Corporation)	1984	–
British Telecom	1984	250 000
Trust Ports	1985	–
British Shipbuilders – various dates from	1984	–
British Gas Corporation	1986	89 000
National Bus Company Subsidiaries	1986–88	30 000
British Airways	1987	36 000
Royal Ordnance factories	1987	–
British Airports Authority (BAA)	1987	7 000
British Steel	1988	53 000
Passenger Transport Executives – various dates from	1988	8 000
Regional Water Authorities and Water Authorities Association	1989	40 000
Electricity distribution	1990	–
Electricity generation	1991	–

Source: 'Employment in the Public and Private Sectors', *Economic Trends*, December 1990.

London Transport. The number of employees in nationalised industries fell from 1.85 million in 1979 to 0.66 million in 1990.

The government was of course not the direct employer of workers in the nationalised industries; nevertheless it could and did exercise considerable influence over pay and employment matters, mainly through financial controls and targets, but also through the appointment of chairmen and board members who were in tune with Thatcherite beliefs and policies. In addition, the development of the policy of wholesale privatisation had a major effect on nationalised boards. In order to be saleable, the industries had first to be made profitable if they were loss-makers and this had implications for pay, manning levels and redundancies. (It was, of course, not true that all nationalised industries were loss-makers. For example, gas, electricity, BAA and BT consistently made surpluses under the government's own rules: the only big and consistent loss-makers were the coal industry, steel and the railways, although others like British Airways had spells in the red.)

For purposes of analysis it is useful to divide the nationalised industries into declining and expanding industries. The main expanding industries were BT, gas, airways, water and electricity and, to nearly everyone's surprise, the Post Office: the main declining industries were coal, railways, shipbuilding, buses and iron and steel. It is clearly impossible to deal with all of these industries or deal with them in any detail, so only a broad picture will be drawn.

Declining Industries

Coal

The coal industry in 1979–80 had 232 500 wage earners on the colliery books and produced 109 million tons. Throughout the 1970s, the British coal industry faced competition from other sources of energy – oil, natural gas, nuclear energy and cheap imported coal. In the early 1980s the demand for coal fell steadily owing not only to competition from other fuels but as a result of the recession. Output and manpower were reduced, as was the number of working pits. The decrease was however gradual until 1984 when the National Coal Board announced that over 30 pits would close in 1984–5. This led to the miners's strike.

With the NUM's complete defeat and subsequent powerlessness, management was free to pursue its own policies with impunity. Growing competition, including that likely to arise from the privatisation of electricity, and tight government financial constraints and targets, meant hard-line management in efforts to attain government targets and to bring down costs and prices. This meant restraint on national pay increases, changes in payment systems with great emphasis on piecework, local pay variations, large-scale closures, and major changes in working methods. As a consequence, by 1990, in the 5 years since the miners' strike, the number of pits had been reduced from 170 to 68 and the number of men employed from 150 000 to 75 000: productivity doubled. Whether this will be enough to meet the competition from cheap imported coal is however questionable. It is also questionable whether the 'macho-management' style adopted by British Coal after the 1984–5 strike was necessary. After all, very substantial reductions in the number of pits, in output and in manpower had been achieved in earlier decades without a major confrontation. However, a senior British Coal executive told us that in his opinion the progress which has been made and the changes in attitude could not have been achieved without the strike.

Railways

Like the coal industry, the railways had experienced secular decline during most of the post-war period, largely as a result of competition from other forms of transport, in particular the growth of car ownership and the growth in the size and the use of lorries. It is true that the railways had an advantage in the movement of bulk commodities, such as coal, iron ore and steel, but these were also areas of long-term decline. The railways' predicament in the face of such competition was accentuated in the 1980s by the government's policy of alleged non-interference, free competition, drastic reductions in financial assistance, tough financial targets and a refusal to consider the social costs of competition. The result in industrial relations terms was a hard-line attitude on pay which meant that pay rates fell below those achieved elsewhere and reasonable average earnings could be obtained only by the working of excessive overtime. It also meant determined drives to change working practices in order to increase efficiency. One such attempt resulted in a strike by ASLEF in 1982 which was unsuccessful from the union's point of view; however in 1989 a series of one-day strikes by the NUR (and ASLEF) over pay and against changes in bargaining structure and other industrial relations procedures was successful in that the pay offer which BR had sought to impose unilaterally was significantly increased and the proposed procedural changes were not imposed, but referred to a joint union–management working party for further consideration, with the assistance of ACAS. The deterioration of industrial relations on the railways was not marked by industrial action, with the exceptions of 1982 and 1989, but by high labour turnover and often labour shortages, particularly in London and the South-East, and by low morale due to relatively low pay, long hours and poor working conditions. How far this contributed to a spate of major railway accidents is debateable, as is the contribution of inadequate investment, although the public support for the NUR during the 1989 strikes could be interpreted as a sign that many people believed railway pay should be improved. What seems certain is that without a change in government policy the future will mean continued financial pressure on British Rail, worsening services, fares going up by more than inflation and problematic industrial relations.

Steel

The steel industry was nationalised for the second time in 1967 and was privatised in December 1988. Its story needs to go back to the mid-1970s when the British Steel Corporation had 230 000 employees. It was suffering from gross overcapacity because it had been building capacity for an estimated

UK demand in 1980 of around 39 million tons, whereas actual demand turned out to be 14 million tons. There was also overcapacity in the world steel industry. However, UK costs were high and productivity relatively low; there were also heavy financial losses. Management then decided that there had to be a strategy for change, the main elements of which included the closure of uneconomic steelmaking plants and the concentration of production on modern technology, the slimming of manpower, decentralisation to increase business identity, improving direct communications with the workforce, and having an active social policy contribution to alleviate the effects of change and to create a climate within which change became acceptable. The first closure took place in the mid-1970s.

In 1980 there was a major national strike lasting some 3 months in an industry which had long been noted for its good industrial relations. The dispute was overtly over pay and it is difficult to avoid the suspicion that the government had played a part in the original low offer. Be that as it may, the strike was also covertly about power. Management claimed that they had not been looking for a showdown: they had not thought it necessary. In retrospect, management now believe that they could not have moved as fast as they did if it had not been for union weakness and exhaustion as a result of the strike.

The reduction in manpower happened rapidly: by 1985 manpower was down to some 65 000, while in 1990 it was some 51 200. Closures were very extensive and included many major works such as Shotton and Corby. Apart from closures there were substantial manpower reductions at surviving plants. For example, at Llanwern between September 1979 and December 1980 manpower was reduced from over 9350 to under 4900 and man-hours per ton reduced from 9.75 to 4.2. This was achieved, according to management, through reducing the number of management levels, increased flexibility between craft and process workers and manual and staff grades, increased mechanisation, greater use of contractors, a higher work tempo and the cutting out of inessentials. These achievements were attained against the background of a threat of complete closure of one of the major plants in South Wales. There was also very intensive local consultation and negotiation. Redundancy pay was relatively generous and was helped by ECSC funds.

Overall, labour costs as a proportion of total costs came down from 35 per cent in 1978–9 to 19 per cent in 1989. From heavy financial losses in the 1970s British Steel made a trading profit of £91 million in 1985–6 and £425 million in 1987–8 – the last year before privatisation. Its latest accounts for 1989–90 showed a trading profit of £708 million. In terms of efficiency and profitability steel has thus been a success story – a success achieved while the industry was still nationalised – but a success achieved by a reduction in the labour force of over three-quarters and hence at a great social cost.

British Steel has favoured a more devolved business structure in order to respond with greater flexibility to the varying commercial and economic pressures which faced the different businesses. There are now five main divisions, of which the two largest employing about 20 000 each are General Steels and Strip Products. Since the beginning of 1990 bargaining has been decentralised to the separate businesses and corporation-wide bargaining has ceased. The unions had been strongly opposed but eventually reluctantly accepted the new bargaining structure. The five businesses have varied in the decentralised negotiating arrangements they have adopted. The two large businesses — General Steels and Strip Products — have established joint bodies at business level, whereas the other three have decentralised further, down to their constituent manufacturing units. Bargaining takes place at business unit level round a 'single table', except that managerial grades are covered by a separate business level bargaining unit. SIMA still represents managers and unlike for example BT and BR there has been no attempt to roll back managerial unionism. There has been no derecognition and the check-off still applies. There was no change in the established grievance and disciplinary procedures except that matters cannot be referred beyond the business unit level. Arbitration arrangements were rationalised and are now in every case by mutual agreement only.

On pay systems, the steel industry has always put considerable weight on local bonuses linked to performance and in recent years more and more emphasis has been put on locally determined bonuses and less and less on industry-wide basic rates. Bonuses are now related both to departmental and plant performance.

Finally, management unquestionably considered that the cause of change was the parlous economic state of the industry: it was not the law, nor Thatcherism, nor privatisation.

Expanding Industries

Electricity

The electricity supply industry in post-war Britain has had a long history of expansion. It also has had a long history of technological advance and rising productivity. Thus the chairman of the Electricity Council in its last annual report (1988–89) stated that it was appropriate to record briefly what the industry had achieved over the past 30 years since the Electricity Act 1957 which set up the Electricity Council twelve area boards and the CEGB.

In this time the number of customers has increased by about 50 per cent, sales have increased by more than 220 per cent, while the number of staff employed has fallen by more than 55 000. Output has trebled, productivity increased more than four-fold and technical efficiency has dramatically improved. Thirty years ago there were more than 250 power stations; today there are only 72 producing three times as much electricity. Thermal efficiency at coal- and oil-fired power stations increased from 26.77% to 35.47%, representing a saving of more than £1 billion per annum at present-day prices.

He added that there had been an operating profit in 1988–9 of £777 million, that the industry was able to finance its capital investment programme entirely from internal resources and that it had reduced its net borrowings by £1779 million.

The industry has also been a model of industrial relations stability. The only significant industrial action taken in the post-war years was an overtime ban by the manual workers in 1972. The effects of this limited action were almost immediately apparent and potentially so serious that the government set up a Court of Inquiry, the action was called off and the Inquiry recommended a significant pay increase. Indeed, so essential is electricity to the economy and to society generally that the unions have overwhelming bargaining power. However, it could be argued that they dare not use it to the full because of the dire consequences of industrial action for society. Nevertheless, it is difficult to argue that the unions have abused their power. They co-operated in technological change, productivity increased steadily and earnings rose significantly, but not noticeably faster than the national average over the years. Moreover, manpower was gradually reduced as a result of technological change and increased efficiency, but without any traumas. The industry had long-established collective bargaining machinery at national level and elaborate consultative arrangements at all levels: it was a pioneer of productivity bargaining in the 1960s and one of the first to engage in moves towards harmonisation of the terms and conditions of blue-collar and white-collar workers. All this was achieved within the centralised bargaining arrangements and there was no move to decentralised negotiations. How far and in what way industrial relations will change under privatisation remains to be seen, although it is likely that there will be separate negotiations in the twenty successor companies, with decisions to be made about bargaining levels within the companies. Certainly it can be argued that in the 1980s in contrast to, say, coal and the railways, industrial relations remained non-confrontational and cooperative, presumably a reflection of the fact that it was a successful and profitable industry, and hence less susceptible to government pressure. The continuation of central bargaining during a period of change and of manpower reductions had also helped to preserve stability.

Privatisation is bringing about alterations in negotiating machinery which may well make the avoidance of disputes more difficult in what is one of the most essential of industries.

Gas

The story of the gas industry has been very similar to that of electricity. had
well-established industrial relations procedures and good industrial rel ions
with a virtually complete absence of industrial action over the yea of
nationalisation. At one point in the post-war period it looked as if he
industry was due to stagnate and indeed decline in the face of its depende ce
on coal as a raw material and competition from oil and electricity. Enterpris g
management, however, sought other ways of obtaining gas, including using
as a feed stock, the extraction of methane from the then National Coal Board
pits and the importation of frozen methane. The industry was subsequently
transformed by the discovery of natural gas in the North Sea. Its history has
been one of growth and high profitability.

The industry bargained at national level, both for manual and white-collar
workers, although particularly for white-collar workers there was flexibility at
local level in the pay scales. For manual workers, incentive schemes have long
been in operation – following NPBI Report No. 29 in 1967. Earnings have
been relatively high, but by no means the highest in industry, and again there
is no evidence of the unions exploiting their strong bargaining position.
Industrial relations in the nationalised gas industry were cooperative and not
confrontational. Like the electricity industry it did not suffer undue interference
from government in the 1980s. Again as with electricity, this was doubtless the
result of its growth, steadily increasing productivity and profitability. To date,
privatisation has not significantly changed industrial relations. Management's
intention was to preserve industry-wide bargaining and indeed to strengthen
national pay structures with national standard job specifications. In a single-
product business, they believed that there must be common terms because the
work was identical wherever it was done. Sufficient flexibililty was provided
through regional bonus schemes related to performance and there was local
control of the amount of overtime and the schedules of standby and call-out.

The Post Office

The Post Office (PO) and British Telecom (BT) were separated in 1981. The
universal expectation was that BT was the growth area and that PO faced
inevitable decline. This latter expectation proved to be false and PO
experienced a boom period – greater than ever before in its history, the
volume of letters increasing from 30 million a day in 1984 to 54 million in
1990. Social mail had gone down but business mail had increased enormously.

The Post Office had been run on civil service lines. In the 1970s one senior
manager, originally from the private sector, stated, 'Management didn't

manage.' He considered that the traumatic postman's strike of 1970, won by management, had the paradoxical effect of management almost bending over backwards to make concessions. They had found the conflict distasteful and wanted to reintroduce 'sound' relationships.

In contrast to the 1970s, the 1980s were a good decade in the sense of the successful achievement of business objectives. It was a period of change. Management faced various restrictive practices, for example a ban on the mechanisation of sorting and a virtual ban on the use of part-timers. Changes had to be achieved and management were determined to achieve them – using persuasion, inducement and, in the last resort, a determinationn to act unilaterally, regardless of union opposition, for example on part-time workers.

Management, the same interviewee stated, had been greatly helped by the new climate of industrial relations – weaker unions and stronger management. They had also been helped by the new industrial relations legislation and government policies. It was not that PO had been a great user of the legislation (although it had done so on at least one occasion) but that the legislation was part of the new climate. In the unions' view it was the government's financial targets and rates of return which had been the main influence and not the legislation. During the 1980s there had been a series of national enabling agreements and details of change were then determined locally. There had been 3 or 4 major disputes and in the late 1980s a series of short-lived local disputes. There had therefore been industrial relations troubles but PO had succeeded in bringing about substantial change and there had been business success.

In 1986 PO had created three separate companies – Royal Mail, with 160 000 employees out of a total PO labour force of 210 000, Parcel Force and PO Counters. Counters was being restructured, with small offices closed so that there would be only 500–600 main post offices. There are now no central negotiations covering PO. Each of the companies conducts its own negotiations. The unions had not liked the separation but had accepted it. It had meant 16 to 18 main bargaining units. According to management, the main pay increases had been similar but it had enabled different grading structures to be introduced as well as different productivity schemes. According to the unions, each of the companies tries to put its individual stamp on its agreements. Thus, for example, there are three different settlement dates and thus three occasions in the year when there could be confrontation. One union leader stated that 'each settlement is used as the foundation on which to build the next'. He firmly believed that 'decentralisation contained the seeds of its own destruction and that the PO Board would eventually insist on pulling back to one agreement on pay. The steady ratcheting up would force this on them.' However, management is planning further decentralisation for 1992 with the establishment of 9 independent business centres instead of 64 divisional districts. Each business centre, it is stated, will be in charge of its own bargaining, pay, its quality of service and its profit and loss.

In the PO there had not been the removal of collective bargaining for managers to the same extent as there had been in BT and BR. Personal contracts had been introduced for the top 30 managers a number of years ago and then extended to 500 senior managers, but there was no intention of going further. The top 250 jobs were managed corporately with pay review and appraisal carried out by the chairman and a central committee. Merit pay is at a maximum of 25 per cent and is in the form of a lump sum and non-pensionable.

Finally, there had been a post-entry closed-shop agreement with the UCW which had been put into cold storage. Union membership however remained at over 90 per cent. The check-off had not been affected.

British Telecom (BT)

BT, with a labour force of some 250 000, was privatised in 1984. It had previously been separated from PO in 1981. Like PO its management and industrial relations were steeped in civil service traditions. Indeed, one senior executive described it as 'more civil service than the civil service . . . at every level throughout the business there was joint management with the unions.'

The major change has been in management, in no small part according to a union general secretary through the importation of people from outside who had brought in a different culture. 'Change used to be gradual and joint. Now it is quick and, if necessary, unilaterally decided . . . . In the past if the union's response to a proposal was "no" the management would drop it. But now they persist and impose it if necessary.'

Major changes had taken place in BT, partly as a result of management, partly as a result of technology and partly because of increased – if so far limited -competition. The labour force was being markedly reduced although, because of turnover, this was without compulsory redundancies.

There have been a number of significant disputes during the 1980s, in particular the 1981 SCPS strike over pay differentials; in 1983 over connecting Mercury and privatisation; and in 1987 over BT's linking of the annual pay increase with demarcation changes. In all three cases management had acted firmly: indeed they had sought to escalate the action in order to put financial pressure on unions. The 1981 strike, which was selective, went on for 21 weeks and achieved no gain for the union on management's last offer. In the 1983 industrial action, staff were not allowed to work their normal hours if they refused to do overtime. They had to sign a document saying that they would work as management directed or not work at all. Management won, but a senior executive admitted that 'industrial relations had been poisoned and scars were left on many managers.' The 1987 industrial action had begun with an overtime ban. Overtime was necessary to run the system without interruptions and working overtime was part of the contract of employment. Management decided that it was best to exclude operational staff from the international exchanges and they were run by managers. The main cost of the action to BT was a large backlog of faults which took a year or more to catch up.

Management had not resorted to the use of the law. 'What matters are the working relationships and they have got to take the responsibility; importing legal decisions would worsen them.' However, it was accepted by both management and unions that the legal changes had altered the backcloth. 'They had made it respectable to stand up to union strength.' Negotiations in BT were still largely centralised. The unions, according to one general secretary, had made agreements which had helped management to reach its objectives. He believed that you 'had to do the best you could and that there was no percentage in just resisting management's pressure . . . So there was acceptance, though reluctant, of changes.' The National Communications Union (NCU) had never had a closed shop but its membership was over 90 per cent. Its clerical section (formerly part of the CPSA) had had a closed shop and had lost membership on its termination in 1983. The check-off was still in full operation. Under the old system there had been collective bargaining for every level of staff up to the board. Individual contracts have been introduced for the top 100, then the next 250 and the next 600 and then the main group of 5000 managers. Going beyond the 5000 would not be done by extending it to a new level but according to whether jobs were suitable for it.

Conclusion

The public sector has been the main area of conflict in industrial relations during the past decade. This has been because the government, either as employer or paymaster, started with the belief that the public sector was intrinsically inefficient: it was over-manned, bureaucratic, a drain on the public purse and the home of powerful trade unions which were unconstrained by market forces. Government policy was therefore to create a more commercial environment through stricter financial controls, increased competition, contracting out or the threat of contracting out, and eventually privatisation in order to achieve greater efficiency. Indeed, as the government's belief in wholesale privatisation developed, this in itself became a major factor in the drive for greater profitability for unless there were a sufficient level of profitability, privatisation would not be possible.

As a consequence of government pressure – above all financial pressure – industrial relations has moved from consensus to confrontation. As Ferner (1989) notes:

> This is not to say that the government has deliberately provoked public sector strikes in order to force a showdown with the unions . . . . But the government's pressure on management has created conditions in which conflict became more likely if not inevitable.

Financial pressure has been applied, both to the public service sector and to the public corporations in order to reproduce the conditions under which the private sector was believed to operate and to introduce what were believed to be private-sector management practices. Consequently, pay moved from being determined mainly by comparability to being determined allegedly by ability to pay and the need to recruit and retain labour. Moves were made to decentralise bargaining and to reduce the importance of national pay scales: merit pay was introduced and so were allowances based on geographical shortages of labour and skill shortages. Staff numbers were reduced and increased flexibility in the use of labour sought. Organisational change was introduced and also cultural change, often driven in the public corporations by the appointment of 'right-minded' chairmen and board members from the private sector.

As a consequence, industrial relations in much of the public sector changed for the worse and almost beyond recognition. While it is true that there were a number of public sector disputes in the 1970s, these were over specific pay claims. There was not the general deterioration and malaise which took place in the 1980s.

Towards the end of the decade there were some signs of change — not in government hostility or basic objectives with regard to the public sector, but in a recognition of certain realities. Thus tightening labour markets and rising inflation mean some relaxation in the policy of holding down public service sector pay: indeed, comparability in the form of the new Civil Service agreements re-emerged in an institutionalised form. There was also perhaps a partial realisation that constant denigration and confrontation was not the way to obtain the best results from employees. However, these limited examples of improvement were dwarfed by numerous examples of continued disregard of 'good' industrial relations practice such as constant refusal to compromise in order to avoid disputes and refusal in virtually any circumstances to permit the help of a third party, in particular arbitration; permitting pay to fall behind that of the private sector and indeed in some cases below the RPI; and reductions in time-off and other facilities for union representatives.

CHAPTER 8

Trade unions

Introduction

During the 1980s the trade union movement experienced greatly reduced membership, reduced influence with government and in society generally, and greatly reduced bargaining power *vis-à-vis* employers. The environment in which unions had to operate was the crucial cause of their problems, although this is not to say that there were not deficiencies in union organisation, policies and behaviour which contributed.

Metcalf (1991b, p. 22) argued that the decline in union membership in the 1980s was 'the result of a complex interaction of five factors: the macro-economic climate, the composition of the workforce, the policy of the state, the attitudes and conduct of employers and the stance taken by unions themselves'. With regard to the first factor, the record post-war level of unemployment in the first half of the 1980s was undoubtedly a major factor in the decline in membership, but the substantial reduction in unemployment and the increase in the labour force in the second half of the 1980s did not lead to an increase in membership. The second factor – changes in the composition of jobs and the workforce with major declines in manufacturing and manual male employment and major increases in the service sector, female part-time employment and in professional, managerial and highly skilled work – unquestionably contributed to the decline in union membership and density. However, these labour market trends were also present in the 1970s when union membership and density grew to unprecedented levels. The third factor – government policy and, in particular, anti-union legislation – was also of some significance; for example the outlawing in effect of the closed shop and the ending of statutory recognition procedures. The fourth and fifth factors – the behaviour of employers and of unions – are of key importance. Unions needed to both extend recognition and to avoid derecognition. While derecognition has not happened on a major scale, there are some well-known examples as well as a number of less widely known cases. Securing recognition in hitherto unorganised sectors has proved very difficult, with many employers taking a much harder line than they did in the 1970s.

Two recent studies on reasons for the fall in trade union density give somewhat contradictory results. Freeman and Pelletier (1990) calculate that changes in UK labour law reduced union density by 1 to 1.7 percentage points per year from 1980 to 1986, which cumulatively amounted to 9.4 percentage points – effectively the entire decline in UK density in that period. They therefore conclude that 'the vast bulk of the observed 1980s decline in union density in the UK is due to the changed legal environment for industrial relations' (p. 141). In contrast, Disney (1990) concludes that it is macroeconomic factors that explain the upturn in union density in the 1970s and the downturn in the 1980s. Employment composition effects moved in a perverse direction (relative to membership) in the 1970s and played little part in the decline in the 1980s. He further concludes that industrial relations legislation of the period seems to have had no direct effect. Neither of these studies is entirely satisfactory. Our own view is that the decline in membership is due to an amalgam of five factors enumerated by Metcalf and that it is impossible to put figures to each of them.

Most of the main environmental changes have been discussed in earlier chapters. In this chapter we consider the effects of these changes on trade union membership, on trade union finances and organisation, on union responses to changes in employers' policies and to changes in the law. We also consider changes in the organisation, role and policies of the TUC.

In many respects the major issue is whether the trend of union decline in the 1980s is a permanent trend which will continue in the 1990s and lead to the marginalisation of unions or whether the events of the 1980s did not basically change the institutions and procedures of workplace industrial relations, and that the future will see a readjustment of union attitudes, objectives and methods to the changing environment and a revival of union fortunes. Connected to this issue is the so-called 'new unionism' or 'new realism' which some have argued is essential if unions are to survive in the future (Bassett, 1986; Roberts, 1987).

Trade union membership

The fall in trade union membership has been dramatic and was made even more so by the rapid increase in membership enjoyed by unions in the 1970s. Between 1969 and 1979 total trade union membership increased by nearly 3 million from 10.5 million to 13.3 million, and union density increased from 45.3 to 54.2 per cent. TUC membership over the same period increased from

9.4 million to 12.1 million. In contrast, between 1979 and 1989 the total number of trade union members declined from 13.3 million to 10.2 million, a fall of 3 million and union density declined from 54.2 to 41.2 per cent. TUC membership over the period 1979 to 1989 declined from 12.1 million to 8.4 million and in 1990 there was a further fall to 8.2 million. So in terms of numbers of members the gains of the 1970s had been lost by the end of the 1980s and in terms of density the position was worse than at the end of the 1960s because the total number of employees had increased.

Union density is actual union membership as a percentage of potential membership. Potential membership can be defined in a number of ways. The traditional method as used by Price and Bain (1983) is to take potential membership as being the number of employees in civil employment plus the unemployed, and this is the method used to produce the figures quoted above. A second method would be to take only those in civil employment and not include the unemployed in the denominator. For the early post-war decades, with very low unemployment, the result of using either method would not be very different. With the high unemployment of the 1980s, however, the result is significantly different and the decline in density if the unemployed are excluded would be from 56.9 in 1979 to 44.2 per cent in 1989, compared with 54.2 to 41.2 per cent if the unemployed are included (see Table 8.1). Price and Bain mainly justified the inclusion of the unemployed on the grounds that many unemployed kept their union membership, at least to begin with. This may have been true particularly of craftsmen, and when periods of unemployment were of short duration, but is arguably less true of the 1980s with mass unemployment and the large increase in the number of the long-term unemployed. Waddington (1991) in a recent article which updates Price and Bain (1983) produces density figures based on both methods. A third method of measuring union density would be to take as the denominator the total civil labour force, thus including the self-employed. There is no one 'right' method: it depends, as Kelly and Bailey (1989) have stated, on the purpose for which the figures are being used.

One further point needs to be made on union membership which also affects calculations of union density. This is that union membership figures have traditionally been taken from the returns made by unions to the TUC, to the Certification Officer and to the Department of Employment. It has long been realised that some of the union membership figures have been exaggerated for a number of reasons – one of the most common being that some unions include retired people in membership. Light has now been thrown on the extent of this exaggeration by the inclusion for the first time in the Labour Force Survey (LFS) for 1989 of a question on union membership. The results for Great Britain give an estimated figure of 9.1 million for membership and a union density of 39 per cent in spring 1989 (Stevens and Wareing, 1990). The membership figure compares with 10.2 million for December 1989 as compiled by the Department of Employment. Among reasons given for the difference

TABLE 8.1   Trade union membership, 1979–89

	Union membership (000s) (1)	Number of unions (2)	Potential union membership (000s)			Union density	
			Employees in employment (3)	Unemployed (4)	Total (5)	(1)÷(3) % (6)	(1)÷(5) % (7)
1979	13 289	453	23 206	1 301	24 507	56.9	54.2
1980	12 947	438	22 386	2 137	24 523	57.8	52.8
1981	12 106	414	21 580	2 782	24 362	56.1	49.7
1982	11 593	408	21 101	2 949	24 050	54.9	48.2
1983	11 236	394	21 169	2 956	24 125	53.1	46.6
1984	10 994	375	21 363	3 106	24 469	51.5	44.9
1985	10 821	370	21 418	3 133	24 551	50.5	44.1
1986	10 539	335	21 389	3 121	24 510	49.3	43.0
1987	10 475	330	21 956	2 569	24 525	47.7	42.7
1988	10 376	315	22 513	2 038	24 551	45.5	41.7
1989	10 158	309	23 004	1 635	24 639	44.2	41.2

Source: *Employment Gazette*, June 1991, for number of unions and union membership.

Employment Gazette, various, for employees in employment and the unemployed.

Employees and unemployed Figures are for UK, seasonally adjusted for December each year.

were that the LFS question was only asked of those in employment and therefore excluded those who were unemployed or economically inactive during the 'reference week' in question; the LFS estimate counted individuals in membership rather than individual memberships – those belonging to two unions would appear twice in the DE figure but once in the LFS figure; and retired people who were currently union members were excluded from the LFS survey.

The LFS figure receives a considerable degree of support from some recent research work (Bailey and Kelly, 1990, p. 9), which sought to adjust the DE membership figures to less inflated ones. They produced revised figures for trade union membership and density, with figures adjusted to account for the inclusion of non-UK citizens, retired members, unemployed members and self-employed members. Their deflators, based largely on a survey of TUC unions conducted in 1988, depend 'on one very important assumption: namely that the proportion of non-Great Britain retired and unemployed workers in trade unions has not varied significantly over the years.' Their estimate for 1987 gave union membership of 9.427 million for Great Britain compared with the DE's 10.475 million for the UK, and put union density at 44.1 per cent. The main reasons for the difference were that union returns in 1986 included an estimated 500 000 retired people, 190 000 unemployed and some membership in Northern Ireland as well as some in the Irish Republic.

For our purpose the measure of trade union density which best indicates the decline of union bargaining power is one which excludes the unemployed from the denominator and retired and unemployed members from the numerator. That measure according to Stevens and Wareing (1990) was 39 per cent in the spring of 1989. According to Bailey and Kelly (1990), it was 44 per cent in 1987 compared with 53 per cent in 1979 – a fall of 17 per cent. The series, which is continuous from 1979 in Table 8.1, shows quite clearly that a decline in density has taken place in every year of the decade.

Table 8.1 also shows that between 1979 and 1989 the number of unions declined from 453 to 309, thus continuing a long decline which goes back to before the turn of the last century. It should be recalled that there are still many very small unions in existence. Thus just under half the unions had a membership in 1989 of less than 1000 each, accounting in total for only 0.3 per cent of total union membership. At the other extreme, there were 23 unions with a membership of 100 000 or more each, accounting for just over 80 per cent of total union membership (*Employment Gazette*, June 1991).

The impact of the overall fall in union membership on individual unions is shown in Table 8.2. which lists the 20 largest TUC affiliated unions – those with a membership of over 100 000 at the end of 1989. It will be seen that the fall in membership is not evenly distributed. Some white-collar unions, for example NCU and BIFU, stand out against the trend, although some other white-collar unions such as ASTMS (before its merger with TASS to form MSF in 1988) experienced a decline of some 20 per cent and APEX (which is not shown in the table) experienced a decline of some 50 per cent before its merger with the GMB, also in 1988. Another union not shown in the table, the NUM, had its membership reduced from 253 000 in 1979 to 59 000 in 1989 as a result of the cut-backs in the coalmining industry following its defeat in the 1984–85 strike, and the breakaway movement which resulted in the formation of the UDM, while the membership of the ISTC fell from 104 000 in 1979 to 65 000 in 1989. Some other smaller unions, for example the National Union of Seamen and the Agricultural Workers' Union (the latter eventually merging with the TGWU and the former with the NUR) were also greatly reduced in size. Outside the TUC, the RCN grew from 162 000 in 1979 to 282 000 in 1988, AMMA reached over 130 000 and a new teachers' union – PAT – built up a membership of some 40 000 by 1988. The biggest union – the TGWU – and the AEU, NUR, CPSA and NUT all declined by a good deal more than the average.

The change in membership of individual unions needs to be treated with some caution. Thus in some cases the loss is understated because of mergers with other unions. This is true, for example, of the GMB. Sometimes a heavy fall is the result of special factors separate from the general trend, for example the NUT, part of whose loss was due to teachers switching to other teachers'

TABLE 8.2   TUC membership, 1970–89 (December, 000s)

	1970	1979	1989	Change 1979–89	% Change 1979–89
1. Transport and General Workers Union (TGWU)	1639	2073	1271	−802	−39
2. General Municipal Boilermakers & Allied Trades Union (GMB)	853	965	823	−142	−17
3. National and Local Government Officers Association (NALGO)	440	729	751	+22	+3
4. Amalgamated Engineering Union (AEU)	1202	1199	742	−457	−38
5. Manufacturing, Science & Finance (MSF)*	−	−	653	−	−
6. National Union of Public Employees (NUPE)	373	712	605	−107	−15
7. Shop, Distributive & Allied Workers (USDAW)	330	462	376	−86	−19
[8. Electrical, Electronic, Telecommunications & Plumbing (EETPU)]†	421	420	−	−	−
9. Union of Construction, Allied Trades & Technicians (UCATT)	−	321	258	−63	−20
10. Confederation of Health Service Employees (COHSE)	90	215	209	−6	−3
11. Union of Communication Workers (UCW)	209	197	203	+6	+3
12. Society of Graphical and Allied Trades (SOGAT)	193	203	176	−27	−13
13. National Union of Teachers (NUT)	311	291	172	−119	−41
14. Banking, Insurance & Finance Union (BIFU)	89	126	170	+44	+35
15. National Communications Union (NCU)	117	121	157	+36	+30
16. Civil and Public Services Association (CPSA)	185	225	128	−97	−43
17. National Graphical Association (NGA)	107	110	125	+15	+14
18. National Association of Schoolmasters and Union of Women Teachers (NAS/UWT)	57	112	118	+6	+5
19. National Union of Civil and Public Servants (NUCAPS)‡	−	−	116	−	−
20. National Union of Railwaymen (NUR)	198	180	103	−77	−43
Total number of TUC affiliated unions	142	112	78	−	−
Total TUC membership (in millions)	10.0	12.1	8.4	−3.7	−31

Source: TUC statistical statements.

* MSF − A merger of ASTMS + TASS; in 1986 ASTMS = 390 000, TASS = 241 000.
† The EETPU was expelled from the TUC in 1988.
‡ NUCAPS − A merger of SCPS + CSU; in 1986 SCPS = 89 000, CSU = 30 000

unions. Again, some unions have been eliminating 'ghost' members as a result of improvements in their record keeping, for example the AEU, while others have their membership figures inflated through keeping retired members on the books, e.g. NALGO.

The variation in the fortunes of different unions reflected to a large extent the varying fortunes of different sectors of the economy. Union membership and density, even in its heyday, had varied in different sectors, with the highest density in the public services and the rest of the public sector, high density in much of the manufacturing sector, particularly in large establishments, and very low density in much of the private service sector. With the severe contraction of manufacturing in the 1980s and the fall in the size of establishments, unions with membership concentrated in that sector suffered the most, as also did parts of the public sector like coal-mining and iron and steel, where there were drastic cut-backs in employment, whereas those in the public services, taken together, suffered the least.

The LFS 1989, based as it is on individuals, gives a wealth of detail on the characteristics of union membership. Table 8.3 gives union density in Great Britain for males of 44 per cent and females 33 per cent; manual density is 43 per cent and non-manual 35 per cent; for manufacturing it is 41 per cent and for non-manufacturing 37 per cent; density of full-time employees is 43 per cent and for part-timers 22 per cent. As the WIRS surveys have shown, there is a strong association of density with size of workplace. Thus density is 11 per cent in workplaces employing under 6, 23 per cent for 6–24 employees and 48 per cent for 25 or more employees. The table shows also that in all categories unionisation is higher in Northern Ireland than in Great Britain.

Turning to the jobs union members do, Table 8.4 (p. 143) shows that for non-manual workers there was little difference in union density for males and females — both were just over a third. For manual workers, however, density was 50 per cent for males and only 31 per cent for females. It is notable that 18 per cent of all union members (who were employees) were skilled craftsmen, whereas 30 per cent were in managerial and professional occupations.

In order to get an idea of the change in industry density levels, Stevens and Wareing compare the LFS results for establishment of 25-plus employees with the WIRS results. They acknowledge that there are obvious difficulties in comparing results from sources with different units of analysis — the one individuals, the other workplaces. With this caution in mind, their comparison shows that union density in non-manufacturing declined from 58 per cent in 1984 to 49 per cent in 1989; for manufacturing industries, the decline was from 58 to 47 per cent. Industries with particular marked falls in density were energy and water (88 to 71 per cent), transport (85 to 62 per cent), public administration (78 to 59 per cent), chemicals (58 to 41 per cent), electrical and instrumental engineering (51 to 32 per cent), and timber, furniture, paper and printing (59 to 44 per cent). Table 8.5 (p. 144) shows union density in 1989 by industry.

TABLE 8.3   Union density, spring 1989 – UK

	Great Britain		Northern Ireland	
	Number (000s)	Density (%)	Number (000s)	Density (%)
Male	11 862	44	262	51
Female	10 187	33	226	47
Non-manual	12 357	35	249	51
Manual	9 659	43	235	47
Manufacturing (2–4)	5 434	41	106	55
Non-manufacturing (0, 1, 5–9)	16 584	37	379	47
Full-time†	17 051	43	397	54
Part-time†	4 995	22	91	28
Size of workplace:				
under 6 employees	2 407	11 ⎫	170	25
6–25 employees	4 378	23 ⎬		
25 or more employees	14 465	48	316	62
All employees‡	22 049	39	488	49
Self-employed	3 425	9	87	*
All in employment§	25 962	34	595	42

Source: 'Union Density and Workforce Composition: Preliminary Results from the 1989 Labour Force Survey', *Employment Gazette*, August 1990, pp. 403–13.

* Sample size too small for reliable estimate.

† The definition of full-time and part-time is based on the respondent's own assessment not on the number of hours usually worked.

‡ Includes those who did not provide information on one or more of the dimensions reported in the table.

§ Includes those on government employment and training programmes and those who did not report their employment status.

Union mergers

Over the years many smaller unions have simply disappeared, while others have merged with larger unions. However, mergers have not simply been between small unions and large ones, but between medium-sized unions and

TABLE 8.4 Union density among employees – occupational status and sex, Spring 1989 – Great Britain

	Males		Females	
	Employees (000s)	Density (%)	Employees (000s)	Density (%)
Broad occupation				
Non-manual	5 547	37	6 810	34
of which:				
Managerial and professional	3 953	37	2 547	49
Clerical and related	760	45	3 224	28
Other non-manual	834	29	1 040	13
Manual	6 286	50	3 373	31
of which:				
Craft and similar	2 749	52	381	38
General labourers	140	56	16	*
Other manual	3 397	48	2 975	30
All employees†	11 862	44	10 187	33

Source: 'Union Density and Workforce Composition: Preliminary Results from the 1989 Labour Force Survey', *Employment Gazette*, August 1990.
* Sample size too small for reliable estimate
† Includes those who did not state their occupation

between large unions. Thus some of the notable mergers of the 1980s have included that of ASTMS (with a membership of 390 000) and TASS (with a membership of 241 000) to form the MSF; the GMB (membership 800 000) and APEX (membership 80 000); and the Civil Service Union (30 000) and the Society of Civil and Public Servants (89 000) to form the National Union of Civil and Public Servants, all three mergers taking place in 1988. In 1990 there was the merger of NGA and SOGAT to form the Graphical, Paper and Media Union (GPMU). Earlier in the decade the Boilermakers (120 000) merged with the General and Municipal Workers (866 000) to form the GMB in 1982; the POEU and the CPSA (Posts and Telecommunications Group) merged to form the NCU in 1985; the National Association of Theatrical, TV and Kine Employees (20 000) and the ABS (16 000) merged to form the Entertainment

TABLE 8.5 Union density of employees by industry, spring 1989 – Great Britain

Industry	All		Full-time males†		Full-time females†		All part-time†		Distribution of union members by industry
	000s	Density (%)	000s	Density (%)	000s	Density (%)	000s	Density (%)	(%)
0 Agriculture, forestry and fishing	264	13	186	15	31	*	47	*	0.4
1 Energy and water supply	560	76	472	78	69	63	19	*	5.0
2 Extraction, minerals etc./ manufacturing metal	777	48	580	54	149	34	49	*	4.4
3 Metal goods engineering	2418	42	1846	46	444	30	127	14	11.9
4 Other manufacturing industries	2237	38	1331	44	627	33	279	22	10.1
5 Construction	1171	30	998	33	92	18	81	*	4.1
6 Distribution, hotels and repairs	4381	14	1589	17	1034	16	1757	11	7.3
7 Transport and communication	1449	62	1065	69	274	46	109	28	10.5
8 Banking, finance,etc.	2364	25	1082	28	927	27	355	13	7.0
9 Other services	6393	52	2145	61	2082	61	2166	34	39.2
All Industries‡	22049	39	11315	45	5736	40	4995	22	100.0

Source: 'Union Density and Workforce Composition: Preliminary results from the 1989 Labour Force Survey (Employment Gazette, August 1990).

* Sample size too small for reliable estimate
† The definition of full-time and part-time is based on the respondent's own assessment not on the number of hours usually worked
‡ Includes those who did not state the industrial activity of their employer.

Trade Alliance in 1984; the Metal Mechanics (33 000) and the Tobacco Workers (16 000) transferred their engagements to TASS; and the Amalgamated Textile Workers (19 500) transferred their engagements to the GMB in 1986. The trend in mergers has been such that more than one general secretary has talked about there being only five or six 'super unions' at the end of the century.

McCarthy, who together with Undy had been conducting a review for the TUC on union mergers (TUC 1991a), makes a number of interesting points, among which is:

> that the underlying motives of most contemporary mergers are defensive, or consolidatory, rather than expansionist. The merger partners wish to recover lost membership, or improve their bargaining position in established areas; many are experiencing financial problems and need the support of larger and more stable organisations. Some wish to bring to an end long-standing and wasteful rivalries in the face of a more effective employer challenge. (p. 20)

Further, he believes that:

> the merger process will continue and grow over the next ten years. It should at least halve the number of TUC unions before the turn of the century. Yet it will not lead to any discernible ideal 'model' or optimum union size. From the outside, according to traditional classifications, British unions will look as illogical and unplanned as before. From the inside, I think, they will be much leaner and fitter; with more effective and improved services, and a greater ability to fight their corner if required. (p. 20)

McCarthy concludes that care must be taken to ensure that the merger trend does not lead to counter-productive rivalry and dissension between unions and that it was here that the TUC has a vital role to play.

Willman (1989) contrasts 'market share' unionism, by which he means unions competing for their proportion of a declining membership base in high-density sectors, with 'expansionary unionism', by which he means attempts to extend union membership into low-density sectors. He argues that competition by unions in the membership market is financially unrewarding and difficult, as is individual recruitment in unorganised areas.

> To the extent that competitive 'market share' unionism dominates over 'expansionary' attempts to extend union membership into low-density sectors, we may expect a long-term stagnation or decline of union membership. Under such circumstances, the limits to membership will be roughly set in the aggregate by employment in the manufacturing and public sectors – assuming no widespread derecognition – while the expanding private services sector characterised by female employment, part-time work, small establishments, self-employment and employer hostility will remain un-unionised. (p. 261)

This is a fair assessment, although 'stagnation' or 'decline' might become a small expansion if services within the public sector like the NHS and education expand and the unions retain their present density.

Trade union finances and organisation

The loss of membership has been accompanied by straitened financial circumstances. The British trade union movement has never been well endowed financially, particularly compared with many West European countries and the United States. This is largely the result of low subscriptions, both absolutely and as a proportion of average earnings. Falling union membership in the 1980s has worsened the position. Willman and Morris (1988) after looking at the period 1975–88 stated that given the loss of members 'the data convey a picture of remarkable financial health' (p. 96). This conclusion, as shown in Table 8.6, does not appear justified. Indeed, in two later papers, Willman himself seems to have had second thoughts (Willman 1989, 1990). In the latter work, he used a number of ratios to measure the financial position of unions and concluded that overall they indicated 'financial health and stability from 1950 to 1966; a period of financial decline during membership growth from 1967 to 1981, and some financial recovery during membership decline in the 1980s' (p. 318). His data further showed that

> per capita income, expenditure and net worth moved broadly in line up to 1968. Thereafter, to 1979, real income and expenditure per capita continued to rise as membership rose, but real net worth per capita fell very steeply. The financial and membership conditions of the 1980s differed again. This was a period of rapidly rising per capita income, expenditure and net worth, but of sharply contracting membership. (p. 319)

He concluded that in 1988 'the financial position remains relatively weak. Reserves are historically low as a multiple of expenditure. There remains, in addition, the structural problem of the shortfall of membership income.' (p. 324)

It will be seen from Table 8.6 that total income between 1979 and 1989 rose by 124 per cent, although income per head admittedly rose by 195 per cent. Total income from members rose by 122 per cent and income per head by 188 per cent. These figures are in money terms and have to be discounted by inflation, which increased over the same period by 96 per cent. They also have to be compared with a rise in total expenditure of 141 per cent and a rise in expenditure per head of 218 per cent. Most of the increase in expenditure was not on benefits, but on pay and administrative costs, which rose from 74 per cent of total expenditure in 1979 to 90 per cent in 1989. The figures show that

TABLE 8.6   Trade union finance, 1979–89

	Total			Per head		
	1979	1989	% Inc.	1979	1989	% Inc.
	£m	£m		£	£	
Total income	230.9	516.5	124	17.5	51.7	195
of which income from members	194.7	432.2	122	15.0	43.2	188
Total expenditure	208.8	502.6	141	15.8	50.3	218
of which						
admin. expenditure	154.6	452.0	192	11.7	45.2	286
expenditure on benefits	45.9	50.6	10	3.5	5.1	46
Total assets	318.5	711.9	124	24.1	71.2	195
of which fixed assets	76.5	245.1	220	5.8	24.5	322
Membership (millions)	13.2	10.0				

Source: *Annual Reports of the Certification Officer*, 1980 and 1990, all listed unions.

expenditure on running the unions was less than income from members in 1979, but more than income from members in 1989. The members were no longer paying enough in subscriptions to cover day-to-day operations and that is a sign of deep financial weakness.

The increase in union total assets looked healthier – from £318.5m in 1979 to £711.9m in 1989 and £24.1 per head in 1979 to £71.2 per head in 1989. In real terms, the increase in assets per head was 51 per cent; the reason for this increase was the decline in membership. While it is perfectly true that assets per head had increased considerably, they were still far too small to finance strike action for any length of time, as they always have been.

Among the consequences of strained finances were, first, that even the largest unions, such as the TGWU, the AEU and the GMB were forced during the 1980s to reduce their staff numbers and make other economies as their membership fell. British unions have traditionally relied for most of their activity on unpaid (by them) lay officials. With the need to provide new services and to recruit new members, as well as having to cope with more local and decentralised bargaining, there is a requirement to provide for more officials, not fewer. Moreover, over-reliance on shop stewards who in turn depend on employers providing time-off and other facillities can be dangerous given changing attitudes and policies by some employers. Similarly, unions rely overwhelmingly for the collection of their income on managements' deductions of subscriptions from pay through check-off agreements. It is for such reasons that Willman (1989) refers to unions as 'employer-dependent'.

The practice of the check-off appears to have grown markedly in the 1980s. WIRS 1984 (Millward and Stevens, 1986) found that the check-off was almost universal in the public sector in both 1980 and 1984. Overall, 80 per cent of workplaces with recognised manual unions operated the check-off in 1984 compared with 75 per cent in 1980 and 82 per cent of workplaces with non-manual unions did so in 1984 compared with 79 per cent in 1980. It is, perhaps, surprising that this should have happened during a period of union weakness and a growth among some employers of anti-unionism. While the check-off is a much more effective way for unions to receive subscriptions than their old methods, it works best when the labour force is relatively stable. There is clearly an argument for direct debit which carries on irrespective of a change in employer. Indeed a number of unions are actively encouraging members to use direct debit. One general secretary argued that the check-off helped to retain members, if only because it took some effort on the part of a member to end it. The argument by employers in favour of threatening to end the check-off if there were industrial action was that it made no sense for the employer to collect subscriptions which the union then used to support strike action. Such a threat had been made in the civil service, but it had not had any practical effect on the unions' position in bargaining. Indeed, there is an agreement which lays down the criteria which, if satisfied, would lead to the restoration of the check-off after it had been withdrawn. In the prison service, the check-off agreement was ended by management because prison officers had taken industrial action in 1988. The POA, however, now have 80 per cent membership paying by direct debit and is not interested in having the check-off restored. On the other hand, when the check-off was suspended for the Health Visitors Association its membership fell from 17 000 to 9 000.

While these two examples of the effect on union membership of ending the check-off differed markedly, it is hard to believe that an end to the check-off would not, in general, have a potentially disastrous effect on union membership. One general secretary admitted as much to us. Unions would have to persuade their members to use direct debit -a difficult task in many cases – or revert to either stewards collecting subscriptions or members going to branches in order to pay. The latter is not very likely while the former would depend largely on employer agreement or acquiescence. It is unlikely that this would be forthcoming if employers had already taken the major anti-union step of ending the check-off. One may well then ask why the check-off not only continued during the 1980s, but actually grew. The answer would appear to be that generally employers have not attacked unions head-on and the ending of the check-off would surely be such an attack. Furthermore, many employers value the role of unions for the part they play in securing orderly industrial relations, and as a partner in obtaining change. Also, as we were told by a leading employers' organisation, if the alternative is stewards wandering around the establishment to collect subscriptions, employers would prefer the check-off. Moreover, the check-off does give the employer information, not only about total union membership in his enterprise, but its distribution – for example, whether it is high or not in certain key areas, such as, computer centres.

A second consequence of strained finances has been that a considerable number of unions have been forced to merge. Examples of such mergers were given earlier in this chapter. Third, financial constraint has often been one of the most important factors in forcing unions to become more efficient. One general secretary of a major union argued that although he would rather not have experienced it, 'Thatcherism had been good for the unions because it had made them face up to the issues'. As a result of financial pressures his union had undertaken drastic changes which included: the number of branches reduced by 20 per cent in 2 years; districts merged and offices closed; income and expenditure had been centralised and channelled through head office; numbers of officials and staff considerably reduced; sophisticated computerisation; 'ghost' membership eliminated; and a revised strategy of moving from a geographical basis for organisation to an industrial one. Fourth, financial constraints have been an important factor for unions in considering their tactics on industrial action. All-out comprehensive strikes are very costly, whereas selective strikes or other forms of action are much less so.

Trade unions and their members

The pressures of the 1980s have caused unions to react in a number of ways in their attitudes to their membership and to their potential membership. First, with regard to their membership, legislation, as we have seen, has ensured that general secretaries, presidents and national executive members have to be subject to election and to re-election at least every 5 years. While it is true that many unions prescribed such elections in their rule books (Undy and Martin, 1984) long before the legislation, the required method of secret postal ballots was important. The legislation also stipulated that lawful industrial action could not be undertaken without a secret individual ballot. These changes were intended by the government to increase the power of the individual rank-and-file members, who were deemed to be sensible and moderate, against that of the leadership, who were deemed to be militant and autocratic. Whether these adjectives were justified or not is another question, but the effect has been to increase the power of the rank and file. Interestingly, it has not necessarily done so at the expense of the power of general secretaries. This point was put to us by a civil service union leader who argued that the power of at least civil service union general secretaries had been enhanced by the legislation, for two reasons. First, they had previously been appointed and now that they were elected they could claim a greater legitimacy; this, he argued, was not so much with regard to the membership, but *vis-à-vis* union activists. Second, the obligatory use of the ballot over industrial action could be and has been extended to other matters, such as determining pay claims and pay settlements, which again enhanced the position of the general secretary *vis-à-vis* activists, by appealing over their heads to the wider membership. Thus, for example, he continued, the power of annual conferences, usually dominated by activists, has been greatly reduced, although conferences are still important as policy-making bodies. Confirmation of this view came in a report that Inland Revenue staff had, at a special delegate conference in 1990, voted to withdraw from a performance-related pay scheme introduced two years earlier. In response the general secretary said that the union's executive would press for improvements to the current scheme rather than seek its abolition. The executive, he added, took its mandate from the membership, which had balloted in favour of a comprehensive settlement, including performance pay. A similar view was put by another general secretary from a large public-sector white-collar union who believed that the move from an appointed general secretary to an elected one had transformed his position.

The general secretary of a large industrial union believed that the legal obligation on unions to keep a central list of members had led to computerisation, more accurate membership figures, greater administrative efficiency and increased power at the centre *vis-à-vis* branches and districts. An additional change in his union, which had also shifted the balance of power, had been the decision to channel all income and expenditure through head office. The check-off had removed the need for branch collections of subscriptions for the majority of members. Their friendly society benefits, which used to be paid out by the branch, were now paid direct from head office to the member.

Another factor which has affected the relationship between unions and their members was the series of cases by 'working miners' (see Chapter 5) taken during the coal-mining strike. The interpretation of the courts that in effect there was a contract between the individual member and his union was of great significance in establishing that at common law members had substantial rights *vis-à-vis* their unions. Additional to the common law position was the legislation of the late 1980s which gave a number of specific rights to individual members (see Chapter 5) and which also established the office of a Commissioner for the Rights of Trade Union Members. However, perhaps more important than the legal position was the eventual acceptance by many union leaders that they were out of touch with their members, that the views of members had often been neglected or taken for granted and that this needed to be rectified. Thus, one leading union official stated that the members had become disillusioned with their leaders in 1977–9, believing that they were getting 'too big for their boots'. 'The Winter of Discontent' had strengthened this belief and was connected with the support by many trade unionists for the Conservative government's legislation. Another leading official said that the votes of trade unionists, especially in the South, were a key factor in the return of a Conservative government in 1979. Consequently, many unions in recent years have taken steps to improve two-way communications, for example, through attitude surveys, internal restructuring, the use of 'consultants' (often academics) to advise on changes and the more frequent use of ballots, even when not required by law. The successful campaign carried out by unions in 1984–5 to secure favourable votes for the continuation of their political funds was an educational process which helped greatly in improving communications.

With regard to potential membership, a number of leading unions have been making conscious efforts to recruit in areas where they have previously been weak. Thus, there have been recruitment drives in the private service sector, for example in retail distribution, hotels and catering and finance. There have also been recruitment drives particularly directed at women, at part-time employees and at ethnic minorities. As part of making themselves more attractive to members and potential members, unions have been developing their individual services, for example, financial services such as advantageous insurance policies, mortgages, loans, holidays, discounts on purchases and legal advice, usually in association with other organisations, for example, Unity Bank.

Unions have also been seeking to improve their image and to make more effort in the field of public relations. Too rosy a picture should not, however, be drawn (see Kelly and Heery, 1989). Union resources are limited and there are great difficulties in breaking into unorganised sectors. As one leading general secretary put it, in the early 1980s the unions were too occupied in coping with redundancies; there had also been a major collapse in union morale. Moreover, unions had not done any real recruiting for 20 years, so they did not know how to do it. Officials had not regarded themselves as recruiters; they had become the providers of services to existing members. In the 1970s members came into unions without much effort. Unionisation was often regarded as inevitable by many employers and as a natural state of affairs. In the 1980s, however, the attitudes of many employers changed and anti-unionism became more prevalent; a feeling was encouraged by government and by some employers that there was a better way to deal with employee relations than through unions. Thus far unions have not shown that they can recruit new members and hold them in the private services sector on a greater scale than they have in the past.

One problem for a number of unions is the high turnover of members; for example, in the TGWU about a fifth leave every year and during the 1980s they had failed to recruit enough to replace those who had left. While it is not usually difficult to get a new employee to join a union in a well-organised workplace, when employees leave and move to another less well-organised one, membership often lapses because the check-off stops. So it is still the case that the continuity of union membership depends on workplace recruitment. The situation has led one general secretary to argue that there needed to be a new basis for joining a trade union so that individuals would remain members wherever they worked. Subscriptions would be paid to head office by direct debit, making the membership long-term, if not permanent. For that, the member would get a wide range of services and membership would be valuable, even if in a particular workplace the union was not recognised for collective bargaining. This 'insurance'-based union membership is a long way from current practice and attitudes. Among the things which stand in its way is the check-off, which as we have seen has been a growing practice in the 1980s.

Trade unions and employers

Employer and management policies in the 1980s were discussed in Chapter 6. According to the TUC, 'Management have sought to achieve changes in working methods and technology, if necessary by imposing them; the belief in management by consent − dominant in many large companies during the 1970s − has lessened and, in its place, more aggressive and assertive management styles have developed.' (TUC, 1984 p. 18) Given that the trade union movement was on the defensive throughout the decade and was forced to react to management initiatives, it is important to recall what these management objectives and policies were. We can then consider how the unions responded.

It was argued in Chapter 6 that managements' industrial relations objectives were to:

1. control the work process,
2. secure cost effectiveness,
3. re-assert managerial authority,
4. move towards a more unitary and individualistic approach.

These objectives were reflected in management policies and attitudes with regard to:

1. unions,
2. collective bargaining,
3. involvement, consultation and participation,
4. human resource management and management style,
5. flexibility,
6. levels and methods of remuneration.

One method of considering the unions' response would be to divide it into (a) traditional and adversarial, (b) cooperative − 'new unionism' or 'new realism' which the media have typified as that of the EETPU. But such a dichotomy is misleading, because it assumes that before 1980 unions traditionally and universally adopted an adversarial attitude and this simply was not true. Employers and managers on the one hand and workers and unions on the other hand have both common and divergent interests. They have to work together to secure the success and survival of the enterprise but this does not mean that their objectives and the means of achieving these objectives are always identical. Divergences arise and these have to be accommodated and reconciled — how they are accommodated is the very heart of industrial relations. To brand such divergences as 'adversarial' is meaningless and indeed can be positively harmful.

In Chapter 6 we argued that management's attitude to unions in the 1980s was not one of frontal assault, except in a number of extreme cases, but often of diminishing the power of unions by restricting the scope of collective bargaining and by bypassing unions and stewards through more direct approaches to individual employees. Derecognition has been limited (Claydon, 1989), but union attempts to secure recognition at greenfield sites and at non-union enterprises have mainly been successfully resisted. Where recognition has been granted it has usually been on management terms, that is to say, it has often been exclusive to a single union; management has chosen the union (the so-called 'beauty contests'); and management has largely determined the procedural agreements, e.g. in some cases no-strike agreements with binding arbitration (conventional or pendulum); an absence of the traditional 'status quo' clause and often a clause stating that management had complete freedom in operational matters including the use of labour. The unions' efforts on recruitment have been mentioned earlier and it is only necessary to repeat that they have increased these efforts to recruit new members in order to claim recognition. They have also developed new services to attract members and they have sought to target specific groups such as women, part-timers, the young and ethnic minorities. One consequence has been increased inter-union competition, which the TUC has sought to keep within reasonable bounds.

On collective bargaining procedures, as we saw in Chapter 6, management, as a broad generalisation, sought first to reduce the importance of industry-wide bargaining or eliminate it altogether and decentralise to company, divisional or establishment level, and secondly to restrict the scope of bargaining by reasserting managerial authority, particularly on operational matters. On the level of collective bargaining, the union response has been mixed. In some instances, unions have sought to defend industry-wide agreements, although rarely to the extent of taking industrial action. Two notable exceptions were in British Rail and in local government (white-collar APTC grades) — both in 1989 — where industrial action (admittedly related to pay as well as to procedural change), was successful in resisting management proposals. In the docks industry, the ending by the government of the National Dock Labour Scheme in 1989 was followed by strike action to try to obtain a national agreement with the port employers in place of the scheme. The port employers refused to negotiate a national agreement, preferring local agreements, and the strike collapsed after a relatively short period. In most other cases union opposition was not taken to such lengths. For example, there was reluctant acquiescence to the ending of industry-wide bargaining in the London clearing banks (1987), in the water industry (1989) and in commercial television (1989).

On the scope of collective bargaining it has long been union policy — formally and informally — to seek to extend the scope of bargaining. In response to employer attempts to restrict the scope, either through changing agreements, or unilaterally changing work practices, there have been a number of well-publicised pitched battles, for example, at British Leyland at the end of the 1970s and early 1980s, in the newspaper industry — particularly at Wapping — but also in parts of the provincial press, at P&O, and in coal-mining, all of which resulted in major union defeats. Elsewhere, for example in the television industry, unions have on the whole had to retreat and accept the assertion of managerial authority. Sometimes this has been expressed in agreements and at greenfield sites it has often been one of management's conditions for recognition; for example the Nissan agreement provides for 'complete flexibility and mobility of employees'. More often it has been less a question of changes in formal agreements, but more by way of changes in the way the establishment was managed.

Some proponents of 'new unionism' have made a positive virtue of the restoration of managerial authority, accepting that management has the right to manage, that unions should not bargain about operational matters; instead unions should co-operate with management to ensure maximum efficiency through consultative and participative mechanisms. However, very few unions would deny management's right to manage or the need for cooperation in order to maximise efficiency. But they would also argue that management's operational decisions can sometimes adversely affect the well-being of their members and that it is their responsibility to seek to protect their members whether it be through participative or bargaining mechanisms. How else can differences be settled other than by unions and employees being forced to accept unilateral management dictat?

On involvement, consultation and participation, unions have long argued for the maximum consultation with employers, although consultation was seen by many as an inferior process to collective bargaining, for the former, however genuine and thorough, meant that in the last resort management had the right to take the final decision. In the 1980s, as outlined in Chapter 6, many employers sought to improve direct communications with their workforce, to involve individuals to a greater degree in the work process, and to some extent bypass established joint consultative and even joint negotiating committees. Such practices — of a varying kind — were on the whole not resisted by unions; indeed unions were often in no position to do so, even if they had wanted to.

There were a few examples of resistance, for example, to the introduction of quality circles at Fords, but these were exceptional. At national level, however, the TUC continued to advocate greater union participation in management decision-making, including the greater disclosure of information, further arguing that without statutory obligations many employers would not pursue such policies. Given government and employer opposition to such a step, TUC hopes for progress switched to the EC and to the European Social Charter, with what results remains to be seen.

The move by employers to more direct communications with individual employees and attempts at greater involvement in job-related tasks may be seen as part of a change in management style and in its most developed form as part of a move toward what has been called human resource management. In the early 1980s, the style and actions of many managements was considered as 'macho-management' as typified by British Leyland and British Steel, albeit that such action was usually the result of recession, falling demand and increasing competitive pressures. This term was used in relation to the mass redundancies and closures which were widespread in British industry at that time. It also related to riding roughshod over established procedures and agreements and to major unilateral changes in working practices. What was perhaps surprising was the absence of strong union resistance, in particular to the drastic cut-backs in the labour force. We do not at this stage go into the reasons for this and there were, of course, some notable exceptions. In part it would appear in some cases to have been due to a feeling of inevitability and in other cases to relatively generous severance payments which at the time were attractive to many of the workforce. Thus even if union leaders had wanted to fight, and thought they could do so successfully, they were unable to carry their members with them. With the more recent apparent change in style and approach, unions, as previously stated, have not generally shown any major resistance, although they have often been suspicious of management's motives and policies which have been a move towards individualisation and away from a more collective approach. A more participative style on the part of management is in any case difficult for unions to resist.

Another aspect of management policy in the 1980s has been the drive for greater flexibility on the part of the labour force. It is of course impossible to generalise about unions' reactions to this, for it varies over thousands of different workplaces. Greater flexibility leading to the more efficient use of resources and higher productivity is difficult to argue against, even if there was a desire to do so. Moreover, if unions and workforce are convinced that greater flexibility is necessary for a given enterprise, to survive in a world of ever-increasing competition, then it is unlikely to be resisted. Open communications and consultation, and a willingness to negotiate rather than impose change, are crucial for the peaceful and willing acceptance of change. Moreover, where management has been willing to compensate for the acceptance of change, there is likely to be more willing acceptance. Having said all this, there are limits to which unions and employees can be expected to accept greater flexibility and suspicions have been voiced. Some practices and agreements developed over the years which might be viewed by employers and government as 'restrictive' are viewed by many employees as 'protective', and may be deemed as essential for social reasons, for reasons of health and safety and for economic reasons. For example, temporary and casual employment is not likely to be welcomed by their recipients, and neither is the absence of any limits on daily hours of work. Unions have therefore been cautious and a more realistic approach is to examine existing working practices on a systematic basis rather than condemn them all out of hand and proclaim that 'flexibility' is the answer to all problems and needs. The achievement of greater flexibility can mean a worsening of working conditions for employees.

On pay increases, these have not in general been a major bone of contention in the private sector in the 1980s. Average earnings have kept ahead of the cost of living throughout the period. On the whole private employers sought to reduce costs by cutting numbers rather than reducing the real pay of their surviving employees. In the public sector it has been a different story. While some of the nationalised (or former nationalised) industries, for example electricity and gas, provided pay increases in line with the private sector, others such as British Rail and coal-mining did not. The main sufferers, as a result of government cash limits, however, were employees in the public service sector with pay increases below that of the private sector, except for the favoured few, primarily the police and firemen and those covered by the review bodies. In this sector, there was union resistance and several notable strikes took place during the 1980s, for example, civil servants, NHS staff and school teachers, but with only very limited success, if any.

Apart from the level of pay increases, there have been attempts by management in both the private and public sectors to achieve the greater individualisation of pay, in particular through performance-related pay schemes. Among unions there are major differences of approach. Many unions have traditionally been suspicious of such schemes on the grounds of possible subjectivity, favouritism and divisiveness and because of their belief in 'the rate for the job'. Some, for example NALGO, in many places including gas, oppose it and will have nothing to do with its operation. Others, for example BIFU, seek to control it and seek safeguards against abuse, through negotiating the size of the kitty and the criteria for the operation and through advising members on how to argue about it with managers. Similarly unions have traditionally had reservations about profit-sharing and employee share ownership schemes, but this has not prevented their growth, and unions have in recent years been more prepared to consider them favourably. The other major pay development in the 1980s has been the very substantial widening of pay differentials and, despite the efforts of many unions to improve the lot of the lower-paid, differentials have continued to widen.

The TUC

The TUC has two major roles, the first being that of spokesman and representative of the trade union movement. During the Second World War and in the early post-war decades this role developed into acting as the representative of unions with regard to:

1. government,
2. employers,
3. the public,
4. international institutions.

The second major role has been that of maintaining order and keeping the peace between unions, as typified by the Bridlington Agreement of 1939 and the work of the TUC's Inter-Union Disputes Committee; the provision of certain services, for example, trade union education and training and research facilities; the provision of guidelines on important issues, for example picketing and disputes procedures; and finally having a regard for the wider interests of the trade union movement.

Before considering the TUC's role and the changes which occurred in the 1980s, one preliminary remark is necessary, namely that it must be appreciated that the TUC is the servant of its affiliated unions and not their master. It was the unions which created the TUC and not vice versa. The TUC's powers over affiliated unions are very limited and in the last resort consist essentially of suspension and then expulsion. Such power has to be used sparingly or it becomes self-defeating. The TUC was often in the post-war years portrayed by the media as all-powerful and this was a far cry from reality. But all trade unions recognise that when they agree to act together through the TUC they can be powerful. It has been the role of the leaders of the TUC to secure that unity in order that the unions' influence should be maximised. The 1980s has seen rather more occasions when they disagreed than when they agreed by comparison with, say, the 1960s.

The role of the trade union movement with regard to its affiliated unions, government and employers is considered in the next three sections. Here we briefly consider internal changes in the TUC and the TUC's role *vis-à-vis* society in general and internationally. The TUC conducted important reviews in 1980 and 1984: *The Organisation, Structure and Services of the TUC* (TUC, 1980) and *TUC Strategy* (TUC,1984). The former was adopted by Congress in 1981 and led to the TUC Development Programme which *inter alia* sought to extend the number of TUC industry committees and strengthen its regional organisation. The latter review discussed the changing environment and its effects on trade union aims and objectives, functions and methods. As a consultative document, it did not make recommendations, but posed a series of questions for unions to consider.

With regard to internal organisation, there was a major change in the composition of the General Council in 1983. Until then, members had been nominated by some 20 trade groups, but with all affiliated unions entitled to vote in their election. However, Congress approved changes, which came into effect in 1983, whereby all unions with a membership of 100 000 or more were automatically entitled to at least one seat (Section A). Smaller unions (Section B) – those with under 100 000 members – were allocated 11 seats for which elections were held, but in which only the smaller unions were entitled to vote. In addition, 6 seats were reserved for women (Section C), in the election of whom all unions were entitled to vote. The change was particularly significant in that it had an effect on the political balance of the General Council in favour of moderation. It also reduced the power of the very large unions in that they no longer dominated the votes in the election of the members from the smaller unions. To a considerable extent the change in the composition of the General Council reflected the changing composition of union membership – relatively more white-collar members, more public-sector members, and more women members. A further change in the composition of the General Council, although a less fundamental one, took place in 1989, creating four sections as follows:

Section A: members from those unions with a membership of 200 000 or more:

```
    200 000–399 999   – 2 seats
    400 000–649 999   – 3 seats
    650 000–899 999   – 4 seats
    900 000–1 199 999 – 5 seats
  1 200 000–1 499 999 – 6 seats
```

Where the total number of women members of any union in Section A was 100 000 or more, that union had to nominate at least one woman.

Section B: members from those unions with a membership of 100 000 up to 199 999. Each such union was entitled to one seat.

Section C: 8 members elected from those unions with a membership of less than 100 000.

Section D: 4 women members, all of whom were members of unions with less than 200 000 members.

The main reasons for this change were first to secure a more even balance of members per seat between the smaller and the larger unions, and second to ensure a larger number of women on the General Council. The composition of the General Council under this new system for the year 1990–1 consisted of 33 from Section A, 9 from Section B, 8 from Section C and 4 from Section D, making a total of 54 members.

In recent years the TUC has suffered from financial problems, basically for the same reason as most of its affiliates — namely the fall in union membership. Moreover, it was not helped by the expulsion of the EETPU and a foregone income of some £350 000. In 1989 the TUC's expenditure was £7.4 million and its total income £6.9 million, leaving a deficit of £0.5 million. The financial difficulties of many individual unions make it hard for the TUC to increase continually its affiliation fee and it has consequently been conducting a major inquiry into its organisation and staffing.

The TUC is the acknowledged spokesman of the trade union movement in relation to society or the public at large. Unlike a number of other countries, where there are separate trade union centres based on religious, political or occupational (e.g. white-collar and manual) differences, the British trade union movement has only one central organisation. It is true that there are a considerable number of unions outside the TUC, but most of these are extremely small and the total non-affiliated membership is of the order of less than 2 million, compared with the TUC's affiliated membership of over 8 million. The only non-affiliated unions of any size are the Royal College of Nursing (282 000 members in 1988), the Association of Assistant Masters and Mistresses (AMMA — 132 000 members) and the EETPU (370 000 members).

In its role of spokesman, the TUC seeks to inform the public of union objectives and policies, not only on trade union matters but also on matters relating to society more generally, for example, education, social security, the economy and international affairs. In the later 1980s, more emphasis has been given to expounding the virtues of trade union membership, and indeed of the necessity for the existence of trade unions in a democratic, pluralistic society. The TUC through its Special Review Body (TUC, 1988b, 1989) has been rethinking its role and purpose in the changing environment in which it has to operate, and among other matters has sought to help unions in publicity and public relations, in the development of services and in co-ordinated recruitment drives.

Internationally, the TUC is a prominent member of the International Confederation of Free Trade Unions (ICFTU), which was formed in the early post-war years and has its headquarters in Brussels. The ICFTU consisted in 1989 of 142 affiliated organisations in 97 countries with a combined membership of approximately 88 million. It is the spokesman for much of the non-Communist international trade union movement and presents trade union views on world economic, social and political issues to the public at large and to relevant international institutions, such as United Nations (UN) Agencies. Second, the TUC represents the British trade union movement at the International Labour Organisation (ILO), an agency of the UN with headquarters in Geneva. The ILO is a tripartite organisation, with each country's delegation consisting of representatives from government, employers and unions. It is concerned *inter alia* with setting international labour standards and guidelines, mainly through conventions and recommendations, on a wide range of matters, such as freedom of association, safety and training, minimum pay, minimum terms and conditions of employment. Third, the TUC is a leading member of the European Trade Union Confederation (ETUC) which is based in Brussels and which in 1989 had 36 affiliated organisations from 21 countries with a combined membership of about 44 million. A major concern of the ETUC is the European Community (EC). The ETUC makes representations to the EC on matters of trade union interest and is consulted on such matters. Indeed, at European level, if not in the UK, the trade union movement is acknowledged as, and treated as, one of the social partners.

In addition, the TUC is represented on the EC's Economic and Social Council and on a range of Advisory Committees, for example, on the Advisory Committee for the Free Movement of Workers, on the Committee for Vocational Training, and on the European Social Fund Committee.

Indeed the TUC has been more enthusiastic about the EC than have some of its affiliated unions. Nevertheless, individual unions have also been playing a significant role in EC deliberations, either through the ETUC or through their international organisations, for example BIFU through its membership of the International Federation of Commercial, Clerical, Professional, and Technical Employees (FIET). Other international activities include membership of the Trade Union Advisory Committee to the Organisation for Economic Co-operation and Development (OECD) and the Commonwealth Trade Union Council.

The TUC on a number of occasions in the 1980s complained to the ILO about Government policy. For example, there were complaints about GCHQ and the ILO committee of Experts determined that the British government had been in breach of Convention 87 on freedom of association; subsequently the ILO Conference deplored the dismissal of trade unionists from GCHQ. A second complaint concerned the Teachers Pay and Conditions Act 1987 which had abolished negotiating machinery and which the TUC argued was in violation of ILO Convention 98 on the right to organise and to collective bargaining. This complaint was also upheld by the Committee of Experts and by the ILO Governing Body. A third complaint concerned the Employment Act 1988. The ILO Committee of Experts, who had conducted a review of British industrial relations legislation since 1980, found that large areas of the legislation were not compatible with Conventions 87 and 98 on freedom of association and protection of the right to organise, and collective bargaining. They asked the Government to have the 1988 Employment Act amended to restore to trade unions the possibility of disciplining members who refused to participate in a lawful strike or other industrial action and to enable unions to indemnify members or officials in respect of fines imposed by the courts. The Committee of Experts also noted that the narrowing, since 1980, of protections in civil law for strikes had virtually excluded the possibility of taking boycott, protest, or sympathetic action and that the definition of trade disputes imposed excessive restrictions on the right to strike. Employers could also take refuge behind subsidiary companies to deprive working people of the possibility of taking lawful industrial action. The experts asked the Government to amend the legislation and to introduce legislation preventing strikers from being dismissed or having other discriminatory treatment taken against them. They also asked the Government to stop the blacklisting of people on grounds of their trade union membership or activities. The experts commented that a positive statement of trade union rights by the Government would be of advantage and asked the government to codify and clarify the legislation of the last 9 years, which was complex and gave rise to uncertainty which inhibited lawful industrial action.

TUC and affiliated unions

In 1987 the TUC established a Special Review Body (SRB) with the task of considering the future role of the TUC. Its first report (TUC, 1988b) identified a number of key areas for investigation, namely:

1. the need to review the problems of securing recognition, the terms on which recognition is gained, the pressures arising from inter-union competition, and the role of the TUC Disputes Principles and Procedures − linked to an assessment of employer attitudes;
2. public perceptions of unions and the promotion of trade unionism generally as well as among specific groups;
3. the need to give further emphasis to consolidating membership and building organisation in the light of the labour market trends in order to protect and to expand the 'frontier of trade unionism';
4. the role of union and TUC services and the scope for their co-ordination, expansion and development.

It then identified three broad roles for the TUC:

helping to improve and regulate inter-union relationships;
helping unions to develop their organisation;
helping unions to provide improved services to members.

With regard to inter-union relationships, the Report pointed out that on a number of occasions in the past the TUC had reviewed the complex structure of the trade union movement, but that Congress had not been able to agree on a particular form of trade union structure as being most desirable and the TUC had no authority to impose general solutions. However, important initiatives had been taken to promote mergers on a broadly sectoral basis, to establish spheres of influence agreements between unions, and other joint arrangements, and, since 1970, to set up TUC industrial committees. Indeed, throughout its history, the TUC has sought to promote cooperation between unions and avoid but, if necessary, resolve inter-union rivalry and differences by discussion, conciliation and arbitration.

To this end, the SRB recommended first that there should be a code of practice designed to set standards for unions seeking recognition, and secondly that there should be a modification to Principle 5 of the TUC Disputes Principles and Procedures. These recommendations were accepted by the 1988 Congress. The background to the review was that there had been rows between the big unions about single-union agreements and the Bridlington Procedure was inadequate to deal with them. In particular, the EETPU had been in the forefront of signing single-union agreements − often no-strike agreements. The purpose of the review was to prevent inter-union difficulties when unions sought to enter into single-union agreements. To this end, a union in the process of making a single-union agreement should notify the TUC and provide relevant details (including whether and to what extent any other union had membership, whether other unions were involved in making presentations claiming recognition to the company, and whether contact had been made with other unions). On receipt of the details, the TUC would aim to tender advice within two weeks. The Code also provided that:

> Unions, when making recognition agreements, must not make arrangements which specifically remove, or are designed to remove, the basic democratic lawful rights of a trade union to take industrial action. This is not meant to deter unions using arbitration, pendulum or otherwise, at the request of one or both parties. Unions must not make any agreements which remove or are designed to remove, the basic democratic lawful rights of a trade union to take industrial action in advance of the recruitment of members and without consulting them. If faced by circumstances where procedures are insisted on which remove the basic democratic right to take industrial action, the union should consult the TUC at the earliest opportunity.

It further provided that:

> Unions are expected to co-operate with any procedures, which have been approved by the General Council of the TUC, which are operated by the TUC, STUC, Wales TUC or TUC Regional Councils in relation to inward investment authorities.

and

> When negotiating recognition agreements which have implications for substantive factors, unions should have regard to the general level of terms and conditions of employment which are already the subject of agreement with the company concerned, or which have been set through recognised arrangements, and take all possible steps to avoid undermining them.

These procedures were to operate on a trial basis for 6 months from October 1988 to March 1989 and thereafter to be reviewed by the SRB. The review reported in 1989 that only three cases had arisen and that a thorough assessment was not yet possible, and recommended that the notification procedure should continue to operate for an extended trial period when a further review should be undertaken.

The SRB pointed out that competition between unions concerning recruitment and recognition could result in the duplication of effort and the wasteful use of scarce trade union resources. It could also adversely affect the standing of unions with members, potential members and employers. To help overcome these problems the SRB considered the possibility of 'designated organising' areas and 'protected' areas which would be considered further in the second report of the SRB. There was also a discussion on the problems of multi-unionism, which would also be considered further in the SRB's Second Report.

With regard to helping unions to develop their organisation and to provide improved services, the SRB's first report proposed enhanced contacts with national employers' organisations, in particular the CBI and the IPM, to discuss practical industrial relations questions. Other proposals included: pilot regional and local labour market surveys which would draw up an economic and employment profile and its implications for trade unions; a development programme on union services; improved public relations in order to promote trade unionism, using modern techniques including advertising, videos and opinion research; and targeting special groups such as women workers and young people. All these proposals were to be considered further in the SRB's second report.

The second SRB report (TUC, 1989) reported on a number of matters, including the work carried out on labour market information, local labour market pilots and joint recruitment drives under the auspices of the TUC at Old Trafford Park, Milton Keynes and Dockland. On trade union services a major initial package of services had been established, available to all TUC unions. It covered pension services (arranged with Unity Trust), insurance and certain other financial services, and legal services on non-employment matters (arranged with the Law Society). On problems associated with multi-unionism, the Report promoted the concept of 'single-table' bargaining and, while acknowledging that it was neither practicable nor desirable in all situations, proposed to develop the concept further.

During the 1980s, there were three other issues concerning inter-union relations which were of major concern to Congress. The first was part of the TUC's reaction to trade union legislation (which is discussed in a subsequent section), namely the question of unions applying for government money to meet the cost of ballots. As part of its opposition to government legislation, Congress had decided that unions should not apply for such funds. However, the AEU and the EETPU both decided that they would do so. This raised the likelihood of a major clash, which if the two unions did not back down could only lead to their eventual expulsion. Rather than face this possibility, Congress altered its policy and no longer sought to prevent unions applying for government funds. Virtually all unions now take public funds to pay for their ballots and £2.3 million was provided for 1990–1 in the Supply Estimates.

The second and third issues were both related to the Bridlington Agreement and perhaps its inadequacies, the second being the policies and practices of the EETPU and the third being the episode of Ford Dundee. The EETPU had for many years been pursuing its own policies, which it was of course fully entitled to do, but in doing so was highly vocal in its criticism of many other unions and of mainstream Congress policy. This, needless to say, did not endear the EETPU to many other unions – particularly those on the left of the political spectrum. Conflict reached its height over the Wapping Dispute (see Chapter 5), when the EETPU was accused of supplying labour to the Wapping plant and enabling News International to produce its newspapers despite the dismissal of the entire labour force (with the exception of the journalists) of the *Sun*, *The Times*, *The Sunday Times* and the *News of the World*. The print unions – SOGAT and the NGA – pressed hard for the disciplining of the EETPU and it was censured (TUC Annual Report 1988, pp. 13 and 14), although its expulsion was avoided by a very narrow margin.

Having avoided expulsion over Wapping, the EETPU was however expelled by the 1988 Congress for refusing to conform with two decisions of the TUC's Disputes Committee, and the subsequent General Council directives, regarding single-union agreements into which it had entered, namely Christian Salvenson (Food Services) Ltd, Salstream and Orion Electric (UK) Ltd, Port Talbot (TUC Annual Report 1988, p. 16). This was the first time that a major union has been expelled from the TUC in recent times (with the exception of the expulsion of a number of unions for registering under the Industrial Relations Act 1971), with the expectation on its part, and that of other unions, that it would not be returning. In an earlier existence, the same union had been expelled for electoral malpractices in 1961, but had returned soon after under new leadership. This time the union marked its long-term departure by setting out to lead a rival body to the TUC, although with little success.

The third issue concerned a single-union agreement entered into by the AEU with Ford Electrical and Electronic Division (EED) at a new plant which the company proposed to establish in Dundee. There were immediate complaints to the TUC by the TGWU and MSF that the AEU's actions were in breach of the TUC's Disputes Principles and Procedures. The TUC sought to solve the problem, but at a meeting with Ford (Europe) was told that the decision to locate the plant in Scotland was not that of Ford (Europe) nor Ford (UK), but of Ford (EED). At a subsequent meeting with Ford (EED), the TUC was told that Ford (EED) saw the Dundee plant as an electronics operation quite distinct from Ford car manufacturing. It would be operating in a highly competitive sector. While the existing EED plants in the UK were legally part of Ford UK and covered by the Blue Book, the Dundee plant would not be. Its wage levels must reflect those applicable elsewhere in the electronics industry in Dundee. To be competitive, team working would be needed and a single-union agreement was regarded as an essential condition for the required working arrangements to be achieved. When concluding the provisional agreement with the AEU, EED had not anticipated the extent of the opposition that would come from other unions. The TUC general secretary subsequently flew to Detroit, having obtained an understanding from the general secretary of the AEU that the union would withdraw from its agreement if that would assist. At a meeting with the company, the TUC sought to persuade the company either to consider putting the plant under the Ford UK agreements or to establish the plant without any agreement and use the intervening period to agree appropriate industrial relations arrangements. EED reiterated that they were competing with low-cost plants in the Far East and needed total flexibility, no demarcations, and wages which were competitive with other Scottish electronics plants. They would only proceed on the basis of a single-union agreement.

At the conclusion of the meeting, no decisions had been reached and it was agreed that contacts would be continued before decisions were taken by either party. However, shortly afterwards EED informed the TUC that they had decided not to proceed with the plant. The TUC general secretary flew again to Detroit to try to persuade the company to change its mind, the General Council having agreed that the Ford–AEU single-union agreement should stand. The Company stated, however, that it would not reconsider unless it was confident that the plant could proceed without the threat of boycotting of the plant by other workers at Ford. On his return the general secretary sought assurances from the other Ford unions and from the Ford NJC, but was unable to obtain them. The NJNC and the staff unions' negotiating group maintained their position that the new plant should operate under the existing agreements. The company therefore abandoned its plans to build the plant in Scotland.

Here was a situation where two of the largest unions were quarrelling. The General Council changed its decision, siding first with the TGWU and then with the AEU. Ford is an employer with whom both unions negotiate as part of a joint trade union side. The main conclusion of the episode appears to be that the TUC was shown to be of little account when two of its biggest affiliates fought each other and when their sectional interests were at stake.

TUC and government

The role of the trade union movement as a 'Fourth Estate' or 'social partner' which existed for most of the post-war period was arguably its most important one. In the TUC's own words, 'For over a century the prime role of the TUC has been to influence the actions of governments over a wide range of economic, industrial and social issues of major concern to trade union members. Since 1940 governments too have increasingly sought a working relationship with the trade union movement. The present government has moved in the opposite direction' (TUC 1984, p. 13). In the 1980s under Thatcher governments the role had been reduced to virtually nothing. Indeed it could be argued that it has diminished even further still in that trade unions are regarded as not even a neutral element, but in Mrs Thatcher's phrase as 'the enemy within'. The reasons for Thatcher governments' attitude to trade unions were discussed in Chapter 4 and it is not necessary to repeat them here. What is necessary is to give a brief account of how the reduction in the influence and participation of trade unions has taken place.

In the post-war decades up to 1980, trade unions had a recognised and accepted involvement in a number of areas of national life, the main areas being:

1. economic affairs and particularly incomes policy;
2. social policy;
3. training;
4. health and safety;
5. ACAS;
6. representation on a range of bodies – from the boards of nationalised industries to Royal Commissions.

First, trade union involvement in economic policy was typified by the existence of the National Economic Development Council in which the TUC had, at least in theory, an equal voice with employer representatives and government, and again in theory at least equal control over the NEDO. The TUC boycotted meetings of the NEDC for a time as a protest against the government's ban on trade union membership at GCHQ in 1984. NEDC's role in a supposedly 'free market' economy was always a questionable one and it was perhaps no surprise that the government in July 1987 should have decided unilaterally to curtail drastically its activities, to reduce the 38 economic development committees to 18 new sector groups, and to cut its staff by half. It was to meet less frequently: the Prime Minister would not again take the chair and the Chancellor of the Exchequer would do so only infrequently.

As a further pinprick the government declared that the convention whereby TUC nominees were accepted as the trade union representatives on the NEDC was ended and it proceeded in 1988 to appoint as a Council member the general secretary of the EETPU, which had recently been expelled from the TUC.

However, in the 1960s and 1970s, the major involvement of the unions in economic affairs was through incomes policy which existed directly or indirectly through most of the period. Although the TUC frequently passed resolutions in favour of 'free collective bargaining', involvement in incomes policies, paradoxically, meant not only influence over pay determination, but some influence over matters relating to pay determination, such as prices, profits, dividends, taxation, and macro-economic policy generally. Thatcher governments of the 1980s condemned incomes policies of the past and declared that they would not be part of their economic policy – pay was to be a matter for free labour markets. Given a declared absence of incomes policy there need be no TUC involvement. However, the declared absence of incomes policy did not mean that there was no policy on incomes. For most of the 1980s there was a policy to keep pay down in the public service sector, primarily through cash limits; and in the public corporations, primarily by strict financial targets. In the private sector, pay was to be restrained by high unemployment and greater competition in labour and product markets.

Second, the trade union movement, as a prime progenitor of the Welfare State, had in the post-war decades a major interest in social welfare, for example regarding pensions, sickness benefit, industrial injuries and unemployment pay, and its view and policies in this area were not without influence on successive governments. However, the Thatcher governments, from the beginning, were concerned to reduce public expenditure as far as possible in this area and a trade union input which sought to protect and indeed improve social welfare was therefore unacceptable. By the third Thatcher government it was clear that Conservative Party policy was not one of merely restricting social welfare expenditure, but one of dismantling the Welfare State, it being deemed incompatible with the 'enterprise culture', the Welfare State characterised as 'the Nanny State'. Examples of the new approach included linking of state pensions to the cost of living and not to earnings, the reduction in benefits from the State Earnings-Related Pension Scheme (SERPS), the encouragement of personal pension plans and private health insurance through tax concessions, the much harsher conditions required in order to obtain and retain unemployment benefit and the refusal to index the value of child allowances.

Third, there had been a long involvement of trade unions in the development of state support for training to remedy the deficiencies of British industry in this respect. From its inception, the Manpower Services Commission (MSC) was a tripartite body with full union representation and this was equally true of the Industrial Training Boards (ITBs) and the Area Manpower Boards. The Thatcher governments progressively abolished these bodies, starting in 1980 with the abolition of most of the ITBs. This increased the importance of the MSC whose then chairman – Sir Richard O'Brien – was succeeded by David Young. In 1985 the MSC was abolished and replaced by the Training Commission, which was still tripartite, but less so, when the Employment Service returned to DE. In 1990 the Training Commission was abolished along with the few remaining ITBs and the Area Manpower Boards and replaced by

82 newly created locally based Training and Enterprise Councils (TECs) and the Training Agency. The Training Agency had hardly got off the ground when it too was abolished and national training policy was back in the Department of Employment's Training, Employment and Enterprise Division (TEED), to be assisted only by a purely advisory body – the National Training Task Force. The government laid down that TECs were to consist of two-thirds senior managers from private industry and one-third from the public sector, education, local authorities and trade unions. At the end of 1990 a Parliamentary answer, quoted in *Personnel Plus* (1991), recorded TEC Boards as consisting of 378 employers, 29 trade unionists, 50 local authority representatives, 59 from the educational field and the remainder from voluntary organisations and employers' federations. The decision to create TECs and the Training Agency was the key to the ending of tripartism in the training field. Nevertheless, what is remarkable is the long and successful record of tripartism in the 1980s in which the TUC exercised considerable influence.

Fourth, since the passing of the Health and Safety Act 1974, and related regulations, recognised independent trade unions have had certain statutory rights at the place of work and the whole field of health and safety has been administered at national level by a tripartite body – the Health and Safety Commission. Trade union involvement in this area has not been changed. Indeed, there is still an annual grant from the government to help finance the training of trade union representatives which is related to the statutory arrangement for elected safety representatives. This increased from the expenditure of £320 000 in 1987–8 to the provision of almost £2m in 1990–1.

Fifth, another area where trade union involvement has not been basically changed is the Advisory, Conciliation and Arbitration Service (ACAS), whose council remains tripartite, consisting of union and employer representatives and independents. Although appointments are made by the Secretary of State, the TUC in effect used to nominate the three union representatives, but in 1989 the government asserted itself and appointed an additional representative from a non-TUC union as well as an additional businessman. However, it could be argued that although ACAS undoubtedly performs invaluable industrial relations functions in the field of conciliation, arbitration and advisory services, its council is hardly a major policy-making body. Thus the ideological disadvantage to the government of union involvement is not so great as the practical advantages.

Finally, there was a widely diverse field of institutions where it was accepted practice for trade union nominees, or at least people with a trade union background, to participate. Such bodies ranged from the Boards of Nationalised Industries and Regional and District Health Authorities to Royal Commissions and numerous quangos. Trade union membership in such bodies was progressively reduced. However, importantly, it is still present on industrial tribunals.

While the government had a general objection to trade union nominees, together with employers, having control of official bodies, it saw the force of the argument in favour of representation from the two major organised employment interest groups in the cases mentioned above. The three most important were the Health and Safety Executive, ACAS and the industrial tribunals. In all three the function to be performed is hardly conceivable except on a tripartite basis. If parties are to be conciliated or to take some responsibility for safety at work, their representative bodies have to be involved.

Reaction to legislation

In the early part of the decade, the unions and the TUC reacted strongly to government trade union legislation. The TUC wanted a rerun of the opposition to the Industrial Relations Act 1971. Thus it proclaimed its complete opposition to the Employment Act 1980 and organised public demonstrations on 9 March 1980 and a Day of Action on 14 May 1980. The support, however, was poor compared with the protests against the 1970 Industrial Relations Bill, and it was clear that the TUC had misjudged the mood of the members. There was not the same hostility to the government's proposals. Further TUC opposition was announced to the government's codes on picketing and the closed shop and subsequently to the 1982 Employment Bill. At a special conference of union executives at Wembley in April 1982, it was decided:

- to campaign widely against the legislation;
- not to take part in membership agreement ballots;
- not to accept government funds for balloting;
- that the General Council would help unions in difficulties, if requested, including financial assistance;
- that a special defence fund would be established.

A major economic recession was in progress with massive redundancies, and public opinion, including the opinions of many union members, seemed strongly to favour the view that unions had become too powerful and that some change in the balance of power was required.

However, a number of unions seemed prepared to ignore the new legislation. A crisis point was reached in the 1983 *Messenger Newspapers* dispute (see Chapter 5). The point came when the TUC's then general secretary, Len Murray, immediately renounced the sub-committee's decision to support the NGA's request for a newspaper strike, and his view was subsequently supported by the full General Council. Len Murray's opposition was based partly on the grounds that this would most likely have exposed the TUC to contempt of court, and partly because it would have meant TUC support for unlawful action. This arguably was the major turning point for the trade union movement. However much the TUC might oppose the new trade union laws, it would not engage in unlawful action. Murray, at this stage, also thought in terms of trying to arrive at a *modus vivendi* with the government, remembering that it had just been returned for another 5 years. However, this was not to be, for there followed almost immediately the derecognition of the civil service unions by the government at GCHQ. Not only was there derecognition, but staff at GCHQ were required to give up their union membership or face possible dismissal. The GCHQ episode convinced Murray that no deal was possible with the government, and indeed it was followed not long afterwards by his decision to take early retirement.

The next major clash between unions and government was the coal-miners' strike of 1984–5. The TUC was not directly involved in the early months of the strike, not least because the NUM preferred it that way (Adeney and Lloyd, 1986). The NUM did not seek TUC help but sought support by direct approaches to certain individual unions, for example, the NUR, ASLEF, the NUS and the TGWU. However, at the 1984 Congress the NUM did seek help from the TUC and a resolution of support was overwhelmingly carried. However, during the debate a number of union leaders, while backing the resolution, made clear that any support in the shape of industrial action would have to be conditional on the approval of whichever of their members would be actually involved, for example at power stations. The request for TUC help came very late in the day and what was given – other than moral support – was very limited and virtually confined to a hardship fund. The only active role played by the TUC was towards the end of the dispute, by which time the NUM was clearly facing defeat. At the request of the NUM, the TUC tried to retrieve something from the débâcle in the form of an agreed settlement, but its efforts were rebuffed eventually by both the NUM leaders and the government.

The complete defeat of the NUM was regarded by many as the low point for the trade union movement. If the NUM – the allegedly most powerful of unions – could not win, then who could? However, other battles did take place. In the public sector, the long-drawn-out action of the teachers' unions resulted in the government removing the bargaining rights of some 400 000 teachers in 1987, imposing a unilaterally determined settlement and taking the power to impose further terms and conditions for at least the following 3 years. In the private sector, the strike of the print unions against News International in 1986 demonstrated that the law, particularly with regard to secondary action and picketing, could be effective, and the same was true of the seamen's dispute with P&O in 1988. In both cases, the unions were fined and had their funds sequestered. Following these events, it can be argued that the unions had learned the hard way the inadvisability of openly defying the law and that they had to operate within the law, as the TUC had determined in 1983. Thus, for example, in the 1989 strikes in British Rail and the docks the unions were meticulous in conforming to legal requirements. It can also be argued that the unions learned to use strike ballots as a bargaining tool and that an affirmative vote gave unions a powerful weapon with which to seek an improved offer from management (see Chapters 5 and 11).

Unions and the Labour Party

First it needs to be recalled that the TUC is not affiliated to the Labour Party: it is individual unions which are affiliated, if they so decide. An increasing proportion of the TUC membership is in unions not affiliated to the Labour Party: of the 20 unions with more than 100 000 members in 1989, 5 public-service unions and BIFU were not affiliated to the Labour Party and they had 18 per cent of TUC membership; in 1979 the proportion in unions not affiliated was 13 percent. Trade union–Labour Party links at national level are, of course, strong, through union presence at the Labour Party Annual Conference and the existence of the block vote; strong union representation on the Labour Party's NEC; the unions' participation in elections for the leadership; and the high dependency of the Labour Party on union affiliation fees and special contributions at election times. All this is not to say that the Labour Party is dominated by the trade unions which are affiliated to it. 'The proof of the pudding is in the eating' and Labour governments in the post-war decades have often differed fundamentally on certain policy issues with the trade unions, for example on incomes policies.

During the 1980s, a number of important issues arose with regard to the trade union/Labour Party relationship, the first of which related to trade union legislation. In the early 1980s, both the TUC and the Labour Party completely opposed the government's trade union legislation, and in the 1983 election the Labour Party pledged its repeal. Towards the end of the 1980s both the TUC and the Labour Party started to reassess their position with regard to the legislation and accepted that much of it was here to stay, for example ballots before industrial action, the election of national executive committee members and national leaders, restrictions on certain kinds of secondary action and secondary picketing and the ending of the closed shop. It was clear that such measures had public support and that a complete return to the pre-1980 legal position would greatly harm the Labour Party's electoral prospects. From the union viewpoint, it was for some an acceptance of the inevitable: for others, there was an appreciation of the advantages to unions of some of the legislation, for example strike ballots and obligatory and secret ballots to elect top officials and executives. Further, in supporting the EC and, in particular, its Social Charter, complete opposition to a legal framework became impossible. Indeed, both the TUC and Labour Party came to appreciate that, given the relative weakness of unions, some of their objectives could be realised only through legislation. The 1990 Congress and the 1990 Labour Party Annual Conference provided the final victory for those who accepted this view.

A second issue was that after the 1987 election the Labour Party had come to appreciate that too close an identity with the unions was harmful to its electoral prospects. The unions, for their part, had begun to appreciate that a considerable proportion of their members did not vote Labour – indeed there is some evidence that in the general election of 1983 more trade unionists than non-trade unionists voted Conservative (Himmelweit *et al.*, 1985, p. 208) – and that the composition of union membership had been changing markedly, in particular the growing proportion of white-collar workers.

A third issue was that of ballots for trade union political funds, in which arguably the unions gained a very rare victory over government legislation. The Trade Union Act 1984 required that unions which wished to retain their political funds or establish such a fund had to achieve a majority by secret ballot. The expectation at that time was that a number of unions would not be able to obtain a majority. In the event, every trade union which balloted secured a majority to continue their fund, and indeed some unions, like the NCU, which previously had not had a political fund, voted in favour of such a fund, and later affiliated to the Labour Party.

A fourth issue which arose during preparations for the Trade Union Act 1984 was the question of 'contracting in' or 'contracting out' of the political fund. The government was considering substituting 'contracting in' instead of 'contracting out' but after discussions with the TUC the Employment Secretary, Tom King, decided not to proceed with a clause to the Bill providing for 'contracting in' if the TUC would issue appropriate guidelines to affiliated unions concerning their political fund arrangements. This the TUC subsequently did, in particular drawing the attention of unions to ensure that no obstacles were placed in the way of members who wished to 'contract out'.

Unions and the European Community

Towards the end of the 1980s there was a marked change in the TUC's attitude towards the EC from a degree of caution to one of positive enthusiasm. At the 1988 Congress the General Council's preliminary report, *Europe 1992: Max-imising the Benefits; Minimising the Costs* (TUC, 1988a), was approved. This stated that the UK government had been able to veto many progressive EC measures because of the need for unanimity in the Council of Ministers. However, the Single European Act now permitted new directives for 'improvements, especially in the working environment, as regards the health and safety of workers' to be adopted by a qualified majority, thus bypassing the UK veto. The report continued by pointing out that this promising development was qualified by the lack of a clear definition of 'working environment' and by the continuinng requirements for unanimity for directives relating to the 'rights and interests of employed persons'. The Single European Act had also asked the Commission to endeavour to develop the dialogue between management and labour at European level which could 'if the two sides consider it desirable, lead to relations based on agreements'. A number of meetings have taken place, in what has become known as the Val Duchesse process, between ETUC and representatives of the European employers' organisations. The Report concluded with a final chapter on 'TUC Strategy – Next Steps', which listed a number of issues for immediate action which the General Council intended to pursue. Also of great significance in 1988 was the invitation to the President of the Commission, Jacques Delors, to address Congress, which he did, arousing much enthusiasm as a result of his emphasis on the need for a social dimension to the Single European Market. He proposed a platform of social rights based on the European Social Charter and *inter alia* the introduction of legislation on European companies which would provide for the extension to working people of information, consultation and negotiating rights and for a permanent right to training.

In December 1989 the Social Charter was adopted by 11 of the 12 member states (the UK being the exception) at the Strasbourg European Council Meeting. The Charter was intended as a general statement of minimum social rights which would be applicable throughout the Community. In January 1990 the Commission unanimously adopted its 1990 Action Programme, which is designed as the first stage of the implementation of the Charter.

Conclusion

The EETPU had been portrayed by many observers as the flagship of 'new unionism'. What was meant by that term was not always clear, but it appeared to include a cooperative policy with regard to employers, the complete acceptance of 'management's right to manage', the renunciation of the strike weapon and 'a right-wing' or 'non-political' stance: in short, a form of 'business unionism'. It was exemplified in some of the EETPU's 'new style' agreements with a number of Japanese and other companies, mainly at greenfield sites. The ingredients were typically recognition of a single union; a no-strike clause, usually with compulsory pendulum arbitration as the final means of settling disputes; the complete flexibility of labour; single status; and a high degree of consultation, for example through a company council. Although such agreements were well publicised their number was relatively limited – about 50 and the number of employees covered was perhaps no more than 20 000.

It is, in one respect, interesting to reflect on how such agreements can be reconciled with any democratic concept of employee choice in that they were typically arrived at between union and employer, before any employees were even on site. However, the counter-argument was that the alternative to such agreements was non-recognition, and that was worse. It is also interesting that there is no indication that the bulk of the EETPU's membership (or its officials) in its traditional strongholds of electricity supply, electrical contracting, local government, the NHS and engineering have adopted such attitudes or such agreements. One might therefore query the depth of the EETPU's devotion to 'new unionism'. One might also query what is new about 'new unionism'. Many unions have sought and often achieved single-union agreements: it has long been the policy of manual unions to seek harmonisation of blue-collar and white-collar terms and conditions of employment: unions have always sought consultative processes with employers, and strikes have nearly always been a weapon of last resort, with many unions, particularly in the public sector, preferring arbitration. It was after all the government and not unions in the early 1980s who ended unilateral arbitration in the public sector, as did most private-sector employers where it existed, for example the clearing banks, and it has been employers who have resisted the harmonisation of terms and conditions.

However, if the 1980s have not seen 'new unionism' on a wide scale, it could be argued that the later 1980s have seen a degree of 'new realism' in the unions if by that is meant a growing acceptance of the realities of the changing environment in which unions had to operate. Thus, unions have had to accept the legal constraints imposed upon them and, in contrast to the reckless disregard of the legal consequences shown, for example by the NGA in the *Messenger Newspapers* dispute and the NUS in the P&O dispute, great care has been taken to abide by the law, for example in the docks dispute and the British Rail dispute, both in 1989. Certainly, balloting before the taking of official industrial action has become widely accepted. Unions have become more aware of the more competitive environment in which firms have to operate and have been receptive to the introduction of new technology. Unions have also recognised that they need actively to recruit new members and that in order to do so they need to market themselves and to make themselves more attractive – hence the new services being offered. In so far as these are offered to individuals, they also pinpoint a change in direction in seeking to meet the needs of individual employees, as well as the more traditional role of collective representation. Most of these services can be provided to members even where employers do not grant recognition. Finally, unions seem to have acknowledged that there are certain objectives which can better be achieved through legislation than through collective bargaining, as illustrated, for example, by the adoption by the TUC for the first time in 1986 of a resolution in favour of a national minimum wage and a statutory recognition mechanism, the 'FLARE' (Fair Laws and Rights in Employment) campaign of the GMB, and above all the acceptance by the TUC in 1990 of a legal framework which includes some key features of the Conservative government's legislation. Not only have many individual unions sought to adjust to the changing environment and look to the future, but so has the TUC. The work of the TUC's Special Review Body is evidence of this, as is a series of TUC consultative documents, for example *Unions in Europe in the 1990s* (TUC, 1991a), *Collective Bargaining Strategy for the 1990s* (TUC, 1991b) and *Towards 2000* (1991c).

How far the 'new realism' is an adjustment to the adverse balance of power in a changed economic, political and social environment and which might be reversed if and when the pendulum swings, or how much it is the result of a fundamental change in attitude, is considered in Chapter 12.

The institutions of industrial relations

Introduction

Some aspects of the institutions and processes of industrial relations have already been discussed, in particular collective bargaining and consultation involvement and participation, in the context of employer strategy (Chapter 6) and in terms of trade union reaction (Chapter 8).

In this chapter we concentrate more on the implications of the changes that have, and are still, unfolding. In the early post-war decades there had been, particularly in much of the manufacturing industry, a great growth in informal and fragmented workplace bargaining, in the importance of custom and practice, in the power of work groups and shop stewards, and in wage drift (see Chapters 1 and 2). Among the consequences were the undermining of industry-wide agreements, of national union officials and of employers' associations. The Donovan Commission described and analysed these developments and by way of remedy recommended management initiatives to obtain formal agreements at company and/or plant level. The NBPI in the 1960s in its reforming role had adopted a similar approach and on the substantive side encouraged, for example, the introduction of job evaluation systems and the reform of payment systems and pay structures. In the early 1970s, the CIR encouraged the development and formalisation of company and plant procedures, including the role of shop stewards and their facilities. Progress indeed was made in the 1970s in the formalisation of both substantive and procedural agreements, although this progress was overshadowed in the public perception by rapidly escalating inflation, the re-emergence of major national strikes and the felt need by government, both Labour and Conservative, for a national incomes policy.

At that time, looking forward to the 1980s, most industrial relations experts and practitioners would have expected a continuation of the trends of greater unionisation, a widening of the extent and scope of collective bargaining and more formalised procedural and substantive agreements. One example of academic thought (McCarthy and Ellis, 1973) was a very large extension of joint decision-making. The fact that most of these trends did not continue must be explained in terms of the changed economic and political climate and the parties' reactions to the changed environment.

What happened, generally speaking, was increased formalisation in many procedures, for example, disciplinary and grievance procedures and increased formalisation of pay structures and systems through the extension of job evaluation and performance related pay. But on operational matters there was a complete reversal of trend, with much greater freedom for managers to take unilateral action.

As stated earlier, what has happened to the institutions of industrial relations has been the subject of debate, with one school of thought arguing that fundamentally there has been little change in that the institutions are still in place despite the traumas of the 1980s – mass redundancies, high unemployment, the decline in union membership and fiercely anti-union legislation (Batstone, 1984; MacInnes, 1987). The second school of thought argues that there has been fundamental change which has, and will continue to, marginalise unions and the joint institutions of industrial relations (Bassett, 1986; Phelps Brown, 1990).

This apparent polarisation of views is much exaggerated. The joint institutions are still in place, although in many industries and companies they have undergone marked change. But what has changed above all has been the balance of power within the institutions. Management has been dominant, and as a result it is the use to which the institutions have been put, rather than their retention, abolition or change, which is the crucial factor. It is also arguable that the changing use of the institutions has been affected by the changing attitudes and behaviour of employees and unions towards more cooperation and less confrontation. This has also been the subject of much debate and is returned to in Chapter 12.

In Chapter 6 it was argued that the main developments in collective bargaining which had taken place in the 1980s had been, first, the change in the level of collective bargaining – away from industry level to company level and within companies to plant/divisional level – and, second, the reduction in the scope of collective bargaining. However, before we pursue these developments it is necessary to look at what has happened to employers' associations.

Employers' associations

Historically, employers' associations were major actors in British industrial relations but they have been consigned in the last two decades or so to virtual oblivion by most academics and commentators. Attention has rightly been focused on individual companies and their industrial relations objectives and policies, particularly in view of changing developments and past neglect. However, like trade unions, whatever the knocks they have suffered, employers' associations still exist. A number of them continue to engage in collective bargaining and all are seeking a new role for themselves in a changing world. The CBI was largely ignored by Thatcher governments in favour of the more politically and ideologically acceptable Institute of Directors, and it distanced itself from the TUC in a reaction against the corporatism of the 1970s. But it has a membership of some 250 000 companies and trade associations and their members. It has no rival as the national representative body of employers.

The major trend towards the decentralisation of collective bargaining continued in the 1980s. As Brown and Walsh (1991) show using 1984 WIRS 2 data:

> Collective bargaining was then being used to fix pay for some 80 per cent of employees in private manufacturing and a little under 50 per cent in private services. These arrangements were still predominantly multi-employer for 30 per cent of manuals and 13 per cent of non-manuals in manufacturing and respectively 50 per cent and 40 per cent in services. These figures imply that even counting in the still dominant industry-wide agreements of the construction industries, multi-employer bargaining was the principal means of fixing pay for only about one private-sector employee in five. (p. 49)

Again, as Brown and Walsh (1991) state, 'the decline in multi-employer bargaining has almost certainly accelerated in the second half of the 1980s. At least sixteen major national bargaining groups, covering a total of over a million employees, have been terminated since 1986' (p. 49), the most important of which was that of the engineering industry. However, industry-wide bargaining still exists, for example in electrical contracting, construction — particularly the building subcontracting industries — printing, engineering construction and the garage trade; and in a number of other industries, mainly characterised by a large number of small establishments and with relatively low capital requirements. Twenty-six wage councils still cover some 2¼ million employees; and there are 5 million employees in the public sector, mainly covered by national agreements.

In these industries employers clearly still see advantages in having industry-wide agreements. Usually there is two-tier bargaining, although in electrical contracting and construction engineering standard rates are successfully applied. In commercial printing, for example, where industry bargaining sets a floor, the industry is dominated by small firms spread all over the country with a wide diversity of products. These are characteristics which, according to the British Printing Industry Federation (BPIF), indicate that a national agreement on pay is required by member firms. There is two-tier bargaining in both large and small companies, although its importance varies between sectors, being particularly marked in periodicals, graphics and reproduction. At domestic level it is mainly associated with measures to increase productivity, and the Federation's staff spend a considerable amount of time in advising member firms on productivity improvements.

In building, again an industry with numerous small firms throughout the country, although with a few very large ones as well, a recent survey of members of the Building Employers' Confederation (BEC) showed 100 per cent support for continuing with the national agreement, despite the rise in self-employment. The individual companies tend not to have formal pay bargaining with the unions, but are largely dependent on the national agreement. The main reason why the big employers still support the national agreement is said to be their fear of strikes. They believe that the industry agreement supports the unions nationally and enables them to exert some control on sites when needed.

The Engineering Employers' Federation (EEF), which still has 5000 member firms, abandoned industry-wide bargaining in 1990 in the midst of its dispute with the unions over a shorter working week. However, the EEF is not resigning itself to a minor role. It sees its role increasingly as an advisory one and as a spokesman and pressure group for the industry. This latter role is becoming more important, it believes, with the approach of 1992 and other EC developments. It has in recent years designed new categories of membership and is seeking to attract more members, including some very large firms. It believes that what the big firms want is a representative voice in Brussels, which it is seeking to provide.

While there is no doubt that industry-wide agreements negotiated by employers' associations have been in decline because they have been abolished or their content has been narrowed, they still continue to be of major importance in some sectors. It is not the case that employers' associations have generally ceased to have a role in industrial relations.

Collective bargaining

For present purposes, collective bargaining can be analysed first in terms of recognition and bargaining agents, and second in terms of bargaining level and scope (Bain, 1971; McCarthy, 1971).

Recognition and bargaining agents

It is widely accepted that the degree of derecognition has been relatively low (Claydon, 1989) although there are some indications that it is more widespread than originally thought (Gregg and Yates, 1991). There have been some widely publicised cases, such as the derecognition of the print unions at Wapping; the NUJ in most of the national newspapers, in parts of the provincial press and in parts of book publishing; the then NUS at P&O the TGWU in the horse-racing industry, and at Tilbury following the 1989 abolition of the National Dock Labour Scheme; some parts of the hotel and catering industry; senior managers at British Rail and British Telecom and groups of white-collar workers elsewhere. Indeed, one senior national union official in the newspaper industry believed that there was a concerted campaign by employers to introduce individual contracts in both London and provincial newspapers with the purpose of making the industry union free.

But derecognition has not been widespread. As one employer representative put it, 'Derecognition has not taken off because it has not been necessary, since the unions do not stand in the way of change.' He added that some employers who are hostile to trade unions have been content to stand aside and watch trade union membership fall. Another stated that 'they had got all the cooperation they needed from their unions to make changes which were necessary to achieve great increases in productivity', while a third company which had made major strides in efficiency said that 'the unions could not have been avoided in making changes on such a scale; they had to be integrated into the process.'

If most managers have not been actively pursuing derecognition, their attitude towards recognition at greenfield sites in unorganised parts of the economy has been very different. They have, on the whole, been unwelcoming with regard to recognition and often positively hostile. There are of course exceptions. Thus we were told by the personnel director of a large company with both retail and manufacturing interests, which recognised unions on the manufacturing side, that on the retail side the union had been given access to employees in company time. The company had offered recognition for any group which achieved 50% + 1 membership and union representation in any shop if they achieved 50% + 1. Despite such a favourable attitude by the employer, the union has only attained between 3 and 4 per cent membership.

One senior union official said that U.S. companies have always been anti-union but that they have been relaxed about it and have an open-door policy. He added that Japanese companies tend to follow whatever is the local attitude – thus they follow the U.S. companies in Scotland and are anti-union, but in the North-East and in South Wales they recognise unions because other employers do so.

What is clear is that employers for the first time in many decades have a choice as to whether they recognise a union or not. They are free to consider the advantages and disadvantages of recognition and to make their own decisions. In the 1970s, apart from a number of exceptions, employers felt that union recognition was not an issue because they fell in with it. By contrast, in the 1980s it became the fashion among managers not to recognise unions where they were not already recognised. Just as employers have the power to recognise or not, in most instances they also have the power, if they decide to recognise, to determine which union should be the bargaining agent for its employees. In most cases,they have gone for single-union recognition, while unions have often been subjected to a 'beauty contest' so that employers can satisfy themselves as to the most appropriate – perhaps the least troublesome – union to choose.

Bargaining unit level and scope

The movement of bargaining level from industry to company, and within companies from corporate to divisional and/or plant level, has already been discussed in Chapter 6. However, it should be noted that alongside the major trend in decentralising collective bargaining there has been a move to widen the bargaining units at any given level. This reaches its extreme in 'new-style' single-union agreements where the bargaining unit is usually the whole of the labour force, excluding only management. In brownfield sites, where several unions may already have recognition and where historically there may be a number of separate bargaining units, for example, for process workers, for craftsmen, for clerical workers and for technicians and supervisors, there are moves in some companies towards the TUC's idea of 'a single table'. This at best means one joint negotiating body and one set of negotiations covering manual and non-manual workers and an integrated pay structure. It may, however, be too large a step in some companies, and a half-way house has been one joint body covering all manual workers and another joint body covering non-manuals. However, one employer's representative thought that the TUC's efforts to get single-table negotiation had not been particularly successful because it is not an issue which greatly concerns management. The important thing for management is whether they have the power to take initiatives and get them through the negotiations. The number of unions is far less important than the power relationship.

Turning to the consequences of these trends, the first is that, with an emphasis on domestic bargaining, the importance of shop stewards is enhanced and the importance of the full-time officials reduced. The one caveat is that with the major swing of bargaining power to employers, shop stewards may feel exposed, with few volunteering to put their heads above the parapet. They may be less likely to put their future at risk by opposing management plans. But discrimination against stewards has not been a major issue and there has been no widespread incidence of complaints of stewards being deprived of facilities. Second, as Brown (1986, p. 165) has argued:

shop steward organisations are proving relatively easy to isolate from the wider union movement . . . they identify their interests more with the success of the enterprise . . . . It is hard to avoid the conclusion that the structure of trade unionism, originally developed for the strategies of employee solidarity, is increasingly being shaped to the needs of employers.

The needs of employers have increasingly been towards 'enterprise-orientated rather than occupationally oriented trade unionism'. It is clear from our interviews with senior managers that they now communicate more directly with employees rather than through shop stewards and that is indicative of the reduced significance of stewards in many workplaces. Third, domestic bargaining has made it possible and meaningful to include productivity elements in negotiations and this appears to have been the case on a widespread basis. Thus the CBI (1989) reported that 'every year during the 1980s, more than one in every five pay settlements in manufacturing has featured changes in working practices as part of the deal' (p. 9) and several of the personnel directors interviewed reported that 'something for something' bargaining had become the norm in their companies. In some ways this is a paradox, for as is argued in Chapter 6, the scope of collective bargaining in many cases has diminished as a result of growing managerial power and assertiveness.

In some cases, management has obtained new procedure agreements which expressly state that it has complete control over operational matters, such as the movement and flexibility of labour. In other cases, it has been less a question of changes in procedures than one of style and method of management and in management's ability to make unopposed alterations in working practices. As one union general secretary put it, managers can certainly achieve more than they used to be able to; they drive things through forcefully. He was not critical of this, but he argued there are two types of manager. There are those who say that certain things have to be done and they go to some lengths to carry the unions with them, even if it means dragging them along. But there are others who adopt a take-it-or-leave-it attitude and therefore impose their will. The vital difference between the two types is that the former pay more attention to longer-term considerations than the latter.

The paradox mentioned above is partly explained by differences in the balance of power. In some industries and companies unions still retain considerable power or influence, which means that management has to negotiate over changes in working practices. In other industries and companies management may never have conceded influence over operational matters to the unions, for example in retail distribution and banking, while in others union power may have been destroyed or greatly diminished, for example, in coal, iron and steel and newspaper publishing.

In the public service sector, management has also been largely in control, and the government has been determined to push through change. Where it is the employer, as in the civil service, or is ultimately responsible for management, as in the NHS, it has sought to institute change directly through weakening centralised bargaining and national agreements, as well as through financial squeeze. In other parts of the public service sector, for example local authorities, it has again sought to ensure change, mainly through financial pressure, but also more directly through legislation, for example with regard to teachers' pay and terms and conditions of employment, through allowing and indeed encouraging the opting-out of schools and local authorities from the national agreements, and through the local management initiative for schools and the enforcing of compulsory tendering. In the public corporations pressure for change has been created largely through the setting of financial targets, the removal or reduction of subsidies, deregulation and ultimately through privatisation.

The conclusion is that the major change in the institutions of collective bargaining is in the use to which they are being put. Management has been taking the initiative and tabling its own requirements, for example in demanning and in changes in working practices, payment systems and pay structures. It is no longer simply a matter of unions putting forward their annual claims for pay increases and improvements in the terms and conditions of employment. The subject matter has become much more focused on what workers do rather than on what they are paid. In a programme of negotiations for change, pay is considered in parallel, or pay claims are met, with a set of required associated changes in workplace practices.

In the private sector, as corporate objectives have required more decentralised operations, so the determination of pay and the management of labour have been decentralised to where management has thought it most suitable. This has made the local agenda more comprehensive and less subject to oversight by, and dependence on, corporate or industry bargaining: this process was under way before the 1980s, and still has some way to go in the 1990s. In addition, manpower matters are increasingly in the hands of line managers because the more efficient use of labour has become a major line management responsibility. Moreover, with more quiescent labour, the case for industrial relations specialists to negotiate has arguably become weaker. Manpower use and labour costs are part of a bigger set of managerial questions. Industrial relations decisions follow behind those made about products and investment. As a starting point, managers ask what changes must be made if such and such are to be the products, rather than what changes the unions will agree to. Managers believe that the negotiations are the means for facilitating the achievement of their objectives. They do not approach them in the spirit that the unions can determine whether or not the changes are to be made.

Indeed, it is clear that the significance of industrial relations in many firms has diminished. It is part of a management-controlled operation – a branch of human resource management. It is no longer a high-profile, problem-ridden part of personnel management as it so often was in the 1970s. The role of the unions has become more centred on achieving the best bargain for the changes which plant management wants. Increases in earnings above inflation have made that enforced strategy one which has paid off for individual members — or at least those who have retained their jobs.

Productivity bargaining

It is interesting to compare the 'something for something' bargaining of the 1980s and early 1990s with the productivity bargaining which had its heyday in the 1960s. There is a strong common thread in that in both cases bargaining is about what is done for pay as much as about what pay shall be; bargaining in both cases is at domestic level and carried out by plant managers and shop stewards; settlements are not normally one-off but are linked together on both pay and work in a stage-by-stage approach; and implementation of the changes is part of the follow-up to a settlement.

However, the strongest common feature is that management is responsible for taking the initiative in bargaining because it can translate the plant's economic objectives — products, costs, investment — into labour requirements. Thus, one personnel director of a large manufacturing company told us that the productivity bargaining of the 1960s and 1970s had 'set the juices running' so that in the 1980s productivity bargaining had become the norm. Another personnel director, also of a large manufacturing company, accepted that what they had been doing in the 1980s could be called 'productivity bargaining' and that it had been remarkably successful. Productivity had increased substantially and the labour force had been reduced by well over a third without a single stoppage and without a single compulsory redundancy. The tribute to productivity bargaining in this case is particularly noteworthy because this was a company which in the 1960s had stood aloof from productivity bargaining on the grounds that the organisation of work and other operational matters were solely the concern of management.

What is missing in the 1980s and early 1990s is an element of joint control, by which is meant the shared, cooperative exercise of control over the uses to which labour is put. For Allan Flanders (1964), the leading advocate of productivity bargaining in the 1960s, its essence included the introduction of an element of joint control, as was shown by his famous dictum that 'In order to regain control management must be prepared to share it.' Flanders also argued that it was management that had to be the key actor in the process: for too long managers had been passive and had taken little interest in industrial relations. It was an essential part of Flanders's message, from his study of Esso's Fawley oil refinery, that management had to take the initiative if labour was to be used more effectively. This message he repeated in his evidence to the Donovan Royal Commission and it was indeed adopted by the Commission (1968) in its final report, which *inter alia* emphasised time and time again the responsibility of management to initiate reform. The Commission also stressed the need for companies to engage in plant or company formal bargaining because 'in most industries such matters cannot be dealt with effectively by means of industry-wide agreements' (1968, p. 262).

In a recent work, Ahlstrand (1990) shows how Esso at their Fawley refinery continued to engage in productivity bargaining through the 1960s and 1970s and into the 1980s. However, he also shows that the gains were limited, that there was a significant creep back to old working practices and that Esso was never really interested in joint control, but solely with the restoration of management authority. It would appear that Flanders was over-optimistic about the effects of the Fawley agreements, but this does not negate his message regarding the importance of management initiative and of domestic bargaining.

Thus, managers have come to be where they are now not only because of what happened in the 1980s. Many of them have been endeavouring since the 1960s to promote the efficient use of manpower to as prominent a place in bargaining as pay. The present bargaining norms owe a great deal to what used to be called productivity bargaining. In the 1980s, productivity bargaining has been facilitated by the decentralisation of management authority. However, it has been given a different drive by management's dominance and the unions' acquiescence. But the important point is that in most cases the unions are involved, not excluded.

In concluding this section, it is clear that it continues to be common practice that where unions are recognised there are elected workplace representatives. These continue to have two broad functions: first, representation of members in grievance and disciplinary procedures and other protective functions like health and safety; second, participation in negotiation with managers. The former function is more orderly than it used to be because, as a result of Donovan and legislation, for example on unfair dismissal and health and safety, procedures have become much more formalised. The latter function is the key to the union's role as an effective representative body. As previously stated, management decentralisation accentuates the importance of plant negotiations and hence of shop stewards. It is the use of negotiations which varies.

One way forward for the unions is to challenge management and seek to establish a rival centre of power. Another is to engage in setting the agenda for negotiation and to have a strategy for manpower which complements that of management, based on an assessment of the interests and aspirations of their members at work. The latter is more in line with the way collective bargaining has developed in the 1980s in response to the swing of power to management, and has been espoused in some unions. This approach rejects the idea of a backlash of union power and argues for a measured strategy of improving the quality of union participation in bargaining, for example by getting training on to the negotiating agenda.

Third-party intervention

Traditional third-party intervention in industrial relations continues to be provided primarily by the Advisory, Conciliation and Arbitration Service (ACAS). ACAS was established in 1974 and put on a statutory basis by the Employment Protection Act 1975. Its duties are as laid down in that Act, which basically transferred to ACAS the functions of conciliation, arbitration and advice which were previously discharged by the Department of Employment, and the inquiry functions which up till then had been provided by the CIR.

ACAS is one of the few tripartite organisations which survived the Thatcher years. Its survival might at first sight seem surprising, particularly its objectives of promoting the improvement of industrial relations and of encouraging the extension of collective bargaining as well as its provision of free advice and services, since these would appear to run across the 'bottom line' philosophy of Thatcher governments. However, every industrialised country has a need for a conciliation, mediation and arbitration service. The mere existence of ACAS has the enormous advantage of enabling government to appear to distance itself from industrial disputes and their settlement.

During the 1980s the use of ACAS's collective conciliation and arbitration services declined significantly. The number of completed collective conciliation cases fell from 2284 in 1979 to 1140 in 1990 and the number of cases referred to arbitration and mediation from 363 to 200 (ACAS, 1980b, 1991).

The 'something for something' approach, especially where earnings rise appreciably, offers many opportunities for compromise. The decline of arbitration is explicable in the same terms as the decline of strikes. The parties have usually been able to reach a settlement themselves. In cases where breakdown would mean arbitration, as well as ones where it would mean a strike, the parties have found an answer for themselves. Management dominance has been the main explanation. In the private sector arbitration has always been a last resort and has normally been voluntary, that is to say it could only be invoked, if at all, in terms of procedures by the agreement of both sides. Similarly ACAS has no power to impose arbitration on the parties without their joint agreement. In the 1980s managements have normally been unwilling to do so and because of their dominance have been confident that their final offers would be accepted. In the prevailing climate unions, if dissatisfied and denied arbitration, would in most cases be unwilling to take industrial action.

In the public-sector, the position was historically different in that arbitration was usually the normal means of solving differences between the parties which could not be settled by negotiation. Sometimes reference to arbitration was the norm as a result of custom and practice. In many other cases there was a right, laid down in procedures, for either party to unilaterally invoke arbitration. In the early 1980s the government sought, and largely succeeded, in terminating public-sector unilateral arbitration agreements. Where resort to arbitration depended on both sides' agreement, the government almost invariably withheld agreement and pressurised other public-sector employers to act likewise.

The government's hostility to arbitration was partly because it alleged that arbitrators split the difference, partly because it alleged that arbitration was inflationary, partly because it believed it wrong to give a third party control over pay and cost decisions which should rest with the employer, and above all because it believed its own view should prevail. The big public-sector strikes of the 1980s would in other times probably have been settled by arbitration. The government thus preferred to settle disagreements by force rather than by peaceful means and, having engaged in a dispute, was determined to win, regardless of cost. In some ways such an attitude is paradoxical, because the government has supported 'new style' agreements, such as those entered into by many Japanese companies, which provided for obligatory arbitration in the event of the parties failing to agree. Many of these agreements provided for 'pendulum arbitration'; that is to say, the arbitrator had to make a choice between the final offer of the employer and the final claim of the union, there being no scope for an award in between. The main stated advantage over conventional arbitration was that it encouraged realism on the part of both parties because an unrealistic offer or claim was likely to lead the arbitrator to award in favour of the other party. The main stated disadvantage was the lack of scope and flexibility given to the arbitrator (Kessler, 1987). To date there have been far too few cases for any kind of judgement to be made.

One further point needs to be made with regard to third-party intervention in the 1980s, namely that it has been of the traditional kind. In other words, it is essentially concerned with helping to keep the peace. It has not had a reforming purpose (although arguably some of ACAS's advisory work could fall in this category), unlike certain earlier third-party institutions such as the NBPI and the CIR (see Chapters 1 and 2). The main reason for this is the government's alleged policy of non-intervention in industrial matters – it should all be left to the parties. In reality, the government has sought reform through changes in the law and in the public sector, also through financial squeeze, privatisation and so forth, while private employers have sought reform through their own policies and through the widespread use of private consultants. However, it is true that ACAS advisory work has flourished during the 1980s, subject only to the severe financial constraints imposed on ACAS by government.

Joint consultation

Theoretically there is a clear distinction between collective bargaining and joint consultation -bargaining is a process which normally results in a joint or agreed decision by the parties, whereas in joint consultation decisions are unilaterally determined by management, albeit after consultation. This theoretical distinction is usually mirrored in practice by the existence of separate machinery for bargaining and for consultation. There are also normally separate agendas. Collective bargaining machinery is concerned with the determination of pay and other terms and conditions of employment, whereas joint consultation is concerned with what are considered non-negotiable matters, such as welfare, health and safety, production and efficiency – matters supposedly of common interest. In practice, there is often an overlap and blurring on certain issues.

It was Flanders (1964) who fiercely attacked the separation of the two processes, arguing that it was not only artificial but positively harmful. If efficiency was left to the consultative machinery and pay was left to the negotiating machinery, a management seeking to improve productivity through the cooperation of workers and their union or unions could only resort to exhortation. However, exhortation alone was unlikely to be successful. Attempts to improve efficiency needed to be linked to increased rewards, hence Flanders' advocacy of productivity bargaining – a process which required the enlarging of the content of collective bargaining and including matters which had hitherto been dealt with by joint consultation.

With the growth in productivity bargaining in the second half of the 1960s, this widening of collective bargaining took place and joint consultation declined somewhat. Indeed McCarthy (1966) has argued that, with the growth of shop steward power and workplace bargaining, joint consultation would inevitably decline, for it was regarded by stewards as an inferior process to bargaining on the grounds that it left decisions to be unilaterally determined by management. In fact, reports of the decline and indeed death of joint consultation were much exaggerated, as is shown for example by Millward and Stevens (1986).

Marchington (1989) has argued that there are four different models of consultation which can be seen in action in Britain. First, consultation may be used as an alternative to collective bargaining and to prevent its establishment. Here management is essentially unitarist, but much more sophisticated than the traditional anti-union owner–manager. Thus, it seeks to promote harmony and the willing acceptance of management decisions. The process is mainly one-way and basically educative in its nature. One large retail chain, whose personnel director we interviewed, does not recognise unions, but has an elaborate consultative system. There are 'communication groups'; in all stores and distribution centres, meetings take place every 6 weeks or so but representatives recognise that decisions are left to management.

Second, consultation may be seen as marginal within the enterprise by employer and employees and as achieving little or nothing for either party. This is likely to be the case where there is little trust, where the parties use opportunistic tactics to undermine each other and where there is little management commitment to joint arrangements.

Third, consultation may be seen as being in direct competition with collective bargaining, with management seeking to upgrade consultation so that negotiations become less meaningful or necessary. In order to succeed, management must make consultation appear more significant. The agenda will therefore cover important topics, such as new products, investment plans, efficiency and marketing. In such companies, there are often developments in other forms of involvement, designed to convince employees of the reasons for management actions, for example, briefing groups, employee presentations and reports, and quality circles.

Fourth, especially where trade unionism is strong and well developed, consultation may be seen as a valuable adjunct to collective bargaining. Here the two processes are kept separate, although the representatives of each committee will be largely the same people. Thus the personnel director of a large manufacturing company, which was highly unionised, told us that their present position is the opposite of macho-management. Competition is severe and they need effective communications to ensure that the competitive threat is understood. That requires a coming together on the details of the business. In the 1970s it was a war described in battle terms. Now they seek common solutions and are constantly asking, 'How do we improve relationships?' There has been much more growing together and recognition of the others' interests. Accommodation has been achieved which, 15 years ago, he would not have believed possible. The unions, he said, could not have been left out in making necessary changes. They had to be integrated into the process. To achieve this, management really did open the books.

In Chapter 6 it was argued that in the 1980s management in many cases had sought better communications and greater involvement because they realised that they required a workforce committed to company objectives. It was also argued that this approach was based on unitary beliefs and on seeking greater individualisation. Thus, much of management's efforts are now focused directly on their employees and not only or mainly through representative channels. Such efforts — aimed as they are at enlisting employee opinion and behaviour behind management's objectives — must inevitably threaten to weaken the union's traditional position.

Joint consultative machinery is therefore, like negotiating machinery, still in place. But the use to which it is now put is often different from what it used to be. Moreover, it is now supplemented by a range of management methods to communicate and influence employees directly and individually. The Conservative governments of the 1980s and employers have strongly resisted any suggestion of a statutory obligation on companies to engage in consultation.

They have also strongly resisted any such development through European Community action. Whether a European directive will be adopted or not remains to be seen, as do its effects, if adopted.

Conclusion

In the 1980s there were significant changes in the institutions of industrial relations, in particular the decentralisation of collective bargaining and the development by employers of more direct means of communication with their employees, often bypassing traditional union channels. However, far more important than changes in the institutions has been the use to which they have been put.

The roles of the parties within the broadly similar institutional framework were substantially different. Management seized the initiative as a result of the change in the balance of power and the changing economic and political environment. The assertion of managerial authority meant in many cases a reduction in the scope of collective bargaining and in the ability to act unilaterally, for example in reducing the labour force, in introducing organisational and technological change and 'something for something' bargaining.

There are two main features which have a bearing on the future and are further discussed in Chapter 12. First, in the 1980s, during the period of economic expansion as well as the recessions before and after that period, the new power relationship between managers and trade unions in the private sector looked stable.

Second, it was in the public sector, and particularly in the public services, where the changed relationship made least progress and where it was least stable. The institutions had of course been put under stress by fierce conflict in some parts. The easy acceptance of continuity in the institutions with changes of purpose, which was extensively achieved in the private sector was not present to anything like the same degree in the public sector. Overt conflict and pay failing to keep up with that of others provided a less congenial background for changes which, in the private sector, could be justified by both sides by improvement in both pay and productivity.

CHAPTER 10

Pay and productivity

In this chapter we look first at government objectives and policy with regard to pay determination; second at the outcomes of policies on pay; and finally at how and why outcomes differed from intentions.

Government objectives and policy

The government objectives with regard to pay were clear and were derived from their fundamental belief in the free market. Britain's post-war record on pay was thought to be poor and was the result of government interference through incomes policy and other regulatory means, such as Wages Councils; the Fair Wages Resolution (FWR); over-full employment; too-powerful trade unions; industry-wide bargaining and consequently industry-wide pay rates; protected product markets; too large a public sector, where the price mechanism did not work and comparability reigned supreme; and too generous unemployment pay and too easy conditions to qualify for benefit, as well as a taxation system which discouraged the will to work. The consequences were high wage inflation, inflexibility, inadequate differentials, and pay increases unrelated to performance and profitability, to the supply of, and demand for labour, which in turn resulted in uncompetitive British goods and services and indeed unemployment itself, because the unemployed had 'priced themselves out of jobs'.

Perhaps the best statement of government views was contained in a lecture given by Kenneth Clarke, the then Minister of State at the Department of Employment, at the City University Business School in February 1987. The Minister stated that:

> the inflexibility of our labour market produced the gradually increased unemploy-
> ment we have experienced post-war . . . greater flexibility in the labour market is

essential to tackle unemployment . . . . At the heart of our economic problems since the Second World War has been the problem of paying ourselves more as a nation than we can afford in higher productivity and output growth.

In pursuit of greater flexibility he argued that we must change the way we bargained about wage levels and wage increases. 'We must move towards a system more clearly based on market forces, on demand and supply, on competition and on ability to pay,' and we must move away from the annual pay round, the going rate, comparability, job evaluation and national pay bargaining. Two particular changes he identified as crucial were, first, a move from national to local bargaining and, second, employers introducing payment systems which rewarded merit and performance.

> If we can move to a system where pay increases are primarily based on performance, merit, company profitability and demand and supply in the local labour market, we will dethrone once and for all the annual pay round and the belief that pay increases do not have to be earned.

The defects of the post-war British system were clear in the eyes of the Government; so were the remedies, which followed directly from this analysis of defects. As far as the economy as a whole was concerned, and the private sector in particular, it was not for government to interfere directly. What government needed to do was to provide employers with the appropriate environment to conduct their own affairs. This involved the following:

- Increased unemployment.
- Laws reducing the power of trade unions.
- Reducing the burden on industry — for example through reducing regulations on hours of work; on the employment of women and young people; changing the burden of proof in unfair-dismissal cases; increasing the period of employment to 2 years before a degree of protection applied to employees, such as unfair dismissal; and increasing the number of hours that part-time employees had to work before they became entitled to a degree of protection.
- Abolishing or reducing legal minimum wages, and terms and conditions entitlements where they existed by the abolition of Schedule 11 of the Employment Protection Act 1975, and of the FWR and the curtailment of the power of Wage Councils.
- Encouraging the break-up of national wage agreements.
- Encouraging a reduction in the pay of young people in the early 1980s, so that they could be priced into jobs.
- Encouraging performance-related pay, profit-related pay and share ownership.
- The ending of 'the wage round' and the concept of 'the going rate'.

In the public sector the government sought to reproduce the conditions and policies which existed — or rather which the government thought ought to exist — in the private sector. Thus, to produce financial pressure in lieu of product market pressure, strict financial limits and targets were imposed; performance-related pay was introduced; local allowances were permitted to provide pay flexibility to meet geographical and skill shortages; industrial action was resolutely resisted — the unions had to be defeated; the right to unilateral arbitration was removed wherever it existed, and recourse to jointly agreed arbitration almost invariably denied; comparability was considered irrelevant (until towards the end of the decade when it partially re-emerged in the IPCS agreement and other subsequent civil service agreements); the need 'to recruit and retain' was paramount — a useful doctrine in the years of high unemployment; finally, there was privatisation either of complete public corporations or of designated services through contracting out; and, by the end of the decade, the policy of hiving off central government functions to agencies, which would have a degree of freedom to determine pay, although the eventual extent of this has yet to be determined.

In the following sections, we consider the results of just over a decade of such policies.

The growth of earnings

Average earnings for all men increased by 192 per cent between April 1979 and April 1990 and average earnings for all women increased by 220 per cent (Table 10.1). The increase in the RPI was 130 per cent, so there was an increase in average real earnings of 27 per cent for men and 39 per cent for women. In terms of reducing the increase in earnings, government policy got off to a disastrous start. Between April 1979 and April 1980 average earnings increased by over 20 per cent, compared with an annual rate of increase of 10 per cent (April 1978 to April 1979) — the last year of the Labour government. The government sought to lay the blame on the awards of the Clegg Comparability Commission, but the real reasons were partly that pay increases had been escalating as a consequence of the 'Winter of Discontent' and partly — and most importantly — there was a very sharp increase in the cost of living as a result of the government's own fiscal and monetary policy, namely a hefty rise in interest rates and a major increase in indirect taxation in its first budget, in particular the doubling of VAT at a stroke. The rapid escalation in the RPI which ensued was followed by an equally rapid escalation in pay settlements.

In the following two years, however, during the depth of the recession, there was a major de-escalation in pay increases, followed by several years of

TABLE 10.1 Average gross weekly earnings, 1979–90 – UK

April	Male						Female						RPI
	Manual £		Non-manual £		All £		Manual £		Non-manual £		All £		
1979	93.0	100	113.0	100	101.4	100	55.2	100	66.0	100	63.0	100	100
1980	111.7	120	141.3	125	125.4	124	68.0	123	82.7	125	78.9	125	121.8
1981	121.9	131	163.1	130	140.5	139	74.5	135	96.7	147	91.4	145	136.4
1982	133.8	144	178.9	158	154.5	152	80.1	145	104.9	159	99.0	157	149.3
1983	143.6	154	194.9	172	167.5	165	87.9	174	115.1	174	108.8	173	155.2
1984	152.7	164	209.0	185	178.8	176	93.5	169	124.3	188	117.2	186	163.3
1985	163.6	176	225.0	199	192.4	190	101.3	184	133.8	203	126.4	201	174.6
1986	174.4	188	244.9	217	207.5	205	107.5	195	145.7	221	137.2	218	179.9
1987	185.5	199	265.9	235	224.0	221	115.3	209	157.2	238	148.1	235	187.5
1988	200.6	216	294.1	260	245.8	242	123.6	224	175.5	266	164.2	261	194.9
1989	217.8	234	323.6	286	269.5	266	134.9	244	195.0	295	182.3	289	210.5
1990	237.2	255	354.9	314	295.6	292	148.0	268	215.5	327	201.5	320	230.0
% increase in real earnings, 1979–90	+11		+37		+27		+17		+42		+39		

Source: NES

stability with annual increases in earnings of between 7 and 8 per cent. In 1987–8, however, the rate of increase started to move up again and this continued in the following 2 years.

Throughout the 1980s pay increases had been above those of our main industrial competitors (Chapter 3), and throughout the decade earnings increased more than the cost of living, so that real earnings continued to increase. What was remarkable was that earnings should have increased to the extent that they did despite very high unemployment for most of the decade and despite the reduction in union power. Whatever the reasons (which are returned to later), it was clear that at the end of the decade, with earnings rising at an annual rate of some 10 per cent, which was far higher than that of our main competitors, 10 years of Thatcherism had not solved the problem of excess increases in money earnings which had been a major feature of post-war Britain.

The distribution of earnings

If the Conservative governments had been unsuccessful in reducing earnings increases to satisfactory levels, it could be argued that they *had* been successful in changing the distribution of earnings. The distribution had changed in two major aspects. First, non-manual earnings increased far more than manual earnings (see Table 10.1): for manual males, between 1979 and 1990 the increase in money earnings was 155 per cent, or 11 per cent in real terms, compared with a money increase of 214 per cent and a real increase of 37 per cent for non-manual males. For manual women, money earnings increased by 168 per cent and real earnings by 17 per cent, compared with 227 per cent and 42 per cent respectively for non-manual women.

Second, the higher paid did better than the lower paid (Table 10.2). Between 1979 and 1990 the lower quartile for all men as a percentage of the median went down from 80 per cent to 75 per cent while the upper quartile as a percentage of the median increased from 125 per cent to 135 per cent. For all women the lower quartile as a percentage of the median fell from 82 per cent to 77 per cent and the upper quartile as a percentage of the median increased from 125 per cent to 138 per cent. Management pay, and above all directors' salaries, as evidenced by various salary surveys, increased at a far faster rate than pay generally, to a point at the end of the 1980s where such increases actually drew a rebuke from Mrs Thatcher and an appeal for restraint.

Supporters of (or apologists for) the markedly changed distribution of income in favour of the better-paid (even without taking into account the income tax cuts for the higher paid) argue that it is all the result of market

TABLE 10.2 Distribution of earnings, 1979–90

| | Males | | | | | | Females | | | | | |
| | Manual | | Non-manual | | All | | Manual | | Non-manual | | All | |
	1979	1990	1979	1990	1979	1990	1979	1990	1979	1990	1979	1990
Median Weekly earnings (£)	88.2	221.3	103.6	312.1	93.9	258.2	53.3	137.3	60.8	191.8	58.4	177.5
Lowest decile as per cent of median	68	63	63	55	66	58	70	68	70	62	69	63
Lower quartile as per cent of median	82	79	79	74	80	75	83	82	82	77	82	77
Upper quartile as per cent of median	122	127	127	133	125	135	118	125	126	138	125	138
Upper decile	149	158	163	182	157	181	141	157	161	173	159	179

Source: *New Earnings Survey*, 1979 and 1990, adult full-time employees whose pay was not affected by absence.

forces and that wider differentials are necessary for the success of 'the enterprise culture'. How directors' pay, normally determined by non-executive directors who primarily owe their appointment to the full-time directors, can be said to be determined by market forces, is not always easy to understand. Certainly, the climate created by the doubling and trebling of managing directors' annual salaries to reach in some cases £1m or more was not conducive to restraint and responsibility in pay claims at lower levels.

Earnings by occupation

The distribution of earnings has thus changed markedly in the 1980s, with the lower-paid getting relatively less and the better-paid getting relatively more, while non-manual employees as a whole gained substantially compared to manual workers. These are very broad categories, however, and we need to look more closely at changes in occupational earnings. A comparison of changes in occupational earnings between 1979 and 1990 based on the New Earnings Survey shows that among non-manual groups which did particularly well were those in 'the professional and related, supporting management and administration', where the overall average increase in earnings was 244 per cent for males and 253 per cent for females, and where, for males, accountants' earnings increased by 237 per cent; finance, insurance and tax experts by 280 per cent; personnel officers and managers by 255 per cent; and marketing and sales managers and executives by 234 per cent. Other groups which did particularly well were nurses, with male earnings up by 229 per cent and female earnings up by 271 per cent; general practitioners, with male earnings up by 247 per cent; and journalists, with male earnings up by 232 per cent. Non-manual groups which did worse than average included clerical workers, with male earnings up by 177 per cent and female earnings by 204 per cent; salespeople and shop assistants, with male earnings up by 177 per cent and female earnings up by 185 per cent; and professions relating to science, engineering and technology where male earnings increased by 198 per cent.

As far as manual occupational groups were concerned, it needs to be repeated that their overall increase in earnings was 155 per cent for males and 168 per cent for females, in contrast with the non-manuals' increase of 214 per cent for males and 227 per cent for females. Indeed, very few of the manual categories exceeded the non-manual average. Among those significantly below the manual average increase were female hospital orderlies with 119 per cent, male hospital porters with 131 per cent, bus and coach drivers with 134 per cent, male railway trainmen with 142 per cent, and face-trained coal-miners with 145 per cent.

Earnings by industry

The average increase between 1979 and 1990 for manual males was 155 per cent for all industries and services and 155 per cent for manufacturing. For non-manual males the increase was 214 per cent for all industries and services and 209 per cent for manufacturing. There was thus remarkably little difference over the decade between manufacturing and all industries and services.

If earnings by industry are arranged in descending order of earnings for 1979 and 1990, they show basically how little change there has been in the 'pecking order' over the 1980s. For manual males, of the top 10 industries in 1979, 9 were still in the top 10 in 1990. Within the top 10, there was some change in order between 1979 and 1990, but the changes were not very significant: the top 3 — oil refining, air transport and coal-mining (underground) were the same in both years. Only one of the 10 top industries in 1979 - shipbuilding — had a lower than average percentage increase during the 1980s.

Of the bottom 10 industries in 1979, 9 were still at the bottom in 1990. The one which moved up was insurance and banking, while the newcomer to the bottom 10 was railways. The bottom 3 remained the same in both years — hotels and catering, agriculture, and educational services. The picture for non-manual males was similar. Eight of the top 10 industries were the same in 1990 as in 1979, while of the bottom 10 industries only one had moved out during the decade.

Looking at average gross weekly earnings for women by industry in 1979 and 1990, there was somewhat more movement but still a considerable degree of stability. For manual women, 5 out of the top 8 industries were the same in both years, while 7 out of the 8 bottom industries were the same. For non-manual women, 4 out of the top 8 industries were the same in 1979 and 1990, while 7 out of 8 of the bottom industries stayed the same. Thus, despite the economic and political upheavals of the 1980s, taking men and women together, pay relativities between industries have on the whole shown remarkable stability.

Public-sector pay

Public-sector pay deserves to be looked at separately for a number of reasons. First, the public sector still remains a significant part of the economy despite cuts and privatisation. Second, it has been the centre of most of the major industrial disputes of the 1980s. Third, it has been the subject of special government treatment, whereas the private sector has been free to make its own settlements, subject to the market and to government-induced environmental changes. In one sense there was nothing new about the public sector receiving special treatment. In effect, this was true of the 1960s and 1970s as well, because incomes policies always bore more heavily on the public sector than the private sector. The difference was that under incomes policies there was not overt discrimination against the public sector. It was just that it was easier for the government as a direct or indirect employer to enforce incomes policy norms than for it to enforce those norms on the private sector: in the 1980s, however, the discrimination was overt. Fourth, despite all the evidence (Bailey and Trinder, 1989), there are myths, misconceptions and indeed prejudices about public-sector pay.

During the 1960s and 1970s public-sector pay fell behind private-sector pay in periods of incomes policy and was then restored to its approximate former relationship. In the earlier decades this was often done by special *ad hoc* Committees of Inquiry, such as Houghton on teachers (1974), Halsbury on nurses (1975) and the Clegg Comparability Commission (1980) which dealt with much of the public-service sector. For most of the 1980s, the public service sector again fell behind, but this time there has not been a body established to restore former relationships. Despite these facts, one senior business executive told us that the real problem area was the public sector, where pay had been allowed to run ahead of the private sector.

Table 10.3 shows the changes in average weekly earnings in the public and private sectors between 1981 and 1990. 1981 has been chosen as the base year rather than 1979 because if one took the latter it would mean including the Clegg awards and the special settlements for many of the public-sector groups. This would clearly be wrong because these awards were a catching-up exercise following the relative loss sustained by the public sector in the second half of the 1970s.

Average weekly earnings for all men increased by 94 per cent between 1981 and 1990 in the public sector as a whole, compared with 120 per cent in the private sector, while for all women the respective increases were 110 per cent and 136.5 per cent (see Table 10.3). There can therefore be no doubt that pay increases for employees in the public sector were markedly less than those in the private sector and that this is true of all broad categories – national government, local government and the public corporations. Indeed a comparison of the movement of earnings from NES data by collective agreement shows that between 1981 and 1990 not a single public-sector negotiating group reached the average level of increase in the private sector.

However, there were considerable variations in the treatment of different parts of the public sector. Among the nationalised industries, some fared better than others, with employees in the more profitable corporations doing the best and suffering the least government interference, for example gas and electricity, while British Rail fared badly.

In the public service sector, those who did worst were lecturers in further education, university academic staff and NHS ancilliary workers, with increases

TABLE 10.3 Average gross weekly earnings – public and private sectors 1981–90

	Manual			Non-manual			All		
	1981 £	1990 £	% Increase	1981 £	1990 £	% Increase	1981 £	1990 £	% Increase
Males									
Public services	110.1	202.9	84.3	166.7	323.1	93.8	146.8	288.9	96.8
Central government	112.7	195.8	73.7	165.0	321.3	94.7	146.9	287.0	95.4
Local government	108.9	206.5	89.6	167.7	324.0	93.2	146.8	289.9	97.5
Public corporations	137.0	251.4	83.5	171.2	352.0	105.6	147.5	274.5	86.1
Public sector	127.2	226.0	77.7	168.0	325.9	94.0	147.1	285.3	93.9
Private sector	119.2	240.0	101.3	158.1	366.9	132.1	135.8	299.0	120.2
Females									
Public services	75.1	145.3	93.5	111.3	231.4	107.9	105.8	221.1	109.0
Central government	77.0	135.8	76.4	97.4	217.5	123.3	94.5	210.5	122.8
Local government	73.5	150.5	104.8	125.7	246.0	95.7	117.3	231.5	97.4
Public corporations	97.2	193.9	99.5	101.0	220.6	118.4	100.3	213.6	113.0
Public sector	78.7	150.0	90.6	109.9	231.0	110.2	105.1	220.8	110.1
Private sector	72.9	147.4	102.2	83.6	204.6	144.7	80.3	189.9	136.5

Source: *New Earnings Survey*, 1981 and 1990, full-time employees whose pay was not affected by absence.

for men of 68 per cent, 71 per cent and 71 per cent respectively, compared with the increase in the private sector of 120 per cent. Other employees doing relatively badly included maintenance workers in the NHS, ambulance staff, local authority manual and APTC workers, government industrials, clerical, administrative and scientific employees. Those who fared best included the police, firemen and nurses.

These relative positions are largely confirmed by NES figures for earnings by occupation. Again, where there are figures available for both years, they showed that among those gaining the highest increases were nurses, general practitioners and telephone fitters: the lowest included lecturers in further education, refuse collectors, hospital porters, road sweepers and welfare workers. These results are not of course surprising. Broadly, of those who did relatively well, the police and the firemen were privileged by having pay agreements, dating back to the late 1970s, which linked their pay to general movements in earnings in the economy as a whole, while others such as nurses and doctors had the advantage of pay review bodies. Of those doing exceptionally badly, further education and university lecturers, as well as being subject to severe government financial constraints, had little bargaining power and what they had they chose not to use for most of the decade, because they put the interests of students first. Others such as local authority manuals and NHS ancillary staff − among the lowest-paid groups in the economy − suffered through their services being made open by the government to private tendering.

Towards the end of the decade there were small relative improvements for some public service sector groups. This was partly because of the restoration of some limited degree of comparability in the civil service (see Chapter 7). For certain other groups, with the economy booming for a period, the relative fall in earnings led to severe labour turnover and shortage problems, so that extra pay was forthcoming, although not so much through national agreements as through local allowances. Whatever else government policy on pay may have achieved, it had certainly not solved the problem of pay determination in the public sector.

Regional pay

The significance of local labour markets has been much discussed since 1979, partly because of large geographical differences in the incidence of unemployment, partly because of the decentralisation of pay bargaining in private industry, but above all because of the Conservative government's policy of seeking to break up national pay bargaining in the public sector and its rhetoric with regard to the virtues of local pay determination in the economy as a whole. Government policy was based on belief in free labour markets, so that if pay determination was locally based then employers would be able to take advantage of labour surpluses in areas of high unemployment and pay lower wages there than in areas of low unemployment. This would, it was claimed, lower labour costs as well as increasing employment in areas of high unemployment. It would also encourage the unemployed in low-paying areas to move to areas of high employment and higher pay unless differences in housing costs prevented it.

Table 10.4 shows gross regional average weekly earnings expressed as a proportion of national average weekly earnings. The outstanding conclusions from the table are, first, that the issue of regional pay is overwhelmingly a London problem. It is London, and London alone, where pay is markedly above the national average. Even the rest of the South-East is only slightly above the national average. The second conclusion is that the amount by which London pay exceeds the national average has increased markedly over the 1980s – for men from 14 per cent in 1979 to 30 per cent in 1990 and for women from 16 per cent to 29 per cent. For the rest of the South-East the increase for men was from being virtually the same as the national average in

TABLE 10.4   **Regional average gross weekly earnings as proportion of the national average, 1979–90**

	All men		All women	
	1979	1990	1979	1990
Greater London	113.9	129.6	116.3	128.5
Rest of South-East	100.5	105.1	100.5	102.7
East Anglia	94.3	95.1	95.6	92.1
South-West	91.1	93.8	95.2	93.4
West Midlands	96.7	91.1	97.5	89.9
East Midlands	95.8	91.2	94.8	90.1
Yorks and Humberside	97.7	90.3	94.3	89.9
North-West	97.8	92.9	96.0	92.8
North	98.3	91.1	96.2	89.4
Wales	96.2	87.5	97.5	89.5
Scotland	99.8	93.5	95.9	92.9
% difference between Greater London and the lowest region	25.0	48.1	23.4	43.7

Source: Based on *New Earnings Survey*, 1979 and 1990, full-time employees, whose pay was not affected by absence.

1979 to 5 per cent above it, and for women from again being virtually the same as the national average in 1979 to 3 per cent above it. An additional measure of the relative increase in London pay is to take London earnings as a percentage of pay in the lowest region. This shows that for men the increase in the percentage was from 25 per cent to 48 per cent between 1979 and 1990, and for women from 23 per cent to 44 per cent. These figures therefore do not support a policy of decentralisation of pay determination in the public sector. The regional problem is specifically a London problem. This conclusion is also reached by Brown and Rowthorn (1990), who argue that the government policy of decentralisation is flawed because it is based on a fallacious view of labour market mechanisms and a misunderstanding of private-sector practice. Where pay bargaining has been decentralised within private-sector companies it has usually been on a product basis and not on a geographical basis.

Productivity

Figures on productivity were given in Chapter 3 (see Table 3.1). Basically they showed that productivity – both for the whole economy and for manufacturing industry – declined at the beginning of the 1980s, during the depths of the recession, but thereafter in manufacturing there were substantial increases in most years until near the end of the period when there was a marked slowdown. Output per person for the whole economy moved in a similar fashion, but increases were at a much lower level than they were for manufacturing. Thus between 1979 and 1990 output per person for the whole economy increased by 20 per cent, while for manufacturing it increased by just over 50 per cent.

The increase of productivity in manufacturing was hailed as a 'miracle' by Conservative politicians, part of the overall so-called 'Thatcher Economic Miracle'. Claims from such a source that an economic miracle had taken place may be treated with scepticism, especially as by the end of 1990 it was clear that the country was heading for a severe recession. However the claim of a productivity 'miracle' has been made in a number of academic articles. In one such article, Metcalf (1990) produced the table shown here as Table 10.5 and commented that 'Great Britain was bottom in the 1960s, still bottom and performing relatively even worse in the 1970s, yet top by a mile in the 1980s.' (p. 65)

Metcalf argued that of the four explanations usually advanced for this turnaround, three were not valid. First there was 'no batting-average effect'. The plants that closed in the recession of the early 1980s did not have low labour productivity, so composition effects did not account for the increase in productivity. Second, the capital–labour ratio did not grow more rapidly in the

TABLE 10.5   Manufacturing output per head – 1960–88 (average annual per cent changes)

	1960–70	1970–80	1980–88
UK	3.00	1.50	5.25
USA	3.50	3.00	4.00
Japan	8.75	5.25	3.00
Germany	4.00	3.00	2.25
France	4.50	3.25	3.00
Italy	5.25	3.00	3.75
Canada	3.50	3.00	3.50
Average	4.50	3.25	3.50

Source: HM Treasury, *Autumn Economic Statement (Red Book)*, 15 November 1989, Table 8.

1980s than the 1970s. Third, the quality of inputs did not improve, comparatively, in the 1980s. For example, spending on research and development and on human capital remained low. Consequently, he concluded that the explanation must be that labour was being used more efficiently. Elaborating on this conclusion, he argued that three major factors and the interaction between them were the major reasons for higher productivity, namely, the shock effects of the recession in the early 1980s, more competitive product markets, and the reduction in union power. The shock effects, which elsewhere Metcalf (1989) called the fear factor, arose on the workers' part from mass redundancies and high unemployment and on management's part from fear of bankruptcy.

This conclusion has not been without its academic critics, in particular, Nolan and Marginson (1990). However, both Metcalf and his critics agreed that whatever the causes of higher productivity in the 1980s, there were grounds for scepticism about its continuation in the 1990s. Sustained improved productivity requires increased capital investment, increased expenditure on research and development, and increased investment in human resources through education, training and development. These were certainly not forthcoming in the 1980s.

Labour costs per unit of output

Table 10.6 shows the movement of labour costs per unit of output during the 1980s. It will be seen that after a horrendous increase of over 20 per cent in

1980, there was a rapid decrease during the early 1980s in the rate of rise in unit wage costs for both manufacturing and the economy as a whole. Thereafter, the rate of increase moved upwards, with the exception of 1986 and 1987, with the increase accelerating very markedly towards the end of the decade. Indeed, by the last quarter of 1990 the increase reached over 11 per cent for both manufacturing and the whole economy. For the complete period 1979–90 unit labour costs rose markedly less in manufacturing (88.5 per cent) than they did for the economy as a whole (130.4 per cent). Thus, the persistence of increases in money earnings in excess of productivity caused increases in unit labour costs throughout the decade, even in manufacturing in those years when productivity was rising especially fast.

TABLE 10.6 **Wages and salary costs per unit of output, 1980–90 – UK (per cent increase on the previous year)**

	Manufacturing	*Whole economy*
1980	22.3	22.7
1981	9.3	9.6
1982	4.2	4.8
1983	0.5	3.8
1984	3.1	4.6
1985	5.8	5.4
1986	4.0	5.4
1987	1.8	4.7
1988	2.4	7.2
1989	4.7	9.4
1990	8.8	10.4
1990 level (1979 = 100)	188.5	230.4

Source: *Employment Gazette.*

Conclusion

A number of features are readily apparent from this discussion of pay in the 1980s. First, there was a significant increase in both money and real earnings during the 1980s. Second, this increase was not evenly spread; rather there was a very marked widening in the dispersion of earnings, the lower-paid doing far worse than the higher-paid. Thus, manual workers did worse, while non-manual workers did much better, and within the white-collar group the higher-paid – managers and professionals – did best. Third, the public service sector as a whole did far worse than the private sector, although there were exceptions, such as doctors, nurses, police and firemen.

What is clear is that the Conservative governments which were in office throughout the 1980s had not solved the problem of wage inflation. As the CBI (1989) put it:

> Inflation in the UK, after an initial rapid decline at the start of the 1980s, has remained stubbornly resilient. Year after year, we have experienced an annual inflation rate higher than most other major countries. (p. 7)

Furthermore, the CBI states that:

> Our unit labour costs in manufacturing are still rising faster than those of our competitors, up by more than 4 per cent in the past year at a time when others have seen little increase or have been achieving reductions in their unit labour costs. And across the economy as a whole, we have been far less successful in containing unit labour costs than in the manufacturing sector. (p. 7)

The CBI concludes that:

> . . . the UK remains a low productivity economy, with levels of output per employee in manufacturing well below the levels [sic] achieved by our major competitors . . . By the standards of our many competitors, the UK remains a low productivity, low pay economy. (p. 9)

Indeed, one of the enigmas of the 1980s is the extent of the rise in money and real earnings, despite very high unemployment, record interest rates and monetary squeeze, and a great weakening in trade union power. This is further discussed in Chapter 12.

What is also clear is that the problem of public-sector pay was not solved in the 1980s. The government early on abolished comparability as the main criterion and replaced it by 'recruitment, retention and motivation'. For most public-sector employees this has meant a substantial decline in their pay relative to that of the private sector. Motivation was forgotten, and certainly not enhanced by the government's berating of public-sector employees, of whom teachers were a prime example. Towards the end of the decade, the government sought to increase motivation through the introduction of performance-related pay. The problem of public service sector pay is one to which we return again in Chapter 12.

CHAPTER 11

Strikes

The litmus test of the Conservative government's objective of curbing the power of trade unions was strikes. Over-powerful unions were, in the eyes of the Conservative Party, too ready to use strikes to get their way – 'strikes are too often a weapon of first rather than last resort' (Conservative Party manifesto, 1979). In the Party's demonology stood the miners' strike of 1974 which had challenged, and some would say brought down, a Conservative government. Moreover, the general election of 1979 which the Party had won with a majority over all other parties in the House of Commons had taken place in the shadow of the 'Winter of Discontent' and extensive strikes among public-service workers. Strikes had become for the Conservative Party the symbol of the abuse of their power by trade unions.

This chapter looks first at the place of strikes in industrial relations and then at the strike record of the 1980s, comparing it with earlier periods and with other countries. It then summarises the changes in the law affecting strikes and the impact on ballots, picketing and secondary action is examined.

Strikes and industrial relations

Before embarking on a detailed examination of strike activity in the 1980s, it is as well to keep a sense of proportion about the significance of strikes. In the 1970s an annual average number of 2.6 milion workers were involved in strike action, about 1 in 8, so it was somewhat more than a once-in-a-decade event on average for employees. In the 1980s the annual average number involved was about 1.1 million and by the end of the decade it was down to less than 0.8 million; going on strike had become less than a once-in-two-decades event on average. The proportion of all days which could be worked but which were lost through strikes was minute in the 1970s – 0.2 per cent – and in the 1980s it became even more minute – less than 0.1 per cent.

Of course, there are some ways in which the statistics underestimate the effect of strikes. The method of counting stoppages ignores other forms of industrial action, e.g. bans on overtime and working to rule; strikes lasting for one day or less causing the loss of less than 100 days work are not counted in the official statistics; and many stoppages, especially short ones, have repercussive effects for which the number of days work lost is an inadequate proxy for the cost.

Going beyond the statistics, strikes have a symbolic significance because they are the open use of power to inflict damage in order to extract concessions or to defend existing positions. The use of terms such as 'militant minority' indicates a belief that strikes are warlike conflict. On that view, if a strike is in breach of agreed procedures and is unofficial, the conclusion to be drawn is that control has passed to the 'militant minority'. For those who see management as the unitary government of workplaces, strikes, especially those in breach of procedure agreements, are challenges to the established order. The government's claim in its 1979 manifesto that 'a minority of extremists in the trade unions had the power to abuse individual liberties' and that 'Labour had enacted a "militants' charter"' gave strikes a heightened importance and made the reduction of stoppages a test of the government's reforming zeal.

The practitioners of industrial relations tend to see strikes in less political terms, although they are well aware that strikes are the most politically charged part of industrial relations. They emphasise that strikes have always to be seen in the context in which they occur. If there are agreements laying down a procedure for resolving disputes then a strike indicates that they — the negotiators — have failed. Most procedures recognise that when they end the unions may call a strike and the threat of it is taken on board in the negotiations. The right to strike is acknowledged in democratic countries because it is a legitimate last resort, the existence of which is part of the balance of the relative power of the two sides. This is well understood by negotiators but for most of them it is a background point remote from day-to-day negotiatons. The lockout and the dismissal of employees are in theory the employers' equivalents of the strike, although as became clear in the early 1980s, it is the closing of a place of work, or the threat of it, and the making of workers redundant which is the equivalent in practice.

For most managers and trade unionists there is a continuing, long-term relationship in which the same individuals have to live together and that shapes the use which both make of the measures available for bringing their maximum bargaining power to bear. In most places of work a strike is a sign of failure because for most of the time the two sides are well enough attuned to each other's potential power to take account of it in bargaining. But if it comes to a strike, though it may be a failure on the negotiators' part, it is not a failure of industrial relations; rights of last resort are there to be used when people feel justified in employing them. Sometimes managers prefer to take a strike because they believe that the eventual settlement will be better for them than the agreement which would have avoided the strike. In the end, virtually all strikes conclude with a negotiated settlement, although the parties may need the help of a third party to reach it. In that sense, strikes are extensions of negotiations beyond the agreed procedure. There are cases where strikes occur in breach of agreed procedures. Exceptional impatience on the part of employees and undue frustrations on the part of managers can cause under-standable explosions. So long as they are rare the procedure can usually survive. But frequent and deliberate breaches of procedure involving strikes indicate some deep-seated problem.

The procedure may itself seek to make a strike virtually impossible. Employers and trade unions may agree that if they fail to reach agreement the dispute will automatically go to arbitration. A milder provision is to require agreement between them on each reference to arbitration. Compulsory arbitration is a fundamental step to rule out strike action. Some unions like the EETPU have set out to make no-strike agreements with employers, judging that the benefits obtained in other parts of the agreement, like exclusive negotiating rights and other aspects of union security, make it worthwhile to sign a no-strike clause. The legitimate hesitation by most employers as well as unions over both compulsory arbitration and no-strike clauses arises because they cannot be sure that there will never be a time when employees might decide to exercise their right to strike.

Strikes are bound to occur from time to time even with the best procedure agreements and the most sophisticated negotiators because there will always be cases where one side or the other miscalculates the determination or bargaining power of the other. This is quite compatible with a general policy of seeking to reduce the use of strike action. It is also compatible with a belief that people on both sides can bring matters to a point where a strike occurs in order to meet objectives which lie outside the current negotiations if they are determined to do so. 'Militant' shop stewards may precipitate strike action and 'militant' managers may provoke it.

In some industries strikes always have a high political profile because of the nature of the product or service they provide. This is particularly so in the public services, where the citizen is a captive non-commercial customer and there is no feasible alternative supply. Strikes in some parts of the private sector, like the sale of petrol and bread, have something of the same significance and the privatisation of utilities like gas, water, electricity and telephones has added to them. An element of cost to the customer is inherent in all strikes. The public look to government in a parliamentary democracy to reconcile the pursuit of sectional interests with regard for the public interest. It follows that, even on the negotiators' view of strikes, governments will from time to time have grounds for interfering in the way in which industrial relations are conducted, and that often means adding to or subtracting from the bargaining power of one side or the other and thus affecting the use of strike action. The argument is then about whether the public interest will be served more by whatever restriction is under consideration than by allowing legitimate sectional interests to run unimpeded. The last decade has seen a government take legislative action directly affecting strikes which has had the objective of changing the balance of power between the negotiating parties to the disadvantage of the unions and the advantage of managers.

The strike record

Table 11.1 shows Britain's strike record since 1950. The number of recorded strikes increased throughout the 1950s, 1960s and 1970s, as did the number of workers involved and the number of working days lost. In the 1980s all three measures of strike activity were very substantially reduced compared with the 1970s. Compared with the 1950s and 1960s the number of strikes was greatly down but the number of working days lost was markedly higher.

A comparison of working days lost in relation to the working population shows that in the 1970s there were only 2 years when less than 300 working days were lost per 1000 workers whereas in the 1980s there were 8 such years.

TABLE 11.1   Strikes, 1950–89 – UK (annual averages)

	Strikes	Workers involved (000s)	Working days lost (000s)
1950–59	2 119	663	3 252
1960–69	2 446	1 357	3 554
1970–79	2 601	1 615	12 870
1980–89	1 129	1 040	7 213

Source: *Employment Gazette.*

Large strikes have always had a disproportionate effect on the number of working days lost and that has been particularly so in the 1980s. Out of the 72 million days work lost in the decade, 26 million (36 percent) were accounted for by the miners' strike in 1984–5 alone. The biggest strike of the 1970s, the miners' strike of 1971, lost 6.25 million days, which was a mere 5 per cent of the days lost in that decade. If to the miners' strike of 1984–5 are added the four other strikes in the 1980s which exceeded 1 million working days lost – steel (1980, 8.8 million), local government non-manuals (1989, 2 million), telecommunications (1987, 1.5 million) and postal workers (1988, 1 million) –

the concentration is even greater, being 55 per cent of the total for the decade in 5 strikes.

The miners' strike was so unusually large that it dominates any comparison with earlier periods. If it is excluded, the annual average working days lost in the 1980s comes down to 4.6 million, which is only about a third of the average for the 1970s, although it is still greater than the averages for the 1950s and 1960s.

Strikes of over half a million working days lost formed a bigger part of the total in the 1980s than in the 1970s. But it is their concentration in the public sector which stands out. Of the 13 such strikes in the 1980s, 11 were in the public sector – local government, the civil service, the NHS, railways, education, the Post Office, steel and coal mining. By contrast, in the 1970s only 6 out of 16 such strikes were in the public sector.

This was a radical change. The 1980s were a decade when big set-piece battles took place in the public sector. There had been major strikes in the 1970s in coal mining, the Post Office, the civil service, the fire service and the NHS, but in the 1980s strikes in the public sector were more widespread and more bitterly fought, with the government and public employers coming out on top.

The private sector had virtually no big strikes in the 1980s, in stark contrast to the 1970s when British Leyland, Vauxhall, Ford and Times Newspapers each had strikes costing more than half a million working days lost, as also did the engineering, construction, docks, and road transport industries. The public sector became the cockpit of industrial conflict in the 1980s as major strike activity in the private sector almost ceased.

At the other end of the size scale, very short strikes formed a considerable proportion of all strikes. As Table 11.2 shows, the number of one-day strikes included in the official figures has not changed much over the past two decades. But such strikes have become proportionately much more significant because the total number of strikes has fallen. The share of one-day strikes in the number of working days lost remains small – 4 per cent in the 1980s compared with 2 per cent in the 1970s.

As already stated, the incidence of strike action – working days lost per 1000 workers – was considerably lower in the 1980s than in the 1970s. In the motor vehicle industry it fell spectacularly. In the second half of the 1970s it had averaged annually 4626 working days lost per 1000 workers but in the 1980s it was 1398; in the second half of the 1980s it was only 760. Although motor vehicles remained one of the most strike-prone industries the decline in the incidence of strikes marked a major change in its industrial relations.

The coal-mining industry experienced average strike incidence in the 1970s in years when there was not a major dispute. But in the 1980s the incidence was much higher than elsewhere, quite apart from the 1984–5 strike. Between 1986 and 1989 an annual average of 1130 working days were lost per 1000 workers, nearly 8 times the national average.

TABLE 11.2   Strikes lasting not more than one day 1970–89 – UK (annual averages)

	Number	Percentage of all strikes
1970–5	601	20.6
1976–80	423	18.0
1980–4	432	31.7
1985–9	393	43.9

Source: *Employment Gazette.*

Some of the causes of strikes are set out in Table 11.3. The major change in the 1980s was the decline in pay as a cause of working days lost; it continued to be the main cause but ceased to be as dominant as in the 1970s, falling from nearly 9 out of 10 working days lost to under 7 out of 10. The main reason was the virtual disappearance of large private-sector disputes over pay.

TABLE 11.3   Working days lost by principal cause of strikes, 1970–89 UK (% of all days lost)

	Pay	Redundancy	TU matters	Dismissal and discipline	Manning and work allocation
1970–4	87.2	n.a.*	n.a.	n.a.	n.a.
1975–9	84.2	1.5	6.5	3.4	5.4
1980–3†	68.5	9.6	2.9	4.0	4.0
1985–9†	69.4	6.6	2.5	2.7	13.5

Source: *Employment Gazette.*
* The definitions changed in 1973.
† The miners' strike was classified under 'redundancy' and since its size outweighs all other factors in the breakdown by cause for 1984 and 1985 those two years are omitted from the comparison in the table.

Redundancy became a more important cause, especially in the early 1980s when unemployment rose fast. But the number of working days lost was not high considering the scale of redundancies; in the late 1970s 133 000 working days were lost annually while in the first 5 years of the 1980s the annual average was 606 000.

Strikes over manning and work allocation became more prominent after 1985, perhaps reflecting stronger union reactions against managers' proposals than had been the case earlier in the decade. Even so, the number of working days lost from this cause in the second half of the decade was only 448 000.

In the late 1970s trade union matters, dismissal and discipline, caused nearly 10 per cent of working days lost through strikes. This proportion fell by nearly half in the 1980s and the number of working days lost annually fell from nearly three-quarters of a million in the late 1970s to about 320 000 in the 1980s. Unions were weaker.

So far the 1980s have been treated as a single decade or as two groups of 5 years. As Table 11.4 shows, important changes have taken place within the decade. The number of strikes fell throughout. It went down in every year but two and in 1989 was little more than half the number in 1980. The 598 strikes in 1990 were the smallest annual number since 1935.

TABLE 11.4   Strikes, 1980–90 – UK

	Strikes	*Working days lost (000s)*	*Working days lost per 1000 employees*
1980	1 348	11 964	521
1981	1 344	4 266	195
1982	1 538	5 313	248
1983	1 364	3 754	178
1984	1 221	27 135*	1 278
1985	903	6 402†	299
1986	1 074	1 920	90
1987	1 016	3 546	164
1988	781	3 702	166
1989	701	4 128	182
1990	630	1 903	83

Source: *Employment Gazette.*
* Includes 22 400 for the miners' strike.
† Includes 4000 for the miners' strike.

The incidence of working days lost was affected by the miners' strike in the middle of the decade. But there is a clear downward trend. The working days lost per 1000 workers annually were 330 in the first 3 years of the decade and 170 in the last 3. So the record shows that strike activity in the 1980s was about half that in the 1970s and during the course of the 1980s, leaving aside the miners' strike, the decline in it was continuous.

The main features of the lower level of strike activity in the 1980s were that large strikes were virtually confined to the public sector, pay was a declining cause of strikes, and one-day strikes did not decline much in number.

Comparisons with the strike record in other countries

Comparisons of the UK's strike record with that of other countries is important for two reasons. The UK's poorer economic performance has often been put down in part to its greater strike incidence, so a reduction in strike activity might be taken to indicate better relative economic performance. The second reason is that the Conservative governments have taken credit for reducing strike activity, mainly by its industrial relations legislation.

Table 11.5 compares the record of the main OECD countries. Reductions in strike incidence between the 1970s and 1980s were a common experience in all countries, while during the 1980s incidence was lower in the second than in the first half of the decade without exception. Moreover, the reductions in the UK's incidence were not larger than those of its main competitors, nor did they bring it anywhere near the extremely low incidence in Germany and Netherlands. The UK's rank order position was unchanged between the two halves of the decade.

TABLE 11.5   Working days lost through strikes per 1000 workers, 1970–89: international comparisons – all industries

	1970–9	1980–9	1980–4	1985–9
UK	570	330	480	180
France	210	80	90	60
Germany	40	30	50	less than 5
Italy	1310	620	950	300
Netherlands	40	10	20	10
USA	n.a.	120	160	90
Canada	n.a.	460	660	280
Sweden	n.a.	180	240	120

Source: *Employment Gazette*, December 1990.

So the UK's strike position did not improve *vis-à-vis* its competitors. The fact which matters is that the decline in strike incidence has been dramatic in a number of countries and not just in the UK.

Causes of the decline in strike activity

The reasons why strike activity declined were the same as the reasons why employers were for the most part stronger and unions weaker in the 1980s than in earlier periods. Strikes are not detachable from the rest of industrial relations; factors affecting the whole affect them as part of the whole. But because of the high political significance attached to strikes, their causes have to be examined separately.

The similarity in the decline of strike activity in most industrialised countries in the 1980s is the appropriate starting point. Halving strike activity seems a remarkable change in Britain until it is set beside the drastic decline in other countries, in some by more than half. So the causes are likely to have included ones which were at work generally, rather than ones which were peculiarly British.

The worldwide recession of the early 1980s was the common cause, tipping the balance of bargaining power towards the employers and away from the unions. Redundancies in British manufacturing were greater than in most other countries, but unions in all countries were confronted with the threat of contractions and closures. Unions tend to be at their strongest in manufacturing even in countries where they are generally weak and so it was the recession in manufacturing which brought unions face to face with employers who said that only if the labour force was drastically reduced and managers' proposals for improved productivity accepted could firms survive. In the USA reductions in real pay were often part of the package. The unions had to choose between resistance, including strikes, probably leading to closure, or survival on employers' terms with fewer jobs. In the UK acceptable redundancy terms helped the unions to choose the lesser evil. That general explanation of the way in which the unions adjusted to their weaker position is widely accepted among practitioners on both sides of industry.

But the recession ended and after a period of stability expansion occurred. Yet the decline in strike activity continued in most countries, as in Britain. So the explanation for the second half of the decade cannot be the continued threat of closures and the need to survive as output fell. The unions' bargaining power was tending to wane. There were perhaps three factors at work. First, the earlier period of widespread redundancies and closures of plants had been a traumatic experience for both managers and employees and their unions. Those who had survived were chary of risking what had been bought at a high price.

Second, the expansion of output in manufacturing did not need more employees. Employment in manufacturing in Britain continued to fall until 1987 and in the next 2 years increased by less than 1 per cent; yet between 1981 and 1989 manufacturing output increased by over 32 per cent. So jobs were still on the line. Firms recruited on only a limited scale, and in the absence of sufficient natural wastage regular programmes of redundancies remained a common feature.

Third, the rising output, with little or no increase in employees, was achieved by higher productivity. Unions had co-operated in implementing managers' proposals for improved use of labour to secure survival. The process continued as investment came on stream and output began to grow. Many managers involved union representatives in delivering the changes needed to improve productivity and they offered pay increases accordingly. The unions in manufacturing found that their members who remained in jobs did well out of local productivity bargaining and threatening strike action was not necessary.

Indeed, looking at the whole of the private sector, it is notable that pay was not a source of major conflict in the 1980s. While higher productivity enabled employers in manufacturing to offer pay increases in excess of inflation, the rest of the private sector was able to offer pay increases as big as those in manufacturing because of the expansion of the whole economy which the government's economic policy facilitated in the second half of the decade and because the rest of the economy was not exposed to overseas competition to the extent that manufacturing was. Even when expansion slowed down in 1989, pay continued to increase at least as fast as prices. The pay pressure underlying stagflation came not from the unions' threatening to strike over pay demands but from employers making acceptable pay offers. In the 1970s attempts to restrain pay increases had caused some of the biggest private-sector strikes, like Ford in 1978. But in the 1980s, when unions were weak by comparison, real wages forged ahead. No wonder there were fewer strikes.

However, as shown earlier, declines in strike activity were not universal, for there were sectors where strikes were at a high level. First, there were the large, set-piece battles in steel in 1980 and in coal mining in 1984–5 over the terms on which the government intended to contract those industries, although in steel the ostensible cause of the dispute was pay. Second, there were strikes over pay in the public services as the government imposed cuts in real pay which its policy required in the private sector too, but which the employers there would not adopt. Most of the public-sector unions were not weakened by falling numbers of employees; the numbers employed in public administration and education increased in every year of the decade and in medical and other health services in every year but one. Trade union density held up well. In the early part of the decade, the strikes over pay were defeated by the government. In the latter part of the decade, the outcomes were more mixed. The local government officers' strike in 1989 secured sizeable increases in the pay offer and the teachers' protracted selective and partial strikes held the position on pay but lost the negotiating machinery.

The reason why the decline in strike activity did not spread to the public services was that it continued to be the case that strikes were resorted to in the absence of settled methods of pay determination.

But was the legislation, particularly in its specific provisions on strikes, a cause of the decline in strike activity? Certainly it was not a major cause. In the first place it was only in the second half of the decade that the main legal provisions were in force and could exercise an influence. Although secondary action and picketing were curtailed in the 1980 Act and the unions' special legal immunity was abolished by the 1982 Act, it was not until the 1984 Act that a majority in a secret ballot was required before a strike could be called with immunity from the law.

Most negotiators believe that the legislation has had little or no effect on the conduct of industrial relations. But in the case of strikes the provision for a secret ballot lays down actual procedures to be followed which are new and so the practice to that extent is different. Later in this chapter the impact of the changes in the law affecting secret ballots, picketing and secondary action is examined. The conclusion drawn is that while they have tended to discourage strikes, and to that extent have contributed to the decline of strike activity, they have not had a clear and unmistakeable effect of their own. There is no record of cases where unions wanted to call strikes, or where outsiders have considered a strike the next logical step in the union's strategy, but where the legal provisions, especially the need for a majority vote, have stopped the strike weapon being used. The law's existence deters the calling of strikes without careful consideration of where the line of legal immunity is now drawn and of the likely result of a secret ballot. But where a strike is the appropriate next step, the law can make it more likely, not less, because the secret ballot offers a way of legitimising it.

The law requires ballots to be held and they take time. So it would be expected that short, lightning strikes would be deterred. But as Table 11.2 shows, despite the fall in overall strike activity, the number of recorded strikes lasting not more than one day was little different in 1989 from what it had been a decade earlier. With such strikes the law is often, even in its more rigorous form, irrelevant. They happen suddenly and are quickly over. Union officials probably only hear of them when they occur and their main concern is usually to bring them to an end. Most employers want work resumed as quickly as possible so that there can be negotiations and resorting to the courts to penalise the unions will seldom help to achieve that objective. It is, therefore, not to be expected that the law would have a powerful restraining effect on the number of short strikes.

Changes in the law affecting strikes

Chapter 5 reviewed the legislation affecting industrial relations. Here the provisions affecting strikes are briefly repeated. Also in Chapter 5 the consequences of the legislation were analysed under the headings of secondary action, picketing and ballots on the basis of actions in the courts. In this chapter the significance of the legislation is examined under the same headings in terms of its impact on the conduct of employers, unions and government. Inevitably there is some overlap and repetition, although references to the content of the legislation and to Court actions are kept to the minimum, the material in Chapter 5 being available.

The stream of Acts of Parliament since 1980 dealing with trade unions altered the legal position of strikers and their unions. Each new piece of legislation reflected responses to the previous ones, the political pressures which built up between the steps, and the preferences of successive Secretaries of State, since each of the Acts was carried through by a different minister.

The provisions of the Employment Act 1980 on strikes were limited to the connected issues of picketing and secondary action. James Prior, who was Secretary of State from 1979 to 1981, was particularly concerned that the law should prevent the extension of disputes beyond the primary employer and the aggressive picketing which often accompanied it. Both had been prominent features of the 'Winter of Discontent'. He had the failure of the Heath Government's legislation – the Industrial Relations Act 1971 – in the forefront of his mind. His 'purpose was to bring about a lasting change in attitudes by changing the law gradually and with as little resistance, and therefore as much by stealth, as was possible'. He was particularly concerned with 'the dangers of having tougher legislation which employers might in practice be afraid to use . . . and which the courts could not enforce, as had been the case with the 1971 Act' (Prior, 1986, p. 158). This cumulative, bit at a time, way of dealing with the problem was applied not only to industrial relations as a whole but to parts of it like strikes.

Broadly, the 1980 Act preserved unions' immunity from legal action where the industrial action and picketing to support it were confined to the employer with whom the union was in dispute. Secondary action was lawful only against employers buying from or selling to the primary employers. Strikers could picket only at their own place of work. The limit on the number of strikers to six was not in the Act but in the Code of Practice and subsequent case law supported it.

The 1982 Act passed through its main stages when Norman Tebbit was Secretary of State for Employment (1981–3) and he regarded it as his greatest achievement in government and 'one of the principal pillars on which the Thatcher government reforms have been built' (Tebbit 1988 p. 185). On strikes it made key alterations in the law which severely reduced trade union immunity from legal action. If the unions were to avoid losing immunity they would have to give up certain types of strike action.

Although the Trade Union Act 1984 fell in Tom King's period of office as Secretary of State (1983–5), it was the product of Norman Tebbit's policy of 'handing the unions back to their members' and had been heralded in his Green Paper in January 1983. Secret ballots had to be held before lawful industrial action could take place. The ballot had to be confined to those likely to be called out and the question on the ballot paper had to allow a simple 'yes' or 'no' answer to strike action, or to whatever other action was proposed.

The Employment Act 1988 gave trade union members as well as employers the right to ask the courts to stop a strike where there had not been a ballot carried out according to law with a majority in favour. Moreover, even where there was a majority in favour of strike action, a union could not punish a member who went to work or who encouraged others to do so.

The Employment Act 1990 made two major extensions of legal penalties for strike action. It made unions responsible for strike action called by lay officials – unofficial strikes – unless repudiated. The other extension was also to do with unofficial strikes. The Act made it possible for employers to dismiss selectively employees involved in unofficial strikes repudiated by unions. Furthermore, action by the unions to protect shop stewards who lead unofficial strikes and are dismissed is outside the law. So leaders of local strikes which flare up and quickly die down run the risk of dismissal. The Act also went back on the government's definition of legal secondary action in the 1980 Act and made all such action illegal.

So by the end of the decade the law on strikes was different in major ways from what it had been at the beginning. The definition of strikes which unions could call without penalty had been narrowed and secret ballots were needed in all cases. Strikes and limited picketing had to be confined to the employer with whom the union was in dispute. Not only could employers go to the courts and get injunctions if these conditions seemed not to be met, but so could trade union members. If union members chose not to strike, despite a majority vote in favour, they could not be punished by the union and the Commissioner was there to protect their rights and pay their costs. Leaders of unofficial local strikes repudiated by unions for fear of loss of legal immunity risked dismissal. No secondary action was legal.

But there was one proposed legal restriction on strikes which was not proceeded with. Strikes in essential services were part of the old order which the Conservative government was intent on banishing. Of course, the definition of essential services was elastic; at its narrowest it was electricity, gas and water, and at its widest it included the health service, the fire service and certain parts of transport. The 1979 manifesto said that the government would 'seek to conclude no-strike agreements in a few essential services'. Some, like the Institute of Directors, pressed for the withdrawal of immunity from unions calling strikes in essential services defined in a variety of ways, and this point of view had supporters among ministers and Conservative backbench MPs. The 1983 manifesto beefed up the 1979 commitment, about which nothing had been done, by undertaking to carry out 'further consultation about the need for industrial relations in certain specified essential services to be governed by adequate procedure agreements, breach of which would deprive industrial action of immunity'.

To the surprise of some, Norman Tebbit was strongly opposed to going down that road. His position was that the narrower definition of strikes which had legal immunity and the requirement for secret ballots in the 1982 and 1984 Acts would be 'the best – but inevitably imperfect – deterrent' to strikes in essential services (Tebbit, 1988, p. 198).

There was a national strike in water supply from 23 January to 23 February 1983 which made the question pertinent and as Norman Tebbit records, resulted in 'heavy pressure' being exerted on him to make such strikes illegal. This was the first national strike there had ever been in water supply and avoidance of such a strike had been the settled policy of all governments for many years on the grounds that the interruption of pure water supplies was unthinkable. It was an indication of the government's tenacity in resisting pay claims in public services that it countenanced a national stoppage in water supply. The gap between the two sides was great. The unions claimed 18 per cent to give them parity with gas and electricity and they were offered 4 per cent. The unions refused to allow the unilateral arbitration provided for in the procedure agreement on the grounds that the employers had not negotiated in good faith. A mediator pushed the offer to 7.3 per cent over 16 months and eventually a Court of Inquiry (a rare event in the 1980s) proposed ways of increasing that to 11 or 12 per cent over 16 months, although this included some consolidation and was not all 'new' money. Since both the employer and trade union members of the Court refused to sign the report, it was issued as the chairman's recommendation and was accepted. The level of the settlement was a clear breach of the government's pay targets in the public sector.

Two aspects of the strike worked in favour of Norman Tebbit's point of view. The feared health hazards had not materialised, although the number of customers needing to boil water steadily increased. Troops had not been required. In an absolutely essential service, a strike lasting for a month had not had the catastrophic consequences which had always been forecast. Although the eventual settlement was more than the government liked, it had learned that the strikers' power was less than had been supposed.

The strike and other industrial action had been conducted in ways which would not have been possible after the 1984 Act. First there was a one-day strike, then an overtime ban and eventually an all-out strike. After 1984, each of these steps would have had to be preceded by a secret ballot on a question framed as was required by the Act with a majority voting in favour and those hurdles might have had a restraining effect.

Norman Tebbit's position was that none of the remedies urged on him, 'which even included the foolish idea of making strikes in essential services a criminal offence, or wildly expensive and unenforceable no-strike agreements, would have been effective' (Tebbit, 1988, p. 198). The logic of his position was that the same legal rules should apply to strikes in essential services as elsewhere, otherwise there was a danger that any special restrictions would be kicked over. The tightening of those general rules limited strikes everywhere, including essential services. The unspoken final stage of the argument was that if strikes nevertheless occurred in essential services, they would have to be robustly resisted by the government and public authorities. Norman Tebbit's refusal to take special action against strikes in esssential services in the wake of the water supply strike effectively put an end to the proposal and it did not appear again in the 1987 manifesto, although it was resurrected in one form or another from time to time.

This example of Norman Tebbit's realistic assessment of what was practicable and what was not, like his opposition to the banning of the closed shop and to making collective agreements legally enforceable on the grounds that the law would not work, showed how his sensitivity to the nature of trade union bargaining power enabled him to sap the unions' position by concentrating on a few essential changes in the law. As he said, 'I had skinned the cat in a better way' (Tebbit, 1988, p. 187).

Strike ballots

As the law now stands, unless there has been a majority vote of those involved in favour of industrial action, unions lose their legal immunity when calling members out on strike in breach of their individual contracts. This was a major change in British industrial relations. It was legal intervention at the heart of unions' ability to damage employers' interests, or threaten to do so, in pursuit of claims or to protect themselves. Yet it did not figure in the Conservative government's early plans, and the 1980 and 1982 Acts had nothing about strike ballots. But they were a main feature of the 1984 Act and came into force at the end of September 1984. That was too late to affect the miners' strike, which began in March 1984 although the absence of a national ballot before that strike was used as justification for compulsory strike ballots during the passage of the Bill. The unions strongly opposed the change, seeing it as a deliberate attempt to weaken them. Not all employers supported the change, fearing that it would introduce rigidities which would make bargaining more, not less, difficult. So secret strike ballots were a political initiative taken by the government. From 1985 to 1987 ACAS published statistics about strike ballots in its annual reports. Of course its information was not complete, because there was no notification system even of an informal kind, but through its regional offices and its monthly collection of strike statistics ACAS was better placed than any other organisation to collect data on strike ballots.

In the first 15 months to the end of 1985 ACAS was aware of only 94 ballots; in 1986 the number was 246 and in 1987 it was 280. The numbers of unions involved were 37, 30 and 53. In the first year the proportion of ballots with a majority in favour of industrial action was 72 percent, rising to 77 and 90 per cent in the second and third years. The turnouts were commonly above 75 percent. In 1985 23 (34 percent) out of 68 ballots with a majority led to no action and in 1986 they rose to 169 (89 percent) out of 189; ACAS gave no figure on this for 1987. In 1988 ACAS was aware of 331 ballots of which 305 supported industrial action; in 1989, 359 ballots with 336 supporting action; and in 1990, 304 ballots of which 280 supported action. Ninety-two per cent supported action in each of those 3 years.

From this meagre information supplemented by the interviews some general features do emerge. Although unions were punctilious about observing the need to hold a ballot before strike action was officially taken, there were large numbers of strikes on which no ballots had been held; in 1987 there were 1074 strikes and ACAS knew of only 280 preceded by a ballot. However, 601 (59 per cent) lasted for no more than 2 days. Short strikes continued to flare up and end without time for balloting. Employers did not go to the courts because they had little or no notice of these strikes and legal action after the event was likely to worsen their relationships with the unions. The provisions of the 1990 Act, which make unions repudiate unofficial action by their members and allow employers to dismiss its leaders, may modify some employers' attitudes to short strikes.

The level of participation in voting is high but there are no doubt cases where it falls short of the 75 per cent which is common. Most ballots produce a majority for action, but in only a small proportion is a strike actually called. Indeed, strike ballots have been remarkably well integrated into union bargaining strategies and ACAS reported this as early as 1985. Unions have learned to use the results of ballots as bargaining counters. Often the employer's offer is put to the members and, as the union negotiators recommend, is rejected. The union then holds a ballot strictly according to the rules of the Code of Practice in which a high proportion vote and there is a large majority for strike action. The union officials return to the negotiating table with authority to call a strike if there is not an improvement in the offer. As ACAS reported, 'some employers have found [this] difficult to counter.' (ACAS, 1987, p. 14). Some employers believe that a strike ballot should not be held until the negotiating procedure has been fully exhausted, but unions tend to hold it when it will help their bargaining position most. The ballot requirement has strengthened the union's hand in many cases and faced with the choice of a strike or a better offer the employer usually chooses the latter.

Everyone understands what is going on. The union members know that rejecting the offer will be followed by a strike ballot. The union officials will only recommend rejection of the offer if they believe there is a majority for strike action. The employer knows that he should keep back enough to be able to improve his offer in response to the likely majority in the strike ballot.

Of course, such neat ploys can go awry. The strike ballot may produce a minority for action, or only a small majority, in which case the union will rapidly settle for the employer's last offer. Even though there is a majority it may not materialise if action is called for; voting for strike action to put pressure on the employer is one thing, actually striking is another. The employer may have meant it when he said his pre-ballot offer was his final offer, so that the expectation that he would give in to the strike threat may be false and the union's bluff called.

All negotiations in a company or plant where there is a settled relationship contain a number of unspoken assumptions about each side's behaviour based on past experience. Strike ballots have been incorporated into these patterns. The word 'final' applied to an employer's offer has to be interpreted and successful negotiations depend on both sides' interpretations being the same. No employer can deny that the offer being put to the employees is 'final', but it may well be that it is not the final 'final' offer. Strike ballots have clarified the role of the strike threat in negotiations. They have brought the possibility of a strike into the negotiations in more cases than formerly, but on the other hand despite ballots the number of strikes has been going down. Strike ballots have become tactics which are well understood by both sides.

These responses to the legal provisions have been different from what the government expected. Penalties for unions where strikes took place without secret ballots were intended to weaken the use of the strike threat and to give the members the opportunity to stop the 'militant minority' calling irresponsible strikes. The government assumed that employers would seek injunctions against unions if strikes were called without a majority in a ballot or if the technicalities of the ballot were not observed. Some employers have challenged ballots successfully, as did the port employers after the dockers' strike ballot in 1989. But in general employers have held back from the courts even when they knew they would win because, for example, those voting were not confined to those who would be called on to strike. Many managers say that they would only resort to the courts in very exceptional circumstances. This reluctance, as on other elements of industrial relations law, can be explained in terms of having to live with the other side afterwards and of believing that legal penalties would damage future relations.

In the Employment Act 1988 the government extended to union members the right to seek an injunction if a strike were called without a ballot or if the ballot were not properly conducted. In the same Act the Commissioner for the Rights of Trade Union Members was created to facilitate these and other actions by individual union members. If the government believed that individuals would be more willing than employers to bring in the law, there is little evidence that this has occurred. In her report for 1989–90 the

Commissioner stated that there were six formal complaints to her about strike ballots between April 1989 and March 1990.

The combination of high turnout and few failures to secure a majority for strike action did not fit in with the government's objective that secret ballots should enable the rank and file to overturn the decisions of militant leaders. So it attempted to turn the screw on the unions by seeking support in the draft Code of Practice on ballots issued in 1989 for 70 per cent participation to validate a strike ballot. Had it been adopted it would have been a high hurdle to surmount in every ballot and a major uncertainty would have been introduced into negotiations. Clearly a low turnout is damaging, even if there is a majority for action but a limit as high as 70 per cent looked like an attempt to load the dice against strike action. The proposal attracted such opposition even from employers that no limit was included in the Code when it was issued in May 1991. It states that those authorising action after a ballot has been held should take account of 'the number of those voting relative to those given entitlement to vote' (Code, p. 25).

A ballot gives legitimacy to strike action. If a union calls a strike it expects its members, including those who have voted against it, to observe the call and there are usually sanctions in union rules which can be applied to those who work when called on to strike. The government decided to separate the issue of the vote in a ballot from that of the union's power to punish those who do not strike. The 1988 Act prevents unions punishing their members for refusing to strike after a majority vote in favour of action, or for encouraging other members not to strike. The provision has sharp teeth. After the strike action taken by NALGO in the summer of 1989 over a pay claim a number of its members were fined for refusing to strike, despite the majority in favour of strike action in the ballot. They took action against the union. The first case – *Bradley* v. *NALGO* – was determined by the EAT in February 1991, when it awarded £2520 compensation to each of the nine former members of the South Tyneside branch who had crossed picket lines. This was the minimum award possible, the EAT deciding *inter alia* that they could not be compensated for loss of union membership because they had attempted to resign.

The practical effect of this provision on unions is that they are even more reluctant to call strikes where the majority is small or where there is a large minority, some of whom may be inclined to work in defiance of the majority. But many managers doubt the efficacy of this provision because they anticipate that the other more informal pressures on those who work during a strike may be more widely used and they could carry over into day-to-day relations between unions and management in an unhelpful way.

Some strikes seemed to be beyond the reach of the law. The strike on the London Underground in the summer of 1989 took the form of one-day stoppages, usually once a week, on eight occasions. The NUR held a strike ballot which produced a large majority in favour of action but the employers succeeded in getting it invalidated on the grounds that the material on the ballot paper was unreasonably complicated. So the one-day strikes were unofficial and the NUR and ASLEF were opposed to them. But rank-and-file groups successfully organised the stoppages and took steps to prevent identifiable leaders appearing. The key point was that strikes to which the law applied were those called by officials of unions; those which were not called by officials were not within the ambit of the law. The government included in the Employment Act 1990 provisions which removed this distinction between official and unofficial action, so that strikes called by shop stewards and committees of lay members are classed as official and are within the definition of strikes for which unions are held responsible.

If shop stewards call a strike without a ballot the union is no longer immune from legal action unless it repudiates the action by notifying every member who could be involved in a specified form of words. The same Act gives the employers power to dismiss selectively union and non-union members taking part in the action. Immunity from legal action is removed from strikes in support of selectively dismissed strikers even if there is a majority in a secret ballot. The only exception to these powers is workers in places where unions are not recognised. If they strike they cannot be selectively dismissed because there is no union recognised by the employer which can repudiate their action.

The unions' repudiation of unofficial strikes is likely to be understood by the members involved as inevitable because of the law, and so it may not cut much ice, but it severs all links between the strikers and their union and leaves them on their own. It does not, of course, prevent the employer negotiating with the strikers but no union official can be brought in to calm things down and get the dispute put into procedure. Unions may seek agreements with employers which rule out the use of selective dismissal. When unofficial strikes occur an early demand is likely to be that the employer will make no selective dismissals, and if it is not conceded the strike may be extended to cover that issue as well as the original cause. In practice, unofficial strikes usually occur suddenly and employers want to get them settled as soon as possible. Selective dismissal makes that harder to achieve. On the other hand, employers may judge that an unofficial strike can be the occasion for a showdown with local union representatives and take the opportunity to get rid of them in the knowledge that the union cannot take action to protect them. It is undoubtedly a powerful weapon in the hands of an employer who wishes to weaken the union's ability to represent the employees, particularly when it is remembered that many unofficial strikes have their root cause in some managerial decision.

The requirement that strikes should be sanctioned by a majority in a secret ballot is based on the clear principle that the decision should be made by the individuals concerned in private. It is a major improvement in the conduct of industrial relations that this is now almost universally accepted. The unions opposed it, as did many managers, when it was introduced and only a Conservative government could have brought it to pass.

However, the elaborations in the 1988 and 1990 Acts on working during strikes and selective dismissal of unofficial strikers are widely seen as unprincipled and as *ad hoc* reactions to particular events. Tinkering with the principle of the right of those affected to decide whether or not to strike tempts both unions and employers to agree not to use the extra powers or to find ways round them. That weakens the force of the principle. The difference is between the government's political objectives and the negotiators' day-to-day concerns. They have come together on the requirement for strike ballots but they have separated on some of the attempts to block loopholes.

Picketing

Action to make strikes effective has always been contentious. If a strike has solid support from a disciplined labour force no picketing may be needed. But in most cases a picket on the entrance to the workplace is necessary to exercise persuasive pressure on those who do not favour strike action and may be willing to go against the majority decision and continue working. Pickets have been required to limit themselves to peaceful persuasion since the Conspiracy and Protection of Property Act 1875.

Where a strike divides a body of employees and where the success of the strike seems to depend on stopping all those directly involved from working and, even more certainly, where the strikers believe that picketing is necessary to stop others like lorry drivers entering and leaving the workplace, there is a recipe for damaging conflict which may turn into a challenge to the police. If people in no way directly or indirectly involved decide to join the pickets out of sympathy for the strike, that may sharpen the challenge.

Picketing only infrequently raises major issues of public order but in the 1970s there were two events, among others, which had a formative influence on the intentions of the incoming Conservative government in 1979. The first was the victory of pickets over the police at the Saltley coke depot in February 1972. A strike in the coal-mining industry was in progress and the NUM wanted to stop the use of stocks in order to bring pressure on firms dependent on the supply of coal, or of coke in the case of the steel industry and some other consumers. On the morning of 10 February the NUM assembled a large number of 'flying' pickets sufficient to prevent the police keeping the Saltley coke depot open. The police were greatly outnumbered. The depot had only one gate in a closely built-up area and the chief constable decided to close the depot.

Several features contributed to this event's symbolic status and to the Conservative Party's conviction that it should never be repeated. The NUM had organised the transport of large numbers of pickets from far away. Arthur Scargill first achieved national fame as the organiser of these 'flying' pickets. The miners were strongly supported by numerous local trade unionists in the west Midlands, many from the engineering industry. The closing of the Saltley depot by picketing happened the day after a state of emergency had been declared by the Conservative government and seemed to cock a snook at the power of the state. Deliberate planning of large-scale picketing had been shown to have the power to prevent the police keeping open places at some distance from the primary dispute and where the picketing was not designed to deter people from working.

The second event was the Grunwick dispute in 1976. There was a strike over recognition at a north London photographic film processing factory. The employer refused to recognise the union when in August 1976 137 employees walked out over his treatment of them and then joined APEX. The employer held that they had dismissed themselves. The union authorised a strike, the factory was picketed and it escalated into a *cause célèbre*.

By March 1977 ACAS had reported under the statutory procedure then available recommending recognition. The employer refused to accept the ACAS recommendation and the TUC called for a boycott of the company to which Post Office workers who delivered a significant part of the factory's work responded. The picketing built up in the summer. The entrance to the factory was in a confined street and the mass pickets tried to stop the police ensuring entry for those of the firm's employees who had continued to work. There were regular scenes of violence and on 13 June 84 people were arrested. Most of the pickets had not worked at Grunwick but were supporters of the claim for trade union recognition. Leading trade unionists and ministers in the Labour government appeared on the picket line. Grunwick challenged the ACAS report in the courts and its challenge was successful in the House of Lords. In August the report of the Court of Inquiry, which had been set up with Lord Scarman as chairman, recommended reinstatement and recognition of APEX while criticising the picketing. APEX then withdrew its support for mass picketing. The company still refused recognition and the dispute petered out; Grunwick had won. Picketing had not been successful but it had brought a running battle to a North London street and it seemed impervious to all the apparatus of the law, ACAS and a Court of Inquiry.

These two events entered the hall of fame of militant trade unionists and became models for extensive picketing during the 'Winter of Discontent' in 1978–9. But no other events achieved the significance of Saltley and Grunwick for both militant trade unionists and the Conservative Party.

Picketing which challenged the police and was violent was a high priority for attention when the Conservative government came into office in 1979 and so legal limitations on picketing were a major feature of the Employment Act 1980. People involved in a dispute were confined to picketing peacefully their own place of work. Unions which authorised picketing beyond that faced legal action. This limitation meant that people could not picket the premises of other employers involved in the same dispute; pickets had to be drawn from those who worked in the workplace picketed. Limits were also placed on the picketing of other employers who, if their employees went on strike or took other action, might put pressure on the employer in the primary dispute. So from the beginning of the 1980s the law severely reduced the scope of legal picketing and it seemed that the ghosts of Saltley and Grunwick had been laid.

Picketing is ancillary to strike action. In the early 1980s strikes declined in number and picketing was not an active issue, the new law being in general observed. But in the autumn of 1983 there was a dispute between the Messenger Newspapers and the NGA which is described in Chapter 5. Picketing was only one feature of the dispute, but it was the scenes of picketing designed to stop the newspapers leaving the plant and the resulting conflicts with the police which claimed public attention. The union chose to defy the law and brought down crippling penalties on itself. The dispute showed that a union could be prevented from operating effectively if it persisted in picketing in the face of injunctions. Newspaper printing does not dominate the mainstream of British industrial relations but, even so, the lesson was plain for all to see. If injunctions against picketing were not observed then the unions' existence was at stake. The new legislation, when applied, could cripple unions.

Picketing was an essential part of the strategy used in 1984 by the NUM and its areas to make the miners' strike effective. At the very beginning the ballots of South Wales lodges were 18 to 13 against strike action. But by the morning after these results were known there were pickets at every pit in South Wales and no one crossed the lines (Adeney and Lloyd, 1986, p. 96). That showed the superior power of picketing over the ballot. However, in Nottinghamshire pickets from Yorkshire unsuccessfully tried to stop miners going to work and that picketing may well have been the crucial influence causing the Nottinghamshire area of the NUM to vote against strike action by a three-to-one majority. As is explained in Chapter 5, the NCB in accordance with the wishes of ministers took no legal action against picketing and it was the initiating of injunctions by a transport company and NUM members against picketing which led to the sequestration of the assets of the South Wales area of the NUM.

But it was the picketing at the Orgreave depot which brought to a head the consequences of the NCB taking no legal action against picketing. On 18 June 1984 10 000 pickets attempted to repeat Saltley and make the police concede the closure of Orgreave. Like Saltley, Orgreave was a source of coke for steelmaking and the intervention was intended to prevent lorries leaving. It was not a picket to prevent people working. A month's picket had not prevented lorries going in and out, yet the Yorkshire miners made it the test of picketing. But unlike Saltley it was surrounded by fields and had more than one entrance. As the pictures on television showed it became a pitched battle. The large numbers of pickets were insufficient to achieve their objective. Determined police, especially those who were mounted, broke the strikers' lines and the strikers left the field defeated. For some, it was seen as the turning point of the strike. In violent exchanges the police were a different proposition from those at Saltley; they used the force necessary to defeat the pickets. Mass picketing was not used again after Orgreave and attempts to bring the Nottinghamshire miners out by picketing their pits withered away.

The 1980 Act had been designed for such events as the picketing used in the miners' strike. Had injunctions been applied for they would undoubtedly have been granted. If ignored, they would have led to fines and the sequestration of the NUM and its areas' assets in the first few weeks of the strike. That might well have caused the areas to try to restrain the picketing. As it was, they were under no such restraint. Whether attempts to impose injunctions against picketing would have caused the Nottinghamshire miners to vote for strike action is questionable, since it was the picketing itself to which they objected. But the decision not to use the law against picketing ensured that violence between pickets and the police became the norm and victory was seen to belong to the side which had the superior force. By foreswearing their own legal remedies, the government failed to do all they could to deter violent picketing.

Since the miners' pickets were defeated by the police, others who used picketing to exert pressure on employers and working employees could expect the same treatment. The Wapping dispute in which News International used the law on picketing against the unions is described in Chapter 5. The print unions staked their future on the success of the picketing at Wapping. They had to prevent the newspapers being sold for a time if they were to make the company negotiate. The pickets had only to close off the exit from the Wapping plant for a few hours each night to secure their end. The stakes were as high for the company as for the unions. After the move to Wapping and the dismissal of all the previous staff, successful picketing might well have brought the company down. In such a case injunctions and penalties for not observing them could not stop the mass picketing on which the union depended and which the company had to overcome. The police were the key and they gave News International its victory. The picketing failed because the police ensured that the newspapers could leave the plant. As one trade union official said to another on the first night that newspapers were printed at Wapping, seeing the lorries come down the ramp and the police successfully making way for them through the pickets, 'We have lost.' As at Orgreave, the police used the force necessary to overcome the pickets, night after night. A report by Northamptonshire police into police conduct at Wapping in January 1987 found that some officers were violent and out of control. Where the law itself was not enough to prevent mass picketing succeeding the police secured its defeat.

Secondary action

Secondary action is that which is taken by a union against other employers than the one with which it is in dispute, to cause them to put pressure on the primary employer to make concessions to the union. It can take various forms like a refusal to handle material or components bought from, or being supplied to, the primary employer ('boycotting'), or action against any employer who might do business of any sort with the primary employer. It may go much wider. Action may be taken against employers at some distance from the dispute to generate pressure on the employer to settle (sympathetic action). Where unions are in a weak position, as is often the case in recognition disputes like Grunwick, or where unions feel that the action of others may tip the balance their way as with the NUM call for support from lorry drivers and railway workers to which there was a partial response in 1984–5, they appeal to the sense of trade union solidarity and to the feeling that others may need their support another day.

The Employment Act 1980 limited secondary action to that taken by the employees of a supplier or a customer who had a contract with the primary employer. That this was a significant narrowing of industrial action was shown in the Wapping dispute referred to above and in the NUS's dispute with P&O Ferries in February 1988 when the union was made virtually bankrupt by the fines and sequestrations of its assets which followed its refusal to obey injunctions against illegal secondary action.

But in the Employment Act 1990 the government changed its position and all secondary action, including wider sympathetic action as well as action against customers and suppliers, was made illegal. This was a major restriction on the right to strike which could penetrate the scope of primary action if employers deliberately divided their activities between legally separate companies, as some did after the 1980 Act in order to reduce the scope of legal secondary action. While most trade unions would go along with the 1980 Act's restrictions on sympathetic action, they are bound to seek the repeal of the illegality of all secondary action introduced in 1990. It is the threat of industrial action which is most often used, not its actual occurrence, and if no supplier or customer of a firm in dispute can be affected then no convincing threats of action can be made and the right to take industrial action is severely curbed. It was for this reason that in 1980 James Prior had opposed making secondary action against customers and suppliers illegal.

The 1990 Act prevents action against employers who are involved indirectly in the dispute because they trade with the primary employer and who will benefit if the primary employer succeeds in refusing the unions' demands. The 1980 Act's provisions allowing secondary action against employers contractually connected with the primary employer would probably have been a permanent settlement of the legal position on secondary action but the 1990 Act reopens the argument about wider sympathetic action as well as about the narrower action against customers and suppliers. For the trade unions the law on secondary action is again unfinished business.

Conclusion

The record shows that strike activity has been halved in the 1980s compared with the 1970s. It continued to decline throughout the decade so that in the second half the days lost through strikes were down by getting on for two-thirds on the first half. But within that dramatic decline the number of short strikes did not fall greatly and a small number of big strikes in the public sector were of considerable significance, with the miners' strike of 1984–5 being the largest since the General Strike of 1926. However, the experience of other industrial countries has been similar to that of Britain, so the explanation of the decline lies more in general factors affecting all of them than in specific ones confined to each.

Although the government's legislation affecting strikes seems not to have been a main reason for the decline in strike action, that legislation has changed the legal framework affecting strikes in major ways. The paradox, that the practitioners claim that the legislation has not been of major importance, although the legislative changes have been very considerable, is explained by the absorption of the new legal rules into the negotiators' practices. The practitioners mostly believe that the reduction in strike action flows from general factors affecting the labour market and the ability of managers to take and keep the initiative in negotiations, with unions being less able to get priority for their claims. Yet government ministers saw the five Acts, all of which affected strikes, as leading directly to a modification of conduct. It is a fair conclusion that the legal changes have been one influence, but by no means the dominant one, making for the reduction in strike activity.

Strike ballots are a good illustration. That the ballots amount to a major change in practices is unquestionable. Secret ballots are now held as a matter of course before strike action is taken, except for local strikes which suddenly flare up. In the vast majority of cases, of course, a majority in favour of strike action does not lead to one occurring. There is a general acceptance that secret ballots before strikes are a permanent feature of the practice of industrial relations. This can be put to the credit of the Conservative government, since ministers had little support initially for the proposal from employers, and they faced opposition from trade unions. Now it is accepted all round. But its practical significance is limited. When ballots are called trade union members seldom reject strike action. Over 90 per cent of ballots are in favour of it with high participation rates in the votes. Ballots have become part of the bargaining tactics of both sides. The union uses the ballot as a means of showing it has rank-and-file support, while the employer expects the union to prove the strength of its members' feelings through a ballot. The requirement for secret ballots on industrial action has improved the quality of negotiations without changing them in a fundamental way.

The ballot makes known to both sides what the majority of the individuals concerned prefer. It gives legitimacy to the union's position, which could previously be said to be that of the active minority. Many more majority votes in favour of strike action are followed by negotiated settlements on an improved offer from the employer than are followed by strikes. Just as a skilled union negotiator will only go to a ballot which he has good reason to believe he will win, so a skilled manager will not make a final offer (or a final, 'final' offer) which risks being rejected in a ballot. It is proof of the value of the strike ballot provisions in the law that the negotiators have integrated them into their procedures so successfully.

The significance of the narrowing of the unions' legal immunity in calling strikes is more difficult to assess, as is that of the legal changes on picketing and secondary action. During the 1980s these changes seemed to be of little consequence except in certain major disputes. Moreover, the miners' strike showed that it does not follow that because the law exists it will be applied. But the major reason why a firm conclusion cannot be reached is that industrial action has been running at such a low level, and one that has continued to fall, so that there have not been enough occasions on which the law might be tested for its practical significance to have emerged. It can be argued that the low level has itself been caused in large part by the legal changes but international comparisons work against that view. If there were an upsurge of strike activity in the future, the significance of the changed legal framework might turn out to be greater than at present appears. However, so long as strike action continues to be insignificant, or even if in future it rises again to somewhat higher levels, the changes in the law may well continue to be of little apparent importance.

After a decade of few strikes, especially in the private sector, it may be that the prospect of any upsurge in strike activity is slight. If it is the case that in many places of work changes are brought about through negotiations and by skilled management preparation and consultation, strike action could continue to be far less on the cards than it used to be. Experience in the car industry points in that direction. Perhaps the changes in the law on strikes came at the time when strikes were ceasing anyway to be significant.

The conclusions so far are subject to a major proviso arising out of the provisions of the Employment Act 1990 on 'unofficial' strikes and the freedom given to employers to dismiss all or any such strikers. The sudden walk-out because of what is in many cases a spontaneous reaction to a management decision is a long-standing problem for unions as well as managers. Making the union repudiate such action by its members and thus exposing its shop stewards to dismissal in circumstances where spontaneous action is often understandable, creates a new area of potential conflict. Most of these 'unofficial' strikes, which have not been declining in number, are settled quickly by negotiations. If stewards are dismissed and unions are 'officially' banned from being involved some of them could become running sores. The Act has been in force for such a short time that there is no experience to refer to. No doubt most employers will not use the Act, and there may be understandings between employers and unions to that effect, but the opportunity has been created by the Act for employers to get rid of leaders of 'unofficial' strikes and some may take it. The same could be said of the 1988 Act's provision forbidding unions from punishing members who work during a strike which is backed by a majority vote.

While for the most part, so long as strikes are at a low level, the legal changes have general acceptance, uncertainty about their efficacy hangs over the last legal changes made on 'unofficial' strikes. There is a widespread view that the law should be regarded as settled and no longer treated as a shuttlecock batted to and fro as governments come and go. There is some danger that the provision on 'unofficial' strikes and dismissal of their leaders could, through actual events rather than debates, bring the law's effectiveness into question. If that were to happen, it could lead to a more widespread challenge affecting those parts of the legal framework which at the moment are broadly accepted.

While the main conclusions form around the decline in strike activity, it is necessary to come to terms with the great importance of strikes in the public sector in the 1980s. Indeed, there was a marked contrast between the private sector in which hardly any strikes of significance occurred and the public sector where there was a long roll of set-piece battles, often in industries and services where strikes had previously been regarded as likely to damage essential services in politically unacceptable ways. In that sense, the 1980s were the years when the government took on strikes far more readily than any previous post-war government had dared to do. The handling of strikes in steel, the civil service, water, the NHS, and above all coal, showed the government's resolve. Strike action was extensively threatened and taken in the public sector because the changes proposed for running down and reorganising the industries and services were such strong challenges by government to union positions. The unions which called strikes all had to accept defeat, some more extensively than others. The government's policy appeared to be that any challenge to it by strike action would meet with as crushing a defeat as could be mounted. Having defeated the miners, the government was not going to lose to the nurses, teachers or ambulance staff.

This is only part of developments in the public sector which are fully covered in Chapter 7. The conclusion on strikes in the public sector is that the government, whatever its view of strikes elsewhere or in legislation, pursued a policy of facing strikes and defeating them. In the 1980s strikes in the public service were promoted to the active agenda. In the event, the government's determination to defeat strikes, given the resources at its disposal, was bound to succeed. That may always have been so, but it was made evident in the 1980s as never before.

CHAPTER 12

Assessment of the 1980s and implications for the 1990s

Introduction

In this chapter answers are given to the questions posed in the introduction to this book and changes which have taken place in the 1980s and their implications for the 1990s are assessed. The first section surveys the changes in the environment of industrial relations – political, economic and social. Next the changes in the objectives, policies and structure of the two parties – unions and employers – are considered. Then the changes in institutions and procedures, in private and public sector pay, in productivity, and changes in the law, including such issues as strikes, recognition, the closed shop and the check-off are assessed. Finally, the future agenda for collective bargaining and the effects of greater EC integration and the Social Charter are looked at.

The environment

The 1980s was a decade of profound economic, political and social change. Consequently, the environment within which industrial relations was conducted was radically different from that of the 1970s and indeed from that of the earlier post-war decades. First, there was the political environment. The UK throughout the decade was ruled by Conservative governments under the prime ministership of Mrs Thatcher. These governments pursued a brand of conservatism which was in marked contrast with that of earlier post-war Conservative governments. Above all, they signalled the end of the post-war consensus, which had included commitment to full employment, the Welfare

State, Keynesian economics, a significant public sector and a degree of corporatism. In its place was a whole-hearted belief in a free market economy, private enterprise, monetarism, individualism, the creation of an 'enterprise culture' and the ending of any form of corporatism. In pursuit of these beliefs, the government passed legislation which sought to restrict union power severely and to limit union ability to take industrial action. The legislation also sought to enhance the rights of individual union members *vis-à-vis* those of the union leadership.

Government hostility towards unions did not however show itself only in legislation. The government no longer treated the TUC and individual unions as social partners and as important participants in society. In its role as an employer and quasi-employer, the government throughout the 1980s sought to resist union demands and in a series of public-sector disputes showed its determination to defeat the unions, virtually regardless of cost. This policy culminated in the year-long miners' strike 1984–5. Once the miners had been defeated no one else was going to be allowed to win, neither teachers nor ambulance staff. The government's conduct against the miners was a sign to others of what would happen to them if they chose to strike. While the removal of the right to union membership at GCHQ in 1984 was perhaps the most spectacular and extreme anti-union measure taken by the government, the resistance to it prevented it being extended elsewhere.

There can be no doubt that the government's early industrial relations legislation had popular public support – there being a widespread belief, not least among some trade unionists, that the unions had become too powerful in the 1970s. However, the government's antipathy to unions went much further than this. Given its ideological commitment to free markets, to managerial authority and to individualism, the existence of unions was considered a hindrance to the proper working of the labour market. Logically, therefore, the government's ultimate objective had to be the elimination of unions or at the very least, their marginalisation. Except in these terms, or in terms of pure vindictiveness or political opportunism, it is difficult to see the rationale for much of the government's later industrial relations legislation. Thus, for trade unions the political environment was an exceedingly hostile one.

If the political environment was bleak for trade unions, so was the economic one for much of the 1980s. As far as the labour market was concerned, unemployment doubled in the first two years of Conservative rule and continued to increase to a peak of well over 3 million in 1987. Thereafter unemployment fell steadily to around 1.5 million by the middle of 1990. However, with a new recession facing the country, unemployment started to move upwards again and passed 2 million early in 1991. The level of unemployment throughout the decade was unprecedented in post-war Britain. While total employment increased marginally in the second half of the decade, the extra workers were mainly female and/or part-time. Some labour shortages developed in the south of the country, in particular in certain skills.

As far as product markets were concerned, there was a great growth in competition, partly as a result of deregulation at home but mainly as a result of growing international competition – the consequence of the European Community, developments in world trade and the growth of multinationals. This growth in competition – particularly in the manufacturing sector – led employers to seek greater flexibility, efficiency and cost effectiveness, with significant consequences for industrial relations.

For employers, the political and economic environment was mixed. On the one hand there was a government throughout the decade which was favourable to business. Direct taxation for individuals (especially the higher paid) and companies was greatly reduced. The government favoured increased incentives for enterprise and the pay of senior managers and top executives rose at an unprecedented rate, not to mention generous tax concessions on share options. Profits, dividends and share prices also increased very substantially for most of the decade. At the same time, unions were put in their place and management authority was restored.

On the other hand, business faced more competitive product markets. Moreover, in the early and later years of the decade business suffered punitive interest rates. It was manufacturing industry in particular which at times felt most beleaguered.

The third major environmental change was new technology, the development and application of which continued apace in the 1980s. Again the consequences for industrial relations were highly significant, affecting the demand for different kinds of labour and skills, blurring distinctions between manual and non-manual workers, and much affecting the location and size of establishments, job descriptions and pay structures.

Finally, there were changes in the social environment. Phelps Brown (1990) has traced these changes, arguing that after the Second World War there was a growth in collectivism 'centred upon a sense of neighbourly obligation and the intervention of government to guide the economy and modify its workings in the cause of material advancement and social justice.' In the 1980s a new view prevailed:

> people are no longer seen as dependent on society and bound by reciprocal obligation to it: indeed the very notion of society is rejected. Individuals are expected to shift for themselves and those who get into difficulties are thought to have only themselves to blame. Self-reliance, acquisitive individualism, the curtailment of public expenditure, the play of market forces instead of the restraints and directives of public policy, the prerogatives of management instead of the power of trade unions, centralisation of power instead of pluralism. (p. 1)

Phelps Brown argues that this change was partly the result of the perceived defects of collectivism, but also and more importantly the result of a new generation for whom 'a quarter of a century of full employment removed

awareness that an unplanned economy was capable of inflicting great hardship
. . . the very success of the welfare state made it seem unnecessary.' There was
also the growth of consumerism; the effect of widespread car ownership and of
home ownership; and the widening of income distribution and changes in the
tax system, with a consequent undermining of egalitarianism. At the same time,
there were as a result of economic change drastic changes in the structure of
the labour force with the decline of the traditional trade union strongholds, the
rise of the service sector and the increase in self-employment with a consequent
change in social outlook.

The whole process is described by Phelps Brown as 'one of downward
extension of the middle class and its values'. The labour movement had been
based on a sense of common interest and purpose: the purpose was not only
defensive but there was the belief that betterment could come through changes
in society. This called for action at national level – hence the formation of the
TUC and the Labour Party. It also meant unity and loyalty which sprang from
the individual worker's sense of common interest. Phelps Brown believes that
loyalty has ebbed away and there has been a 'dissolution of the labour
movement'. This was the result of the social changes mentioned above and, in
effect, of the 'localisation' of interests – of interests in the home and in the
workplace as against solidarity with fellow workers and policy at national level.
While some might think that this conclusion goes too far, there can be little
doubt that the social changes he describes have had a significant effect on
industrial relations in the 1980s.

During the 1990s environmental pressures on industrial relations are
unlikely to be greatly changed. The political environment for trade unions
would become significantly more supportive if a Labour government was to be
elected. However, the Labour Party has made clear that there would be no
wholesale reversal of the legislation of the 1980s. There would still be
restrictions on secondary action and picketing, and there is no doubt that
lawful industrial action would continue to require a prior individual ballot.
Equally, there would be no return to the corporatism of the 1970s, although
trade unions could expect at least to have their voice listened to.

However, there would be some changes in legislation, in particular the
introduction of a statutory mechanism for unions to attempt to gain
recognition, an end to *ex-parte* injunctions, and a strengthening of the rights
of individual employees. Above all, there would not be a consistent anti-union
campaign led by a hostile government, as has occurred throughout the 1980s,
and which was clearly meant to have an effect on employer attitudes and
behaviour. The return of a Conservative government would presumably mean
more of the same menu provided in the 1980s, although there might well be
some softening of the edges. However, the growing effects of Britain's
membership of the EC could not be ignored whichever party was in power.

With regard to the economic environment, product markets are certain to
remain highly competitive, and indeed with '1992' and the removal of the

remaining barriers to the movement of trade, likely to become even more so. The position in the labour market is likely to be more problematic. On the one hand, demographic changes mean that there will be a very substantial fall in the number of young people entering the labour market. On the other hand, Britain has started the 1990s with a much more severe recession than the government expected and the consequent high and rising unemployment will persist after output begins to recover as happened in the early 1980s. Technological change will continue unabated and there is evidence that its effects on the service sector in the 1990s may equal that on manufacturing in the 1980s. Finally, with regard to social change, it may well be that there will be some reaction to the extreme individualism of the 1980s. However, the main social trends are unlikely to be reversed and all political parties now place 'the market', and hence the consumer, high on their list of priorities.

For employers, it is likely that the environment in the 1990s will continue to mean competition and technological advance, which will make manpower reductions, especially in manufacturing, a continuing feature, with redundancies in recessions. Pressure for improved labour utilisation will continue to be a high priority. While employers have been freer to exert their power over employees, they have not done so as enthusiastically as the government wished. They have not thrown unions out as the government hoped they would. Under a Labour government, private employers would no doubt exert themselves to resist any attempt to curb their authority in the workplace (as they did over the Bullock Report in the late 1970s), and they might cause more confrontation than the unions did under the Conservatives in the 1980s.

Trade unions

For unions, there have been two major developments in the 1980s. First, there has been the dramatic and continuous fall in overall union membership — from 13.3 million in 1979 to 10.2 million in 1989 and in the membership of TUC-affiliated unions from 12.1 million in 1979 to 8.4 million in 1989. Second, there has been the drastic decline in union power in relation to government and employers.

There can be little argument about the change in the relationship between government and unions. At best, unions have been viewed as an irrelevance and at worst as 'the enemy within'. Thus the TUC was seen as having no public role; tripartism was virtually eliminated, for example, in the field of training after 1985; the NEDC was emasculated; TUC advice and policy statements were ignored; and the practice of TUC nominees on a range of public bodies was ended. Complete elimination of a public role for unions was, however, not achieved. NEDC, although emasculated, was not abolished; ACAS is still in the hands of a tripartite council; union presence still exists in the health and safety field and in the composition of industrial tribunals.

The changed relationship between unions and employers is a more debatable question – certainly among academics. One school of thought has argued that the structure and process of collective bargaining has been maintained in the 1980s: there has been no widescale derecognition of unions; the check-off has been maintained; and shop stewards not only still exist but, with the further decentralisation of bargaining, their role has to some extent been enhanced. Another school of thought argues that although the machinery of collective bargaining has been kept in place, the power relationship between the parties has changed to such an extent, that management authority has been almost complete and it is management which sets the agenda. The unions are thought to be in a state of almost terminal decline, management has taken control and 'individualism' will become dominant.

Similarly, there is a major academic debate about the other side of the coin, namely, the position of management. The second school of thought believes that management is now supreme, that unions have largely been marginalised and that their power and effectiveness have been minimalised. Management, it is argued, has been transformed. Human resource management is being widely adopted; unions are being bypassed, with management communicating directly to individual employees; and employees are being directly motivated, not least through the growth of individual performance-related pay. Cost effectiveness rules and management has been free to innovate, to adopt technological and organisational change, to reduce the labour force when required, and to achieve virtually complete flexibility. Moreover, it is claimed, that attitudes and behaviour of both unions and employees have significantly changed. There is a greater realisation of economic imperatives and, consequently, a willingness to co-operate with management initiatives.

The first school of thought, although accepting that many of the changes mentioned above have occurred, emphasises that they are neither universal nor immutable. The fact that unions are less powerful does not mean that they are powerless or that they are bound always to be as acquiescent as many now are. They certainly have an effective presence in most places which still exist where they were present a decade ago. That there is so little overt conflict does not mean that they do not exert any pressure.

The true situation is somewhere between the positions taken by the two schools of thought: moreover, and most importantly, it varies in different sectors of the economy. Thus, overall, generalisations are to be treated with caution. There can be no doubt that unions have lost power and influence and that management authority has been asserted. There has been some derecognition but its extent has been limited, although perhaps somewhat greater than was originally thought (Gregg and Yates, 1991). However, unions have had great difficulty in gaining recognition in new plants and breaking into service industries, where they have traditionally been weak. On the other hand, there has been an extension of the now widespread practice of the check-off. Employers bent on weakening unions might well have ended their check-off arrangements, but they have not done so. Nevertheless, there is as yet no sign of a halt in the decline in union membership which continued unabated during the 1980s.

Turning to the unions themselves, by the end of the 1980s there was a very significant change in attitude and behaviour in most unions. The basic objective of unions has always been and still is the protection of their members' interests. This is an entirely legitimate objective in a democratic and pluralist society. Moreover, a strong and healthy trade union movement is an essential component of such a society. Unions throughout their history have not generally sought confrontation but have sought to achieve their objectives through securing recognition from employers and then establishing procedures for negotiation, consultation and grievance handling, so that issues and disputes could be handled peacefully. Industrial action has never been other than a last resort in most cases.

While the unions' basic purpose has not changed, they have certainly sought to adapt, rather belatedly perhaps, to the realities of the changing environment in which they have had to operate. As stated in Chapter 8, there has been a growing acceptance of some of the legal constraints imposed upon them. There has been a greater awareness of the more competitive environment in which firms have had to operate and they have been more receptive to the introduction of new technology. Unions have also recognised that they need actively to recruit new members and that in order to do so they need to make themselves more attractive and to provide new services. They have also under the pressure of falling membership and financial difficulties sought to make themselves more efficient. Computerisation among the large unions is now universal: and in many unions there have been changes in internal structure to meet changing circumstances, for example a strengthening of local and regional organisation to meet the needs of decentralised bargaining and the problems of individual members.

As part of the process of adaption to changed circumstances, there has been a spate of union mergers in the 1980s which was discussed in Chapter 8. More are in the pipeline, most notably a merger between NALGO, NUPE and COHSE and between the NCU and the UCW: other possibilities include the AEU and the EETPU and the TGWU and the MSF. Whether these will all take place is uncertain, but there seems little doubt that the trend towards mergers will increase, with the possibility of no more than six or eight major unions by the turn of the century. This should lead to stronger unions, the more efficient use of resources and the better provision of services. However, a note of warning should be struck. Such gains are not automatically achieved. A merger between incompatable unions could be disastrous, competition between large general unions could be self-destructive, and giant unions could become bureaucratic and remote from the membership. A scenario of a few big unions might also call in question the present role of the TUC.

Will further new attitudes and behaviour develop throughout the 1990s? In so far as the dichotomy between new unionism and old unionism is a false one, there is every reason to expect a continuation of the changing attitude and behaviour of the 1980s. In so far as there have been changes, however, they have not been due to changes of heart, but to the adaption by unions and their members to the environment. As was said earlier in this chapter, those environmental changes can be expected by and large to continue and they will carry on affecting attitudes and behaviour. This does not mean that there will never be strikes, nor that unions will not seek to strike hard bargains.

With regard to the unions' role in society and *vis-à-vis* government in the 1990s there will not be a return to the corporatism of the 1970s whichever party is in power. A Conservative government is unlikely to change the policies of the last decade, although they might be softened slightly. As far as the Labour Party is concerned, it is already apparent that there has been a reduction in union influence within the party, and indeed that further constitutional changes will reduce union influence still more. Most significantly, these changes are being achieved with union agreement. A future Labour government would not mean a return to the sort of political influence that unions wielded in the 1970s. Their views would be sought, as would their cooperation in handling the problems facing the British economy. Excessive union power and influence, however, is extremely unlikely. The Labour Party seems to believe that it will be unelectable if it is seen to be dominated by the unions. The unions, for their part, now realise that their own excesses in the 1970s contributed to a decade of Conservative Party rule with disastrous consequences for themselves. They also realise that with social and economic changes in the labour force – in particular the growth of non-manual, female and part-time employment, as well as a more highly educated and professionalised labour force – too close political ties with the Labour Party would hinder recruitment in areas where they must recruit in order to remain a significant voice in society.

Will trade union membership continue to fall in the 1990s? Will it resume an upward path or is an end to the decline the best that unions can expect? Many of the adverse factors which have contributed to the fall in union membership in the 1980s will still be present in the 1990s, for example continuing changes in the structure of the labour force away from manufacturing to services, the decline in manual employment and the growth of white-collar employment, the decline in the employment of men and the growth in the employment of women and of part-time women in particular. However, these trends were also present in the 1970s and did not prevent union growth. More important will be the policies, attitudes and behaviour of government, employers and the unions themselves. A Labour government would mean an atmosphere more conducive to growth and even a future Conservative government might well be less hostile than have been the Conservative governments of the 1980s. Employers vary in their attitude to unions from complete hostility to active cooperation. Their attitude is influenced in no small part by the attitude and behaviour of unions themselves. In this respect unions have to a large extent shown that they have absorbed some of the lessons of the recent past (Metcalf, 1991b). In the workplace they are seeking to play a more constructive role, while in an effort to attract membership they have sought to provide new services and have increasingly appreciated the importance of providing individual services as well as collective ones. Whether the favourable factors will be enough to overcome the unfavourable ones is uncertain, but a major advantage for the unions should be the implementation of the Social Charter and Britain's greater integration in the European Community. Unions are unlikely to return to their peak membership but a halt to the fall and some modest recovery would seem possible.

Employers

How have employers used their increased power? Many large organisations have drastically reduced their labour force, without any significant union resistance. This is particularly true of manufacturing, but is also true, for example, of coal-mining, the railways, the clearing banks, the large insurance companies and the civil service. Employers have regained control over operational matters – where it had been lost. Most agreements in those greenfield sites where unions have managed to gain recognition have included a clause providing for flexibility of labour. The old 'status quo' clause, typical of the engineering industry, whereby there was no change unless mutually agreed, has disappeared. Many employers have strengthened direct communications with their workforce and ceased to rely upon the union channel and shop stewards. There have also been many attempts to secure greater employee involvement, not in the old sense of increased worker participation, but in the sense of moulding workers to employer objectives and policies. There has been a very marked widening of pay differentials and a growth in the application of performance-related pay. All these changes can be typified as a growth in the 'individualisation' of industrial relations and a move away from 'collectivism'. What employers did not do in the 1980s, despite their greater power, increased competition in product markets and the need for cost effectiveness, was to cut real pay. On the contrary, on average it increased significantly and to a greater extent than it did in the 1970s, although no greater than it did in the 1950s and 1960s.

Among a number of employers, the 1980s saw an increase in hostility to unions, fostered in part by the government's anti-trade unionism. An overtly anti-union stance became seemingly respectable during the second half of the 1980s in a way that had not been true in Britain for the last half a century, and in a way which more resembled the American scene than the West European one. Such a view was enhanced by the large influx of American firms, by the growth of the financial sector, by other parts of the service sector and by the general weakness of unions. It took the form, as we have shown earlier, not of widespread union derecognition, but of the frequent refusal to recognise unions in greenfield sites, some derecognition of managerial unionism and a greater reluctance with regard to white-collar unionism in general. Above all, however, there were attempts to marginalise unions or bypass them through direct communications with individual employees, through performance-related pay and other measures of 'individualisation'.

Such attitudes have not been universal. Many of the personnel directors interviewed paid tribute to the cooperation of unions in increasing efficiency and productivity in the 1980s, some going so far as to say that without union cooperation such improvements would not have been achieved. However, others saw the unions as a declining force and believed that the future rested entirely with management. Some such companies laid great stress on the development of human resource management, although what they meant by this was not always made explicit. As we pointed out in Chapter 6, the fragmentary evidence which exists suggests that very few firms have espoused HRM in the full meaning of the term. Nevertheless, in looking forward to the 1990s, this is the direction in which many major British firms claim to be moving.

There is some difficulty in reconciling such claims with the practice of large-scale cut-backs in the labour force of many such companies and the patently obvious inadequacy of their investment in training and development. In answer it may be argued that HRM practices are meant to be applied to the 'core' workforce and not to the periphery. This begs many questions, not least how the core and the periphery are to be defined. Even if this is done satisfactorily, and different policies applied to each, does this mean that we are institutionalising a two-tier labour force? If so, what are the implications for 'team working', 'a common purpose', and loyalty to the organisation? Presumably such attitudes would only be expected of the selected 'core' workforce and nothing expected from those on the periphery. It is a cliché to say that management gets the unions and employees it deserves, but if responsibility and cooperation are expected from unions and employees, then management for its part must exercise an equal degree of responsibility and cooperation. The record of British management in this respect, with a few notable exceptions, has not been outstanding.

Changes in institutions and procedures

As described in Chapter 9, the two major changes in collective bargaining have been the further erosion of industry-wide bargaining and decentralisation to company level and within companies to divisional or plant level; second, there has been a reduction in the scope of collective bargaining. In addition, as already stated, there has been no widespread move towards derecognition. New procedures – where introduced – have tended to be more favourable to management: for example, in many cases the end of the closed shop, the end of the 'status quo' clause, the inclusion of managerial prerogative clauses, and the ending of obligatory arbitration clauses, where they existed, particularly in the public sector. Paradoxically, many of the so-called 'new-style' agreements have compulsory arbitration clauses, usually pendulum arbitration.

There have been moves to single-union agreements, above all on greenfield sites, although there have been cases in established organisations, for example, Midland Bank's derecognition of the MSF, leaving BIFU as the sole bargaining agent. Where, in established organisations, single union agreements have not been deemed advisable or possible, there have been some moves towards 'single-table' bargaining, that is to say, management bargaining with a single joint union side, consisting of all recognised unions. There has been the ending of many national agreements, for example, engineering, banking, shipping and commercial television, and the decentralisation of bargaining and other procedures to company, divisional or plant level. Decentralisation within companies has largely been the result of organisational changes made for purposes of business strategy and financial accountability, rather than for purely industrial relations purposes.

As Brown (1989) and Brown and Rowthorn (1990) have shown, such decentralisation has usually been on a product basis and not on a geographical basis, to take advantage of different local labour markets. To the extent that the government has sought to enforce local variations from national agreements in the public sector, it appears to have misunderstood what has been happening in the private sector. Those companies interviewed who produced a single product or who had integrated production spread over a number of plants, insisted that the maintenance of company-wide bargaining was essential.

There has been an end, where it had existed, to the 'single union channel': that is to say, employers no longer accept that communications and consultation should be solely or even mainly through elected union representatives. They proclaim that it is their right – indeed duty – to communicate directly with their own employees and this they have increasingly proceeded to do. In a number of cases, joint consultative committees now consist not only of elected union representatives, but of directly elected individual employees.

These trends are unlikely to be substantially reversed in the 1990s. However, it may be, particularly if union strength recovers somewhat, that the dangers of leapfrogging in too decentralised a system of bargaining may lead to some reconsideration of a role for more centralised bargaining at industry or company level.

Substantive changes

On the substantive side, the first and perhaps the most important change was the significant increase in average real earnings which took place, although the increase by no means applied universally and was largely absent in much of the public service sector. Given the weakness of unions throughout most of the decade, it is difficult to blame (or praise) the unions for the average rise in real earnings. Pay went up as fast as it did more because employers offered it than because unions pressed for it. The key question must therefore be, why did employers act in this way during a period when there was high unemployment, a surplus of labour, cuts in the size of many companies' labour forces, weak unions, strong competition – certainly in manufacturing, constraints on public sector pay, and the need to be cost-effective? The answer can only be that employers, individually, considered that it was in their best interests to do so. Once the worst of the recession of the early 1980s was over, company profits increased dramatically; labour forces were drastically cut and productivity – at least in manufacturing – increased significantly. Employers seemed to believe that their remaining employees should share in their company's prosperity. Employees had earned higher pay by accepting cuts and by accepting organisational and technological change, while flexibility had increased and had been generally accepted, so that increases in labour costs per unit were small for much of the decade – again, at least in manufacturing. In much of the private service sector, international competition was absent, thus making higher pay less of a problem. In addition, some employers believed that higher pay was necessary to achieve involvement and agreement with management objectives. Towards the end of the decade, additional reasons for higher pay were labour and skill shortages in some parts of the country and a resumption of the upward movement in the cost of living. In the public sector, after many years of enforced restraint, there had to be some 'give', if not on grounds of social justice then on grounds of high labour turnover and growing labour shortages in at least some areas and in some occupations.

Second, although there were substantial increases in average real pay, there was also a marked widening of differentials, as shown in Chapter 10. Non-manuals did better than manuals, the higher paid did better than the lower paid, skilled and professional workers did better than the unskilled and semi-skilled. Above all, management pay, particularly top management pay, soared. Such increases were justified at the time on a number of grounds including that it was performance related and that as profits grew significantly, top management deserved significantly higher pay. This did not prevent at least one chief executive justifying a large pay increase, despite falling profits, by arguing that in difficult times the strain on top management was greater. Another common argument was that of comparability, despite all the government's efforts to play down comparability as a factor in pay determination in the public service sector. If comparability with other British companies did not produce the required results, then comparisons were made with overseas companies, particularly American ones. In the former nationalised industries, one of the first steps after privatisation was substantial pay increases for top management. Even in polytechnics, with the ending of any local government influence, a first step in many was a doubling of directors' pay. While government queried the evidence produced by universities, the Association of University Teachers (AUT) and independent consultants about the 'brain drain' caused by inadequate British academic salaries and facilities, no evidence at all of the flight of British managers to America or elsewhere was required to justify large managerial pay increases.

The third significant change has been the growth in the popularity of performance-related pay (PRP) and to a lesser extent in profit-sharing and employee share ownership. While PRP had always been common for management in the private sector, during the 1980s it spread to lower-level white-collar employees and in a growing number of cases to manual workers. In the public sector PRP had been rare, even among management grades, the most common system being incremental point scales with incentives provided by promotion prospects. However, the 1980s saw the introduction of PRP for management grades in the public corporations, such as British Rail, and in the public service sector, including the civil service, the NHS and universities. In addition to its spread, the size of the 'merit' element in pay has been increasing, and indeed some companies have declared that there would be no general pay increases at all and that all increases would be based on 'merit'. Such a policy however might be easier to achieve in times of low inflation than in times of high inflation. While there is an arguable case for pay to be related more to performance, before management adopts such a policy there are some questions which it should consider. There is as yet little evidence of the effects of PRP on performance. Is management satisfied that performance can be accurately measured in every job so as to base pay increases on it? How much of the judgement is objective and how much is subjective? Is it possible that PRP can be divisive and is the need in many cases not to encourage group performance as well as individual performance? It also needs to be remembered that PRP can be demotivating for those who are judged not to have done well. If performance assessment for pay purposes is linked to the appraisal interview, as increasingly it seems to be, what has happened to the previously strongly held belief that the two should be separate in order that the appraisal interview can be conducted honestly and frankly, so that deficiencies could be admitted and hence the first step taken to secure improved performance? With regard to profit-sharing and employee share ownership, while they may have great potential value, unless they are to be merely a trimming on the cake, or a façade, management needs to be clear as to their purpose and their effects on employees. Objective evidence is so far limited. There are, of course, fashions in pay and PRP is the latest in a long line. In the 1990s, it is likely that team-based bonuses will be introduced for many of those who had PRP in the 1980s.

Other changes in pay systems have included simplification in pay structures, for example fewer grades through banding, usually in the cause of greater flexibility and the reduction of job demarcations. Along with the simplification of pay structures there have been doubts in some quarters about traditional job evaluation. For one thing, job descriptions can inhibit flexibility and there is a trend towards paying people for what they can do and how they do it, rather than what they do in a specific job at a specific point of time. There have also been a number of examples of integrated pay structures (that is to say, manual and white-collar) — in Midland Bank, Pilkingtons and a number of Japanese and American companies. The main reason appears to have been harmonisation in order to encourage teamwork and to acknowledge the blurring of boundaries between blue-collar and white-collar work. An added advantage relates to avoiding equal pay actions and this was certainly the major factor in the case of Midland Bank.

There have been developments in other terms and conditions of employment. In 1979, the engineering unions had just won a reduction in weekly working hours from 40 to 39 per week, and the staggered introduction of a fifth week's holiday. During the early years of the 1980s these concessions spread to many other industries. Coincidentally, at the end of the decade, the engineering unions conducted a campaign, including selective industrial action, for a further reduction in the working week, originally for a 35-hour week and then in practice for a 37-hour week. They have had a considerable degree of success, which is likely to lead eventually to similar reductions in other industries.

As far as the 1990s are concerned, given the state of the British economy and our membership of the ERM at a high exchange rate, the prospect of significant increases in real pay are limited. Moreover, it is clear from the experience of the 1980s that the government's 'free market' and monetarist policies have failed to solve Britain's wage–price spiral. It is therefore conceivable that the need for some form of more co-ordinated policy on pay may come to be acknowledged in the not-too-distant future.

The difficulties in the way of such a policy are great. Both unions and employers are presently against it, as are the Conservative and Labour Parties though to different degrees and for different reasons. Past attempts have not been outstandingly successful, although their failures have been more dwelt upon than their achievements. Moreover, in the 1990s, given the decentralisation of bargaining, it would be even more difficult to make a pay policy effective than it was in the 1960s and 1970s.

However, the Labour Party has committed itself to

> develop regular discussions between government, employers, trade unions and others about Britain's economic prospects and the competing claims on national output, taking account of the need for investment, exports and public spending. . . . A new independent statistical unit will provide detailed information on pay and prices in Britain and other EC countries. . . . The central aim of providing this information will be to develop a broad understanding of what is feasible in the light of economic realities. This will be an important element in collective bargaining and other decisions on incomes, taxation and spending. (Labour Party, 1990, pp. 10, 11).

Similarly, TUC policy, based on proposals by Edmonds and Tuffin (1990), in favour of concerted bargaining was endorsed at the 1990 Congress.

Whatever a government may proclaim, it must have an incomes policy not only because it is a large employer or quasi-employer, but above all because it is ultimately responsible to the electorate for the performance of the economy. One alternative is a 'free-for-all' (with a special agenda for the public sector), but with the government seeking to restrain pay increases by affecting demand through monetary, fiscal and exchange rate policy – in other words through high unemployment. The economic and social cost of such a policy is high and it does not necessarily work, as the experience of Britain in the 1980s shows. The other alternative is some form of concerted bargaining policy.

Public-sector pay

Increases in public-sector pay with only a few exceptions fell markedly behind those of the private sector in the 1980s. The absence of agreed guidelines for the determination of pay in the civil service, local government and the NHS leave open the possibility of the sort of pitched battles which occurred in the 1980s. However, government measures for decentralisation such as the widespread establishment of agencies in the civil service, self-governing trusts in the NHS, and the power of local authorities and schools to opt out of national agreements may make this less likely.

In all three services, changes in the 1980s reduced the scope for future conflict. In the NHS, the inclusion of the nurses and some professions ancillary to medicine in the review body procedure means that more than half of the staff now have review bodies and do not have their pay determined by collective bargaining. The decision in 1991 to have school teachers' pay determined by a review body was of major importance, although inexplicably a review body was denied to university teachers.

In local government and the NHS, the obligation to put manual services out to tender means that there is acute pressure to adjust pay and staffing to meet competition. In the civil service the new agreements provide for periodic studies of comparative pay levels to bring pay back into line with that for comparable outside jobs. Since civil service pay (apart from the grades covered by the review body) has fallen badly behind, this provision will be an important test of the comparability element in the new agreements. If the use of the comparisons fails to bring pay into line, the position will be even worse than it was before the Megaw report at the time of the 1981 strike after pay research had been unilaterally abandoned by the government.

The central questions are the same throughout the public services – how should pay relate to that of comparable work outside? What should be the relationship between pay in decentralised units which are part of a national or regional service and how should the contributions of individuals and groups be rewarded? The public services include some professional groups for whom the government is almost the only employer as well as a wide variety of occupations similar to that found in the private sector. It is their financing from public funds which makes them different. In the 1980s the government took advantage of that characteristic to hold back their pay, as had its predecessors from time to time.

It may be that what is needed in the 1990s is a comprehensive approach to all public service pay – those covered by review bodies (doctors, nurses, armed forces, *et al.*), those with formulae (police and firemen), those with an as yet partly untested degree of comparability (civil servants), all local government employees (manual and non-manual), the NHS outside the review bodies, and university and polytechnic staff. They total about 5.25 million employees.

All those listed need settled, regular and permanent access to independent pay comparisons. During the 1980s only the groups covered by the review bodies had such comparisons fully taken into account. A single pay review body solely devoted to providing such information would have to be set up by the government with terms of reference which ensured that it delivered its findings impartially to both sides or to the review bodies. The viability of such an approach would depend on governments acknowledging that reviews of comparable pay were necessary because the settlement of public service pay had to take the results into account. Until that is accepted by government as the employer or chief paymaster, there is always the likelihood that, in the absence of such data and an agreed intention to take it into account, parts of the public services will fall so badly out of line that strikes will occur or a special catching up exercise will have to be mounted. Any government intent on improving the quality of public services could not escape facing the need for some commitment to ensuring that public service pay keeps up with the pay for comparable work outside (see Brown and Rowthorn, 1990).

The actual outcome depends essentially on whether governments in the 1990s put improving the services above the holding back of levels of expenditure. So long as public service pay is left to be settled piecemeal and without a framework of agreed guidelines, as it was for most groups in the 1980s, the pitched battles may well recur. Even if such battles are avoided, the public services will continue to deteriorate as a consequence of low morale, high turnover and a failure to attract an adequate share of the best people.

Productivity and labour costs

Movements in productivity and labour costs per unit of output during the 1980s were discussed in Chapters 3 and 10. Reasons for the marked increase in productivity in manufacturing industry during much of the decade and the fall in the rate of increase in labour costs per unit in manufacturing were considered. By the end of the decade, with the recession as a result of the government's high interest policy, there was also a slowdown in the improvement of productivity and labour costs per unit. Indeed, by the first quarter of 1990 the improvement of productivity in manufacturing was down to an annual rate of 0.5 per cent and in the second half of 1990 it was negative. The increase in labour costs per unit in manufacturing, which was 3.0 per cent in the first quarter of 1989, had risen to 11.6 per cent in the last quarter of 1990. The figures are considerably worse for the whole economy, for it should be remembered that manufacturing accounts only for some 20 per cent of GDP.

The 'productivity miracle' of the 1980s appears less of a miracle at the beginning of the 1990s. Mayhew (1991, p. 14) states that:

it is generally agreed that the improved productivity performance in manufacturing was the result of a more effective use of resources rather than of a significantly greater investment in physical or human capital. The improved efficiency stems from better working practices and a more flexible use of labour.

As far as the UK's comparative position is concerned, as Brown and Walsh (1991, p. 47) state:

Britain had in mid-decade relatively low hourly labour costs. But because its average labour productivity was also relatively poor, its competitive position was weak. It might have been thought that rising labour productivity during the course of the decade would have turned the tide. But it has not. Productivity growth has continued to lag behind wage growth and during the 1980s Britain's competitive position in the world has continued to decline.

The prospects for the 1990s are therefore not good, nor are they helped by a decline of fixed investment in 1990 and a further forecast decline in 1991. While changes in organisation and working practices are important, sustained improvement in the British economy can come only from increased investment in physical and human capital.

Changes in the law

Throughout the 1980s Conservative governments have acted through legislation to reduce the power of trade unions and to make trade union leaders more accountable to their members. The philosophy behind Conservative government policy was discussed in Chapter 4 — namely a belief in free markets and hence the need to deregulate and to marginalise unions. The stream of legislation was described in Chapter 5. Suffice it to recall that in a series of Acts — the Employment Acts 1980 and 1982, the Trade Union Act, 1984, the Wages Act 1986, and the Employment Acts 1988, 1989 and 1990 — trade unions' rights to take industrial action were severely constrained; secondary action and secondary picketing were made unlawful; industrial action could not be taken without a prior individual secret ballot; unofficial strikers could be selectively dismissed; union chief officers and national executives were made subject to secret individual ballots and to obligatory re-election; the closed shop was made unlawful and unenforceable; unions, as organisations were made subject to financial penalties and their funds subject to sequestration, so that potentially they could be made ineffective and indeed bankrupt. The nature and extent of restrictive legislation has been such that the International Labour Organisation (ILO) has ruled that it *prima facie* amounts to a breach of the ILO's conventions on freedom of association, to which the UK is a signatory.

Has the legislation of the 1980s been successful in achieving the Government's objectives of weakening trade union power and making union leaders more answerable to their membership? The answer must be in the affirmative. The incidence of strikes and working days lost through strikes diminished substantially, as the strike statistics in Chapter 11 show. However, as that chapter also shows, most other leading industrial countries experienced a similar decline in strikes, without the introduction of a series of restrictive laws. The use of ballots before the taking of official industrial action has been virtually universally adopted by unions except in local flare-ups. Unions have accepted that their leading officials and national executive committees have to be elected and subject to re-election by individual secret ballots and their rule books have been altered accordingly. They had also by the end of the 1980s.

largely accepted significant restrictions on secondary action and secondary pickets, not necessarily because they agreed with such restrictions, but because earlier attempts to defy the law had proved disastrous for the unions concerned, for example the NGA in the *Messenger Newspapers* dispute, SOGAT in the Wapping dispute, the NUS in the P&O ferries dispute and the NUM in the miners strike. In each of these cases, union funds had been sequestered.

Some caveats must however be recorded to this apparent success story. There is an assumption that the law is of prime importance to the conduct of industrial relations. Our evidence from many major British companies suggests that this is not the case. While not denying that the law must be observed and that it was an important background factor, they considered that other factors were far more important to the way they conducted their industrial relations. By the end of the decade unions had found ways of mitigating the effects of some of the new restrictions. One particular and important example is the way in which ballots prior to industrial action have often been turned to the advantage of unions. A successful ballot for industrial action is a powerful bargaining factor for the union to argue for, and employers concede, an improvement on their earlier offer; also, a successful ballot legitimises the proposed action in a way that a show of hands or a decision by an executive committee cannot.

As Lewis (1991, p. 60) says:

> Formal legal rules and procedures may of course impinge significantly on the employment relationship, but their precise role and impact are likely to be affected if not determined by social attitudes, economic circumstances and the balance of industrial power. The complexity of this interaction makes it difficult to measure or even identify law as an independent factor in the conduct of industrial relations.

Moreover, the work of Brown and Wadhwani (1990), as does our own (see Chapter 11), concludes that the effect of the legal changes on the movement in strike statistics is highly questionable and that the legislation had not produced the economic effects, for example in limiting wage increases, anticipated by free-market theorists.

In considering the future of legislation it is first necessary to accept that the legal position of trade unions prior to 1980 could hardly be described as satisfactory, as a number of leading cases showed. Moreover, as a former senior trade union official argued, although legal changes cannot easily be imposed on people who do not want them, many trade unionists (not to mention non-unionists) wanted a number of the changes which have been made. 'Trade unionists' support for the legislation is the main reason why so much of it is here to stay.' It is therefore not a question of the complete repeal of the Thatcher governments' legislation, but of deciding what is important to retain, modify and add to.

From Labour Party (1990) and TUC (1990) policy statements, it is clear that much of the Conservative legislation would not be repealed by a Labour government. Thus, the provisions for the election of top union officials and national executive committees would be retained, as would ballots prior to the taking of industrial action. In addition, there is the Labour Party's decision to support the ending of the closed shop on the grounds that the European Social Charter enshrines the freedom to join or not to join a trade union, and the party is pledged to support the Social Charter in its entirety. Restrictions on unlimited secondary action and unlimited secondary picketing would also be retained, although modified in some degree, for example to deal with employers who have placed many of their activities in the hands of a series of separate companies in order to protect them from otherwise lawful industrial action. Where industrial action is lawful, individual employees would have the right, as in other European countries, not to be dismissed for that action. Also, the courts would no longer be allowed to issue *ex parte* injunctions to an employer without the union being able to put its case. A new rule is further proposed to ensure that where a court grants an interlocutory injunction then, at the option of either party, a hearing on the full merits of the case would have to follow immediately. Finally, although unions would still be liable for damages, legislation will prevent the total sequestration of a union's income and assets in a way which paralyses the union in all its lawful business.

As well as retaining much of the 1980s legislation, the Labour Party is pledged to expand individual rights. Indeed, the Labour Party's starting point is the vulnerability of the individual employee in relation to the employer, which continues to be the fundamental justification for trade unionism.

Lewis (1991) argues that there are three main approaches to labour law. The first is a return to 'collective *laissez-faire*', where unions would have maximum autonomy within a non-interventionist legal framework. This he firmly rules out because it fails adequately to recognise that the state's responsibility for tackling economic problems includes establishing a structure of labour law that strikes a balance between the interests of the parties and the public interest in industrial peace and an efficient economy. The second is the Conservative Party's approach based on 'free-market' beliefs which we have discussed at length in Chapter 4. The third is the Labour Party's approach, i.e. a 'reformist' strategy which endorses the legitimacy of trade unionism but aims to ensure that the power of unions (and also of employers) is exercised responsibly. He further argues that Labour's approach goes with the grain of European social policy and is in marked contrast with the free market approach of the Conservatives.

With regard to the future, regardless of which political party is in power, there can be no doubt that the law will have an important part to play in regulating industrial relations. This is clear, as has already been stated, from the Labour Party's new policy and from the decisions of the 1990 TUC congress. As a leading TUC official told us, by the time of *In Place of Strife* (1969) and the

Industrial Relations Act 1971, the voluntarist consensus had gone. It had shown itself to be incapable of providing the controlling framework which was necessary. So the law had to become the new source of rules. We are in for a legalistic system. He added that in the future regardless of whether we have a Conservative or Labour government, as a result of our membership of the European Community, we shall move to more individual and collective rights prescribed by law. Thus, for example, rights to recognition and to information and the establishment of representation on works councils are likely to be regulated by law. The 1990 TUC congress had been momentous in that it had crossed the Rubicon by accepting the move away from the old, traditional, voluntarist system. This is the most likely direction of development in the 1990s. Below some of the key legal and procedural matters are considered in more detail.

Recognition

The Labour Party and the TUC are committed to the statutory recognition of unions. The two main reasons are, first, a willingness to depend on the law, including the acceptance of the main elements of the 1980s legislation, a statutory minimum wage and an extension of individual rights, and second, the acceptance of the European Social Charter.

Legal provisions for recognition are seen as one rung in a hierarchy of legal rights to do with union membership and the operation of unions. The hierarchy has the following rungs – the rights of the citizen to join, not to be dismissed for joining or being active, to be represented, to have terms and conditions negotiated with the employer and to have a procedure for resolving disputes. The case for statutory recognition is that if there is a right to join it has to be made effective by the recognition of the union by the employer.

The voluntary method will never get union recognition for large numbers of employees, especially those in small establishments and in weak labour market positions so that those most in need of union protection are least likely to get it until there is legal backing. Although there are few disputes about recognition there ought to be a clear and settled method for dealing with claims for recognition.

The unions which want it are mainly in the service trades where small establishments predominate, recruitment from cold is very difficult when there is little prospect of success, and employer resistance is monolithic. However, there are large and powerful unions, mainly in the public sector, who would get nothing positive out of it and are impressed by the disadvantages. If there are legal rules about recognition there would have to be rules about derecognition and those would impinge on unions which would not be gaining from the recognition procedure. The form of implementation will therefore be important.

In the 1980s recognition was secured on some greenfield sites by prior agreement between employer and union before there were any employees. A statutory procedure would work against that approach because the employees would have both a choice of whether or not to have a union, and which union.

The Bridlington Agreement may creak but it is the TUC's instrument of control. The law would largely replace it and that would weaken the TUC in relation to its member unions. Unions would be divided about whether that were a good thing or not.

With regard to employer attitudes, the CBI says it would oppose such legislation. However, it might become reconciled to it as the unions have to parts of the 1980s legislation. But the employers are less in favour of a comprehensive legal framework connected with the Social Charter than are the unions. Employers argue that they cannot be forced to negotiate 'in good faith', to use the US term. If managers choose to they can prevent the legal rights having substance. However, under the defunct ss. 11–16 of the EPA 1975 a refusal to recognise at the end of the procedure meant the union could resort to unilateral arbitration of matters of dispute. That is the position in Canada today, while in the USA there is a legal obligation on employers to bargain 'in good faith'. Legal recognition is designed to shift the balance of power towards the unions and some argue that it will stimulate greater active hostility to unions by employers in order to compensate. Derecognition would become a much more active subject. This mirror image of the provisions for recognition would be successfully demanded by employers and they might well be used.

The principle of a statutory recognition procedure is deceptively simple. However, in practice, implementation would be complicated as the experience of ACAS in dealing with section 11 of the Employment Protection Act 1975 cases showed. It could possibly result in either a procedure which collapsed under its own weight or one which failed to make much difference. To be effective, the law should only set a framework of guidelines with the details left to a tripartite Commission with its own staff. The suitability of ACAS or some new body would have to be considered. The Commission should have the establishment or support of effective collective bargaining as its yardstick: there should not be a set proportion of votes like 50 per cent plus or minus one for recognition and derecognition.

The employer's preference of union and the unions' choice of beauty contest candidates should be taken into account as well as the wishes of the employees. The conduct of ballots and collection of evidence about the parties should be carried out by the Commission's independent staff, that is to say, the Commission's knowledge should not be confined to what the parties choose to tell it. A minimum of matters should be left to the courts. There should be the minimum of opportunity for procrastination and legal technicalities on both sides. The Canadian procedure for automatic arbitration should be built in and come into force sooner rather than later. To conclude, while a mechanism for statutory recognition is needed, the proposal is only likely to be successful if the views of employers and unions, as well as those of employees, can be taken into account in each case. Cases where employers are intransigent or the union ,ineffective should be dealt with speedily and on a practical basis.

The closed shop

By stages the law was changed to making the closed shop illegal. Under the 1980 Act new closed shops needed 80 per cent support in a ballot, and under the 1982 Act existing closed shops needed an 85 per cent majority every 5 years. The 1988 Act made industrial action to enforce a closed shop unlawful, and the 1990 Act made pre-entry closed shops unlawful. In practice few ballots were held. According to the DE, the coverage of closed shops halved from 5.2 million to 2.65 million between 1978 and 1988 when it was said to be approximately half and half pre-entry and post-entry (*Removing Barriers to Employment*, 1989). The estimate of such a large number in pre-entry closed shops, however, is highly dubious and flies in the face of all previous knowledge.

The decline in coverage had a number of origins mostly similar to those connected with the general decline of union membership. Places of work where the closed-shop was in operation have fallen in number as steel, coal and manufacturing have contracted and the number of large establishments has fallen. Technological change has broken down old skills and new establish-ments are set up away from old centres of employment. In the public sector, the government has expected managers to end closed-shop agreements, for example in the Post Office and on the railways.

There have not been claims that the law on the closed shop has itself caused losses of trade union membership or that it has weakened the authority of collective agreements. It is another aspect of the legal changes which have been absorbed into the negotiators' strategies. The Labour Party's decision not to repeal this part of the legislation is in line with practical experience and its decision to support the Social Charter in its entirety.

The significance of the legislation for the future is not what the negotiators' acquiescence in it might seem. The interviews showed remarkable agreement between managers and trade union officials who previously had closed shop agreements about what has happened. Behaviour has not changed. Employers accept that the unions are strong enough to ensure that virtually all new recruits join and existing members do not leave and the unions believe that if a few refuse to join or cease to be members (as was often the case in closed shops) then managers will discourage such behaviour. Both sides know that in the absence of an agreement it is the informal methods used by union representatives and junior managers which will be the real determinants of how individuals behave. They are not going to be drawn into disputes because a few recruits refuse to join the union. It is because there has been no transformation of the position as closed-shop agreements were 'put on the shelf' after the 1982 Act that explains the relaxed attitude of both sides.

It always was the case that many managers preferred all employees to be in the union. The check-off ensures that they know who are the non-members. Because the unions know from experience that many managers will not use the legislation to prevent them keeping very high levels of membership, they do not feel threatened by it. To the extent that the closed shop was regarded as making union membership compulsory, its formal end improves the unions' collective reputation and there are some trade union leaders who positively welcome its abolition. But informal methods will be almost as effective, though they will be less open and perhaps more subject to underhand pressure. Asked about attitudes to a non-unionist entering what had been a formal closed shop, a researcher was told that he 'might perhaps be "made uncomfortable"' (Metcalf, 1991a, p. 176). The end of the formal closed shop does not mean that new employees will feel no pressure to join unions or that existing members will experience no penalties if they leave.

The legislation has put an end to agreements enforcing the closed shop. In practice the 1980s have shown that in future recruits will still be expected to join unions and existing members to remain. The compulsion has only been nibbled at and those, including many managers, who were opposed to making the closed shop unenforceable or unlawful on the grounds that it would not change behaviour have so far been proved right in the main. The informal has taken over from the formal and that will continue to be the case in many places of work where there was a closed shop agreement before 1979.

The newspaper industry used the pre-entry closed shop extensively and it is exceptional in that the Wapping dispute enabled News International to put an end to the practices associated with it and that has been carried over into other newspapers. But in this respect, as in many others, the newspaper industry has been atypical.

The check-off

The check-off bears the hallmark of the 1980s. The unions have come to depend extensively on employers to collect their members' subscriptions. One respondent expressed the opinion that without the check-off the TUC unions' membership would be halved. It gives unions some security at a time when the employer is in the stronger position. Once a member has signed the check-off it takes a deliberate decision to leave the union to end it; if the member does nothing, the subscription goes on being deducted from his pay like his

National Insurance contribution. The unions are plugged into the administration of the pay-packet and receive regular and steady income via the employers. The employers like it because it makes the unions dependent on them. They know who is in the union and who is not. They no longer have shop stewards regularly asking members to pay up and inquiring what grievances they have, a way of doing it which unions used to believe was essential to keeping in touch with the members.

There is a great inertia in the check-off. It is certainly extremely popular with unions and most employers are happy with it. The longer it is in operation the greater the unions' dependence on it because an alternative becomes more and more difficult to organise. There will soon not be many union activists where the check-off operates who remember how subscriptions used to be collected in the workplace or at the branch meeting. The alternative of union members almost universally paying their subscriptions by direct debit lies some long way in the future.

The employers know that they can exert pressure by threatening to end the check-off, especially if industrial action is contemplated, on the grounds that it would be illogical for them to collect money which could be used to pay strike benefit. The longer the check-off operates and the more extensive its use, the greater is the possibility that it will act as a restraint on unions' actions.

The selective strikes in the engineering industry for a shorter working week in 1989 and 1990 were from the unions' viewpoint one of the most sustained disputes of the 1980s. The AEU ran a highly successful special levy to pay for strike benefit. The significant fact was that the employers affected considered ending the check-off, as was to be expected, but decided not to do so on the grounds that it would sour future relations with the unions. This was evidence that the threat to end the check-off if strikes are called is not always to be believed and that unions can still raise money by asking members to put their hands in their pockets where their subscriptions are deducted from their pay-packets.

The popularity of the check-off operates strongly against certain proposals for a long-term reform of the place of the individual member in the union. John Edmonds, the leader of the GMB, proposes that membership should transcend job mobility and that is incompatible with the check-off. His proposal is that the individual would join and would pay his subscription by direct debit on his bank account, and that the union would protect and advise him wherever he worked and in all circumstances. But the check-off is limited to the member's current employer. Payment of the subscription stops when the member leaves the job and is usually only resumed in another job where there is a check-off and perhaps in another union. The idea of long-term membership was, of course, universal 20 years ago. Now the check-off stands in the way of restoring it.

Another danger in the future will be interference with the check-off by a government seeking to weaken the unions directly, precisely because it is so widely used. The suggestion that by law the check-off should require annual renewal by every individual has been proposed by ministers, only to be strongly resisted by employers as well as unions. It is generally agreed among employers and unions that only political motivation would lead to interference with the check-off. Yet, ironically, only such interference is likely to reduce unions' dependence on it and cause them to consider alternatives. Since both sides want to keep it, it is likely to remain.

Strikes

The 1980s saw a marked decline in strikes except for small, short ones. There was a similar decline in other countries. In the UK, strikes in the private sector, which had four-fifths of the employees, were infrequent, and with a few exceptions were local and short. However, large strikes occurred in the public sector over pay, contraction and reorganisation. More than half the days lost in the decade were in five public-sector strikes.

The reasons for this marked difference were that in the private sector the initiative had passed to managers; there were increased real earnings; there was individualisation; and the unions took a cooperative stance. In the public sector, the set-piece strikes were the result of government challenges to union positions and the unions lost or had the worst of it. The law is not believed by those interviewed to have been of much influence, yet the extensive legal changes affecting strikes are for the most part accepted as virtually permanent. The explanation is that the legal changes have been absorbed into the methods and procedures of the negotiating parties. The best example of this is strike ballots, where unions have increasingly called for these ballots (and over-whelmingly won them), not with the intention of calling a strike, but as a part of their bargaining tactics, to secure a higher offer from employers.

When we look to the future, whether the low level of strike activity in the private sector continues into the 1990s depends more than anything on the general state of industrial relations − strikes are not independent occurrences. When unemployment fell to low levels in the south in 1987–89, there was no increase in strike activity and so it does not follow that strikes would come back if the level of unemployment became low. But higher levels of unemployment in the 1990s than in the late 1980s would make it even more certain that there continued to be few strikes.

One reservation to these generalisations relates to the 1990 Act on unofficial strikes, of the working of which there is so far little experience. The unions are bound to want it repealed, but if it continues in force it could give rise to some nasty disputes. If an employer sacks leaders of an unofficial dispute which the union has repudiated there can be no official action to secure their reinstatement without loss of immunity. It would be seen as victimisation of union activists, an issue on which unions are always sensitive even if the original conduct of the shop stewards or members is difficult to defend. The union might feel that it had to risk its very existence rather than accept such behaviour by an employer. If it did it would have to throw everything into the fight and there would be the possibility of another Wapping and dependence on the police. If the union kept out of it, the strikers might hold out for the reinstatement of their leaders and they would look for unofficial support from wherever they could get it. The employer could sack more of them. Again, it looks like a recipe for violent trouble. Most employers would steer clear of these possibilities but it only needs one intransigent employer to take advantage of the 1990 Act to precipitate a battle into which others get drawn.

So long as the law is framed as if it has the ability to stop small local strikes by making unions repudiate them, which is unlikely to bring them to an end, and by allowing employers to sack their leaders with impunity from the unfair dismissal procedure and official union action, there is a danger that the legal traces will be kicked over. That might put the whole of the legal framework on strikes back into the melting pot just when both sides are inclined to accept most of it.

The public sector is likely to continue to be the possible site of pitched-battle strikes so long as there are no agreed guidelines forming the basis for the settlement of pay and changes in working practices. Some of the big strikes of the 1980s could never be repeated in the same form because the industries are privatised (steel) or because they are so much smaller and different (coal). What happens in the public service sector in future depends mostly on what is done about pay determination in three main areas — the civil service, local government and the NHS. In all three, measures of decentralisation and fragmentation are taking place which may well reduce the likelihood of major national strikes, but could lead to leapfrogging and disorientation.

The agenda for collective bargaining

In the 1980s the trade union agenda for collective bargaining did not change greatly. The unions pursued their traditional aims of higher pay and improved terms and conditions. On pay we have seen that significant increases in real pay were achieved, but we have also argued that this was largely management's doing. Ingram (1991a, p. 103) in his analysis of manufacturing settlements in the CBI data bank, shows that in the years between 1979 and 1989 the threat of industrial action as an upward pressure on settlements only occurred in 2–3 per cent of cases. He further shows that in every year bar one, the average settlement percentage increase for non-bargainers was higher than that for bargainers.

As has been shown, during the 1980s there was a very substantial widening of differentials, particularly those of top and senior management and those between white-collar and manual workers: these were certainly management led. On hours and holidays, the only significant breakthrough, despite the TUC's objective of a 35-hour week, was the result of the engineering strike in 1979 and the eventual settlement which led to the 39-hour week for manual workers and the phased introduction of 5 weeks' holiday. These union gains spread to other industries in the early 1980s. No other major changes occurred during the rest of the decade until the end of the 1980s when there was another breakthrough by the engineering unions which achieved the introduction of the 37-hour week in most large federated engineering companies. Again, this is likely to spread to other industries in the early 1990s. These gains apart, the unions were essentially on the defensive in the 1980s and were on the receiving end of events and management initiatives. On reductions in manpower, unions could do no more than try to get the best redundancy terms possible. On the introduction of technological change, TUC and individual union attempts to attain technological agreements were a resounding failure. In a number of individual companies there were moves towards harmonisation of the terms and conditions of manual and white-collar workers, but these were mainly on the initiative of management. Incoming Japanese and American companies usually had harmonisation as a matter of company policy.

The collective bargaining agenda was thus firmly set by management. This agenda for much of the period included, first, the reduction in the size of the labour force, changes in working methods and increased efficiency and flexibility; and, second, revised pay structures, for example fewer grades and more integrated structures, and revised payment systems, in particular the spread of performance related pay. Above all, management set the agenda through the introduction of 'something for something' bargaining. Ingram (1991b, p. 4), again using the CBI data bank, found that in the 1980s the working practices of three-quarters of manufacturing employees covered by agreements between unions and employers were altered during the 1980s. More than half of all bargaining groups experienced more than one wage settlement involving changes in working practices, while nearly a third of annual wage settlements throughout the decade included changes in working practices.

One of the few innovations in the agenda in the 1980s was the introduction of the Education and Development Assistance Programme (EDAP) in an agreement at the Ford Motor Company in 1988. It instituted an after-work education programme for employees unrelated to the company's training schemes, paid for by the company. Each plant had a joint committee with a budget of £45 per employee per annum from which employees could draw class fees up to £200. It organised the programme of classes in accordance with

the wishes expressed by employees. The take-up has exceeded the expectations of both sides by far and was above 50 per cent in most plants in 1990.
Languages are the most popular courses (Mortimer, 1990).

The scheme has a crucial position in management's strategy for enlisting
employee commitment on the basis of the long-term development of
individuals. The unions see it as a major development because it provides
their members with a popular service in a convenient form. It fits in with the
way the tide is running because it has an appeal to individuals and it develops
learning in ways which have spin-offs for the company but which are driven by
individual preferences. It genuinely extends people's opportunities, since most
have had no formal education since leaving school.

Similar schemes, though with less union involvement, have been running for
several years at Rover and Jaguar plants, also with high rates of participation.

In the future it is to be expected that these schemes will spread, although
they are so far slow to do so. It may be that they are specially relevant to
employers with large plants which make possible the comprehensive class
programme with plenty of choice and facilities for meeting after work. It may
also be the case that anonymous employees in a large establishment are
particularly appreciative of these opportunities.

These developments reinforce the other evidence that unions need to
develop the bargaining agenda in ways which have an appeal to individuals
and that employers have an interest in employees improving their capacities by
pursuing formal courses. Training, with its associated benefits for skill
acquisition and promotability, is the main candidate for addition to the
bargaining agenda. It is usually seen as an exclusively management matter.
EDAP shows that there is an appetite which could be partly diverted towards
vocational training. It amounts to career development for the individual and
the improved performance of the internal labour market as the source of supply
of skilled workers for the employer. What needs to be agreed between the two
sides are training opportunities supported by counselling and arrangements for
linking the training of employees to the labour needs of the firm. Such
developments would probably be most suited to large establishments and
equivalent arrangements for middle-sized firms should be explored.

There is some possibility of employers going ahead on their own. This
indicates that the unions should be laying claim to joint action on the grounds
that the individual's needs will often be at odds with the employer's short-term
requirements. Unless the union is in a position to bargain for what the
individuals want, the employer is likely to fail to do other than offer only
what is in the company's immediate or preconceived interest. Firms should
recognise that what the employees want can be as important an ingredient as
what the firm wants.

Following the same route, the agenda for negotiations could be extended in
other ways which put a high value on what individuals prefer. One group of
possibilities is wider choice of the mix of work and leisure, with time off being

taken in more varied forms to match changing family circumstances, for example paternity leave, and individual preferences. It may be that an annual individual contract for a specified number of hours, without a distinction between full- and part-time would provide the right framework. The annual contract could be for more hours at some periods of family life, and fewer at others. The hours could be evenly or unevenly spread throughout the year, since holidays would no longer be fixed amounts. This flexibility would give individuals more control over their personal lives and at the same time improve the supply of labour to the employer. Towards the end of the 1980s, partly as a result of union initiative, but mainly because of fears of labour shortage as a result of the publicity given to the changes in demographic trends, some employers started to provide crèche facilities and a few explored the giving of extended leave for mothers of young children and school-term employment contracts of a kind which have long existed in local government.

The European Community

Two aspects of the EC are especially relevant to British industrial relations. The first is the economic effects of 1992 and the second is EC law, the Social Charter and its Action Programme.

On the economic effects, 1992 will mean the removal of the remaining barriers to the free flow of goods and services, in other words more competitive product markets. It will also mean the removal of remaining restrictions on the movement of labour and hence freer and more competitive labour markets. The first effect will be of major importance, which combined with the free movement of capital and a relatively fixed exchange rate through the ERM, will significantly affect the economic environment in which industrial relations takes place. On the other hand it should not be exaggerated, for Britain has already faced for many years highly competitive product markets with a relatively open economy. By contrast, the effects of the free movement of labour are likely to develop slowly. The social barriers to the mobility of labour even within Britain are well known and these barriers will be all the greater across national boundaries. This is not to say that in certain parts of the labour market there will not be greater movement and competitiveness, but it will be gradual.

The biggest potential effect of 1992 may well be Britain's membership of the ERM and the consequences of a relatively fixed exchange rate and indeed one which many commentators have argued is too high. It is too early to say what constraints this will impose in practice on wage bargaining, but to judge by the experience of other member countries, for example France and Italy, they may well be considerable.

As to the legal effects of the EC, to date they have not had a major effect on British industrial relations, except in a few selective areas. The most important by far have been the Directives on Equal Pay (1975) and Equal Treatment (1976). Of significance, but relatively less important, have been the Directives on Collective Redundancies (1975) and Employee Rights on Transfers of Businesses (1977). However, looking to the future, the effects are likely to be very significant indeed as a result of the adoption of the Social Charter by the Strasbourg Summit in 1989, with only the UK in dissent, and the commencement of the Social Action Programme to put the principles of the Charter into effect. The Action Programme will make various individual rights a matter for Community laws. Proposals put forward in 1990 include working time, atypical contracts, health and safety and information, consultation and participation.

Conclusion

The main feature of industrial relations in the 1980s was that managers were firmly in charge. This happened because of the economic necessity to increase productivity and efficiency under pressure from domestic and above all international competition. It also happened because the unions were weakened and that occurred mainly because of the periods of extensive redundancies and high levels of unemployment in most years. Management sought greater cost effectiveness through the use of new technology, through increased labour flexibility — both numerical and functional — and through changing reward systems and changing contracts of employment.

But things did not turn out entirely as expected in two main ways. In the private sector, where the redundancies and falling union membership were mainly concentrated, management's accession of power was at its most pronounced but it was not used to achieve what might have been expected. As the initiative passed to managers most of them did not seek to end collective bargaining by derecognising unions or by taking deliberate action to weaken them further. Unions found it difficult to gain further recognition and their role was cut back in numerous ways but there was no outright, concerted policy of scrapping negotiations with unions. Indeed, many employers sustained unions and protected them against further falls in membership, for example by extending the check-off and continuing with practices associated with the closed shop.

Nor did managers make reductions in earnings an objective in a period of union weakness. In many firms managers were highly successful at proposing and securing improvements in labour utilisation through negotiations; labour flexibility was a successful policy. But that was often accompanied by increases in pay over the decade which left many firms with unit labour costs rising at rates still out of line with those of foreign competitors.

There are two contrasting interpretations of these events. The first is that employers allowed the short-term to dominate their thinking and as a result they missed an opportunity to make a greater long-term improvement in their competitive position. On that view they should have used the increases in productivity mainly to reduce unit labour costs by settling for lower increases in pay. As it was, weaker trade unions found their members' real incomes rising faster than in the 1970s when they had been stronger. The productivity improvement was in part used to increase dividends and managerial pay and in part distributed among the remaining workers. Other firms often followed such pay increases without achieving the same productivity gains.

The government must have felt that private employers were letting it down by offering such large pay increases when the unions were not capable of extracting them. But the expression of that criticism was muted because ministers were committed to believing that managers were the best judges of their firms' interests. So because the government believed in the paramountcy of free markets, it could not tell employers that they were shooting themselves in the foot and that there were benefits to be gained by all of them if they put external gains above internal ones and co-operated in restraining the rate at which pay increased.

The other interpretation is that the short-term views of managers fitted in with long-term internal labour market considerations. If managers in large establishments and companies wanted to make changes they looked at ways of doing so within the existing arrangements and if those could produce the goods, they used them. Because managers found that the unions did not stand in their way they saw no reason for getting rid of them. Indeed, continuity with the past and the knowledge that they had to continue to live with them in the future provided an acceptable basis for getting the flexibility they wanted using the existing institutional framework. Once this approach was found to work, it was reinforced by the desire to hold together the labour force remaining after redundancies and ensuring their cooperation by avoiding confrontations over pay. The manager who wanted to pay up to make sure he avoided a confrontation, even if he knew he could win, had a powerful argument. The unions' acquiescence received its reward because resistance by them would be costly to the employer, even if he was certain he would prevail in the end. That approach has meant that there has not been a fracture in the system of collective bargaining in the private sector. It may be that an opportunity to reduce unit labour costs was missed but the achievement of labour flexibility on management's initiative and terms has been peacefully negotiated.

The second thing which did not turn out as expected concerns the public sector. Although the government used its power to defeat the unions in strikes yet the unions are still relatively strong and the public employers have to deal with them or find ways round them. Consider three groups. The civil service unions were defeated in the strikes over pay in 1981 and GCHQ in 1984 but following the lead given in the Megaw report, agreements covering all civil servants were made in 1987 and 1988 which depended heavily on comparability to which the government had previously been opposed. In the NHS after the 1982 dispute, where again the unions were defeated, nurses' pay determination was passed to a review body so that now over half of the staff of the NHS have their pay determined by the findings of review bodies. The teachers took prolonged industrial action in 1985 and 1986 only to have their negotiating machinery abolished yet they too were given a review body in 1991.

Of course, a series of other changes, like the contracting out of services, cash limits, local management of schools and restructuring of the NHS, have all tended to reduce the ability of unions to protect the interests of their members. But generally the unions have not been gravely weakened, hard as the government has tried to push them aside. Union membership continues to be high in the public service. The negotiating machinery is still there and is relied upon by managers.

Continuity is the main factor which has been at work. Despite the government's victories over the unions in strikes the basic nature of the public services has not changed. The pay of their staff has to be settled according to some principle and that of comparability cannot be avoided. The government is responsible for the services to the electorate in the end. Unlike commercial employers, it cannot threaten to close down schools or hospitals on an extensive scale and declare the staff redundant unless the unions reach agreement. The services have to be kept going and the voters can choose a government according to how well the services perform. In that sense the government won pyrrhic victories in strikes. Having won, the government still had to find a basis for managing and paying the staff and there has been a partial return to comparability.

There were many exceptions to these generalisations but two were notable. In the private sector two companies in newspaper printing — the Messenger Newspaper Group and News International — chose to take on the unions and they beat them. From having closed shops in the News International papers the NGA and SOGAT ceased even to be recognised. The individual employers — Eddie Shah and Rupert Murdoch — were both outsiders compared with most corporate managers because they had a big enough personal stake in the firms to make the key decisions and they wanted to get their hands on the gains which would flow from defeating the unions. The law helped them considerably; as did the police, so the government's action and support contributed to the demise of the unions in those newspapers. What was left unsaid was that what happened there could have been made to happen elsewhere if other employers had taken a similar line. Of course, newspaper printing was waiting for a technological revolution to take place and so the prospective gains were large. Moreover, the unions had had it their own way for a long time. It was said by many, including some trade unionists, that the newspaper unions had it coming to them. But newspaper printing did not set a precedent.

In the public sector the exception was coal. The 1984–5 strike not only broke the power of the NUM but it was the prelude to the dismantling of the industry. The previous consensus had been that coal was essential; the government's response to the strike and its aftermath was based on the belief that the country could manage without it. Both sides were intransigent. The government knew that if it defeated the miners it could defeat any other group. The miners believed that they had brought down the previous Conservative government and they failed to read the signs that the foundation of their conviction that they were invincible had crumbled. They so managed the strike that their ranks were divided and some worked while others were on strike. A senior trade unionist said that they too had it coming to them.

So these exceptions support the generalisations. Had the unions in the private sector chosen to be less quiescent they would probably have been completely defeated like the newspaper printers. In the public sector by learning to live with defeat rather than going down fighting like the miners the unions eventually found the government moving in their direction.

But what of the influence of the legislation, the government's chosen way of taming the trade union tiger? Here too matters turned out differently from what was expected. The legal changes were extensive. Though they were always opposed by the unions and many employers were sceptical about their efficacy, they are now, for the most part, accepted as a permanent part of the legal framework of industrial relations. This volte-face occurred for two main reasons. On the union side the changes, including the abolition of the closed shop, were absorbed into their operations. On the employers' side their use of the law was defensive. They have hardly ever used it to prevent unions taking action, although there have been many occasions when they could have done so successfully, most notably in the miners' strike when the government itself prevented the NCB and other public employers from using the law against the NUM. The employers know that the law is now tipped in their favour but they are disinclined to use it. So although the law is now vastly different from what it was in 1979 its direct effect on industrial relations behaviour has been relatively small. However, its potential importance in the background should not be underestimated.

The government reacted to these developments by giving individuals the power to take proceedings against unions, as they did in the miners' strike, and a Commissioner was appointed with funds to pay for their court actions. But it was a forlorn hope that individuals would make good the employers' reluctance to take legal proceedings. For the most part aggrieved union members look for other opportunities to earn their living rather than spend their time caught up in the tentacles of the law.

On the basis of these conclusions about the 1980s, what is likely to happen in the 1990s? Abrupt changes in industrial relations do not occur. The same underlying relationships are likely to continue but that does not mean that there will not be further changes.

Take the law. In the 1990s the law may well be more important than it was in the 1980s. However governments respond to the EC Social Charter, its effect is going to be transmitted through the law. The TUC and the Labour Party are committed to major extensions of the law in industrial relations on protecting and improving individual rights, on recognition and on a national legal minimum wage, and they would use the Social Charter to secure legislation on the right to belong to a union and be represented by it, and on greater participation and disclosure of information. Indeed, the unions have responded to the experience of the 1980s by coming down in favour of the law as a substitute for bargaining power. As one trade union leader put it, 'the union's job will be to see that members get their legal rights from employers.'

Managers will continue to hold the initiative. But one issue unresolved in the 1980s will have to be grappled with in the 1990s. In the 1980s the failure of employers to use their initiative to bring unit labour costs into line with those of foreign competitors was compensated for by creeping devaluation. Entry to the ERM has closed that escape route for our European trade and the open market from 1992 will add to the difficulty. Employers in the 1980s preferred redundancies and closures to effective control of the relationship between pay and productivity, and that was politically acceptable at the time. In the 1990s the likely level of unemployment, even in periods of expansion, may well be politically unacceptable. Employers may find that the alternative route — some organised restraint of the rate of pay increases — becomes a political imperative.

In the public sector there are two somewhat contradictory trends. One is more moves towards formalised, broad comparability as the principle under-lying pay determination. Such developments could be accommodated in a comprehensive attempt to regulate the broad movements of pay. The other direction is towards more decentralisation and fragmentation as for example in schools, NHS trusts and civil service agencies.

The unions' role in the 1990s is uncertain. In the 1980s they were embattled, but a new generation of leaders has replaced the 'barons' of the 1970s and they have a more realistic appreciation of the unions' position. The characteristics of the trade unions are different from what they were. Some of the biggest trade unions are either in the public services or have large sections of membership there. The unions which declined most catered for manual workers in basic industries. The unions which have increased in size or held their ground were for white-collar workers, mainly in the public services.

There are two key questions. Can the unions break out of their strongholds and organise the unorganised? Some counsel concentrating on what they know and mopping up pockets of unorganised employees in organised trades and only expanding into adjacent sectors. This is the approach which fits in with the traditions of British trade unions and employers would not resist it. But in the 1990s it would mean stagnation because the labour forces in many strongholds are going to continue to decline and few will expand.

A policy more in tune with the times is to attempt to break out into the unorganised areas in the private service sector. If that were attempted the new union members would have to be treated more like consumers who judge a product by its quality and price. The difficulties would be considerable. British trade unions are not used to recruiting members by the same methods as the Automobile Association. So there has to be a major change in the attitude towards members. Greater dependence on the law would help; consumers are used to having legal protection, and a union which ensured that employers delivered it would be understood. But employers would be likely to resist. They would take a stand against extending recognition and if there were a legal requirement to concede it they would insist on a legal right to derecognise anywhere which they might actively pursue. Many of the workers whom trade unions would have in their sights would never be easy to organise because they are employed part-time and work in small enterprises, and the turnover would be high. But this is the direction in which unions must go if they are to achieve a position which entitles them to be regarded as representing more than a minority of employees, mainly in the public services.

The second question is, can unions make the agenda of collective bargaining more relevant to their members' aspirations? Members have interests at work which go beyond standard pay and conditions. The focus for the future is likely to be the potential of the individual. In the field of pay, if the employers offer individuals performance related pay, unions will need to look after the individuals' interests. Individuals want careers supported by training and the planning of their progress. Some will do better than others. The unions should see that all their members have their aspirations catered for. That means extending the agenda of bargaining to cover new subjects. This emphasis on the individual works against the old notion of solidarity and is another aspect of consumerism in trade unions.

The 1980s were a period of extensive legal change in industrial relations which the parties have been at pains to claim did not break the continuity in institutions and basic attitudes. By contrast, in the 1990s the legal changes may be even more significant and the changes in behaviour and in the arrangements for representation and bargaining more extensive.

General elections and governments, 1945–91

General election	Government	Prime Minister	Government overall majority in the House of Commons
1945	Labour	C. Attlee	146
1950	Labour	C. Attlee	5
1951	Conservative	W. Churchill	17
		A. Eden (April 1955)	
1955	Conservative	A. Eden	60
		H. Macmillan (January 1957)	
1959	Conservative	H. Macmillan	100
		A. Douglas-Home (October 1963)	
1964	Labour	H. Wilson	4
1966	Labour	H. Wilson	96
1970	Conservative	E. Heath	30
1974 (February)	Labour	H. Wilson	−33
1974 (October)	Labour	H. Wilson	3
		J. Callaghan (April 1976)	
1979	Conservative	M. Thatcher	43
1983	Conservative	M. Thatcher	144
1987	Conservative	M. Thatcher	100
		J. Major (November 1990)	

References*

* Books, articles and official papers to which reference is made.

ACAS (1980a) *Industrial Relations Handbook* (London: HMSO).
ACAS (1980b) *Annual Report 1979* (London: HMSO).
ACAS (1987) *Annual Report 1986* (London: HMSO).
ACAS (1991) *Annual Report 1990* (London: HMSO).
Adeney, M. and Lloyd, J. (1986) *The Miners' Strike 1984–5: Loss Without Limit* (London: Routledge & Kegan Paul).
Ahlstrand, B. W. (1990) *The Quest for Productivity: A Case Study of Fawley after Flanders* (Cambridge: Cambridge University Press).
Atkinson, J. (1984) 'Manpower Strategies for the Flexible Firm', *Personnel Management*, August.
Atkinson, J. and Meager, N. (1986) 'Is Flexibility Just a Flash in the Pan?', *Personnel Management*, September.
The Attack on Inflation (1975) Cmd 6151 (London: HMSO).
The Attack on Inflation: The Second Year (1976) Cmd 6507 (London: HMSO).
The Attack on Inflation After 31 July 1977 (1977) Cmd 6882 (London: HMSO).
The Attack on Inflation After 31 July 1978 (1978) Cmd 7293 (London: HMSO).
British Journal of Industrial Relations (1968) *The Royal Commission on Trade Unions and Employers' Associations 1965–68*, Vol. VI, No. 3, November.
Bailey, R. and Kelly, J. (1990) 'An Index Measure of British Trade Union Density', *British Journal of Industrial Relations*, Vol. 28, No. 2.
Bailey, R. and Trinder, C. (1989) *Public Service Pay Over Two Decades* (London: Public Service Foundation).
Bain, G. (1971) 'Management and White Collar Unionism', in Kessler, S. and Weekes, B. (eds), *Conflict at Work* (London: BBC Publications).
Bassett, P. (1986) *Strike Free* (London: Macmillan).
Batstone, E., Ferner, A. and Terry, M. (1983) *Unions on the Board: An Experiment in Industrial Democracy* (Oxford: Blackwell).
Batstone, E. (1984) *Working Order: Workplace Industrial Relations over Two Decades* (Oxford: Blackwell).
Beaumont, P. B. (1987) *The Decline of Trade Union Organisation* (London: Croom Helm).

Blackwell, R. and Lloyd, P. (1989) 'New Managerialism in the Civil Service: industrial relations under the Thatcher Administrations 1979–86', in Mailly, R., Dimmock, S. J. and Sethi, A. S. (eds), *Industrial Relations in the Public Services* (London: Routledge).

Brewster, C. and Connock, S. (1985) *Industrial Relations: Cost Effective Strategies* (London: Hutchinson).

Brown, W. (1986) 'The Changing Role of Trade Unions in the Management of Labour', *British Journal of Industrial Relations*, Vol. XXIV, No. 2, July.

Brown, W. (1989) *The Evolution of Regionally Differentiated Pay* (London Public Finance Foundation, Discussion Paper No. 24).

Brown, W. and Rowthorn, B. (1990) *A Public Service Pay Policy*, Fabian Tract 542 (London: Fabian Society).

Brown, W. and Wadhwani, S. (1990) 'The Economic Effects of Industrial Relations Legislation Since 1979', *National Institute of Economic and Social Research Economic Review*, February.

Brown, W. and Walsh, J. (1991) 'Pay Determination in Britain in the 1980s: The Anatomy of Decentralisation', *Oxford Review of Economic Policy*, Vol. 7, No. 1, February.

Bullock Report (1977) *See* Report of Committee of Inquiry.

CAC (1976, 1977 and 1988) *Annual Reports 1976, 1977 and 1978* (London: CAC).

CBI (1989) *Pay and Performance 1989–1990* (London: CBI).

CIR (1969a) Report No. 1, *Associated Octel Co Ltd*, Cmd 4246 (London: HMSO).

CIR (1969b) Report No. 2, *General Accident Fire and Life Assurance Company Ltd*, Cmd 4247 (London: HMSO).

CIR (1970a) Report No. 4, *Birmid Qualcast*, Cmd 4269 (London: HMSO).

CIR (1970b) Report No. 9, *First General Report*, Cmd 4417 (London: HMSO).

CIR (1971a) Report No. 17, *Facilities Afforded to Shop Stewards*, Cmd 4668 (London: HMSO).

CIR (1971b) Report No. 22, *Shipbuilding and Repairing*, Cmd 4756 (London: HMSO).

CIR (1971c) Report No. 23, *The Hotel and Catering Industry: Part I Hotels and Restaurants* Cmd 4789 (London: HMSO).

CIR (1972a) Report No. 30, *Approved Closed Shop Agreement British Shipping Federation/ National Union of Seamen* (London: HMSO).

CIR (1972b) Report No. 31, *Disclosure of Information* (London: HMSO).

CIR (1973a) Report No. 37, *Annual Report for 1972* (London: HMSO).

CIR (1973b) Report No. 40, *Approved Closed Shop in Theatre, Independent Television and Film* (London: HMSO).

CIR (1973c) Report No. 53, *Con Mech (Engineers)* (London: HMSO).

Certification Officer (1977) *First Annual Report 1976*, (London: HMSO).

Clarke, K. (1987) Lecture at City University Business School (unpublished).

Claydon, T. (1989) 'Union Derecognition in Britain in the 1980s', *British Journal of Industrial Relations*, Vol. XXVII, No. 2, July.

Clegg, H. A. (1979) *The Changing System of Industrial Relations in Great Britain* (Oxford: Blackwell).

Clegg, H. A. *See* Standing Commission.

Committee of Inquiry (1977) *Report on Industrial Democracy* (Bullock), Cmd 6706 (London: HMSO).

Court of Inquiry (1972) *Report into a Dispute between the National Coal Board and the National Union of Mineworkers*, Cmd 4903 (London: HMSO).

Cross, M. (1988) 'Changes in Working Practices in UK Manufacturing 1981–1988', *Industrial Relations Review and Report*, 415, May.

Crossley, J.R. (1968) 'The Donovan Report: A Case Study in the Poverty of Historicism', *British Journal of Industrial Relations*, Vol. VI, No. 3, November.

Department of Employment (1991) *Code of Practice – Trade Union Ballots on Industrial Action* (London: Department of Employment).

Disney, R. (1990) 'Explanations of the Decline in Trade Union Density in Britain: An Appraisal', *British Journal of Industrial Relations*, Vol. 28, No. 2, July.

Donovan Report (1968) *See* Royal Commission.

The Economic Implications of Full Employment (1956) Cmd 9725 (London: HMSO).

Edmonds, J. and Tuffin, A. (1990) *A New Agenda: Bargaining for Prosperity in the 1990s* (London: GMB/UCW).

Edmund Davies, Lord (1978) *Committee of Inquiry on the Police: Report on Negotiating Machinery and Pay*, Cmd 2837 (London: HMSO).

Edwards, P. (1987) *Managing the Factory* (Oxford: Blackwell).

Efficiency Unit (1988) 'Improving Management in Government: The Next Steps' (London: HMSO).

Evans, S. (1987) 'The Use of Injunctions in Industrial Disputes May 1984–April 1987', *British Journal of Industrial Relations*, Vol. XXV, No. 3, November.

Fells, A. (1972) *The British Prices and Incomes Board* (Cambridge: Cambridge University Press).

Ferner, A. (1989) *Ten Years of Thatcherism: Changed Industrial Relations in Public Enterprises*, Warwick Papers in Industrial Relations, No. 27 (University of Warwick).

Flanders, A. (1964) *The Fawley Productivity Agreements* (London: Faber).

Flanders, A. (1967) *Collective Bargaining: Prescription for Change* (London: Faber).

Fox, A. (1974) *Beyond Contract: Work, Power and Trust Relations* (London: Faber).

Freeman, R. and Pelletier, J. (1990) 'The Impact of Industrial Relations on British Union Density' *British Journal of Industrial Relations*, Vol. 28, No. 2, July.

Gregg, P. and Yates, A. (1991) 'Changes in Wage-setting Arrangements and Trade Union Presence in the 1980s', *British Journal of Industrial Relations*, Vol. 29, No. 3, September.

Griffiths, R. (1983) *NHS Management Inquiry* (London: NHS).

Guest, D. (1987) 'Human Resource Management and Industrial Relations', *Journal of Management Studies*, Vol. 24, No. 5 September.

Guest, D. (1989) 'Human Resource Management: Its Implications for Industrial Relations and Trade Unions' in Storey, J. (ed.), *New Perspectives on Human Resource Management* (London: Routledge).

Halsbury, J. (1974) *Report of the Committee of Inquiry on the Pay and Related Conditions of Service of Nurses and Midwives* (London: HMSO).

Himmelweit, H. T., Humphreys, P. and Jaeger, M. (1985) *How Voters Decide: A model of Vote Choice Based on a Special Longitudinal Study Extending Over Fifteen Years and the British Election Surveys of 1970–1983* (Milton Keynes: Open University Press).

Houghton, D. (1974) *Report of the Committee of Inquiry into the Pay of Non-University Teachers*, Cmd 5848 (London: HMSO).

In Place of Strife (1969) Cmd 3888 (London: HMSO).

Incomes Policy: The Next Step (1962) Cmd 1662 (London: HMSO).

Industrial Democracy (1978) Cmd 7231 (London: HMSO).

Ingram, P. (1991a) 'Ten Years of Manufacturing Wage Settlements 1979–89', *Oxford Review of Economic Policy*, Vol. 7, No. 1, February.

Ingram P (1991b) 'Changes in Working Practices in British Manufacturing Industry in the 1980s', *British Journal of Industrial Relations*, Vol. 29, No. 1, March.

Inns of Court Conservative and Unionist Society (1958) *A Giant's Strength* (London).

Jenkins, P. (1970) *The Battle of Downing Street* (London: Charles Knight).

Kelly, J. and Bailey, R. (1989) 'British Trade Union Membership Density and Decline in the 1980s', *Industrial Relations Journal*, Vol. 20, No. 1, Spring.

Kelly, J. and Heery, E. (1989) 'Full-time Officers and Trade Union Recruitment' *British Journal of Industrial Relations*, Vol. XXVII, No. 2, July.

Kemp, P. (1990) 'Can the Civil Service Adapt to Managing by Contract?', *Public Money and Management*, Autumn.

Kessler, I. (1989) 'Bargaining Strategies in Local Government', in Mailly, R., *et al.* (1989).

Kessler, I. (1990) 'Flexibility and Comparability in Pay Determination for Professional Civil Servants', *Industrial Relations Journal*, Vol. 21 (3), Autumn.

Kessler, S. and Weekes, B. (1971) *Conflict at Work* (London BBC Publications).

Kessler, S. (1983) 'Comparability', in Robinson, D. and Mayhew, K. (eds) *Pay Policies for the Future* (Oxford: Oxford University Press).

Kessler, S. (1987) 'Pendulum Arbitration', *Personnel Management*, December.

Kinnie, N. (1987) 'Bargaining within the Enterprise: Centralised or Decentralised?', *Journal of Management Studies*, Vol. 24 (5).

Labour Party (1976) *Report of the 70th Annual Conference* (London: Labour Party).

Labour Party (1990) *Creating a Dynamic Society* (London: Labour Party).

Leopold, J. W. (1988) 'Moving the Status Quo: The Growth of Trade Union Political Funds', *Industrial Relations Journal*, Vol. 19, No. 4, Winter.

Lewis, R. (1991) 'Reforming Industrial Relations: Law, Politics and Power', *Oxford Review of Economic Policy*, Vol. 7, No. 1, February.

Lodge, D. (1987) 'Working Equality into Manual Job Evaluation', *Personnel Management*, September.

Machinery of Prices and Incomes Policy (1965) Cmd 2577 (London: HMSO).

Mackay, L. and Torrington, D. (1986) *The Changing Nature of Personnel Management* (London: Institute of Personnel Management).

Mailly, R., Dimmock, S. J. and Sethi, A. S. (1989) 'Industrial Relations in the NHS Since 1979', in Mailly, R. *et al., op cit.*

Main, P. (1986) *Committee of Inquiry Report into the Pay and Conditions of Service of School Teachers in Scotland*, Cmd 9893 (London: HMSO).

Marchington, M. (1989) 'Joint Consultation in Practice' in Sisson, K. (ed.), *Personnel Management in Britain* (Oxford: Blackwell).

Marginson, P., Edwards, P. K., Martin, R., Purcell, J. and Sisson, K. (1988) *Beyond the Workplace* (Oxford: Blackwell).

Mayhew, K. (1991) 'The Assessment: The UK Labour Market in the 1980s', *Oxford Review of Economic Policy*, Vol. 17, No. 1, February.

McCarthy, W. E. J. (1966) *The Role of Shop Stewards in British Industrial Relations*, Royal Commission on Trade Unions and Employers' Associations, Research Paper No. 1 (London: HMSO).

McCarthy, W. E. J (1971) 'Changing Bargaining Structures', in Kessler, S. and Weekes, B. (eds), *Conflict at Work* (London: BBC Publications).

McCarthy, W. E. J. and Ellis, N. D. (1973) *Management by Agreement* (London: Hutchinson).

McInnes, J. (1987) *Thatcherism at Work* (Milton Keynes: Open University Press).

Megaw Report (1982) *See* Report of an Inquiry.

Metcalf, D. (1989) 'Water Notes Dry Up: The Impact of the Donovan Reform Proposals and Thatcherism at Work on Labour Productivity in British Manufacturing Industry', *British Journal of Industrial Relations*, Vol. 27, No. 1, March.

Metcalf, D. (1990) 'Industrial Relations and the "Productivity Miracle" in British Manufacturing Industry in the 1980s', *Australian Bulletin of Labour*, Vol. 16 (2), June.

Metcalf, D. (1991a) 'Smithfield Market: The Ultimate Pre-entry Closed Shop', *Work, Employment and Society*, Vol. 5, No. 2, June.

Metcalf, D. (1991b) 'British Unions: Dissolution or Resurgence?', *Oxford Review of Economic Policy*, Vol. 17, No. 1, February.

Millward, N. and Stevens, M. (1986) *British Workplace Industrial Relations 1980–1984* (Aldershot: Gower).

Mitchell, J. (1972) *The NBPI* (London: Secker & Warburg).

Mortimer, K. (1990) 'EDAP at Ford: A Research Note', *Industrial Relations Journal*, Vol. 21, No. 4, Winter.

NBPI (1966a) Report No. 16, *Pay and Conditions of Busmen*, Cmd 3012 (London: HMSO).

NBPI (1966b) Report No. 23, *Productivity and Pay During the Period of Severe Restraint*, Cmd 3167 (London: HMSO).

NBPI (1967a) Report No. 29, *The Pay and Conditions of Manual Workers in Local Authorities, the National Health Service, Gas and Water Supply*, Cmd 3230 (London: HMSO).

NBPI (1967b) Report No. 36, *Productivity Agreements*, Cmd 3311 (London: HMSO).

NBPI (1968a) Report No. 65, *Payment by Results*, Cmd 3627 (London: HMSO).

NBPI (1968b) Report No. 83, *Job Evaluation*, Cmd 3772 (London: HMSO).

NBPI (1969) Report No. 161, *Hours of Work, Overtime and Shiftworking*, Cmd 4554 (London: HMSO).

Nolan, P. and Marginson, P. (1990) 'Skating on Thin Ice? David Metcalf on Trade Unions and Productivity', *British Journal of Industrial Relations*, Vol. 18, No. 2, July.

Period of Severe Restraint (1966) Cmd 3150 (London: HMSO).

Personal Incomes, Costs and Prices (1948) Cmd 7321 (London: HMSO).

Personnel Plus (1991) Vol. 2, No. 1, January (London: Personnel Publications).

Phelps Brown, H. (1990) 'The Counter-Revolution of Our Time' *Industrial Relations*, Vol. 29, No. 1, Winter.

Pollert, A. (1987) *The Flexible Firm*, Warwick Papers in Industrial Relations, No. 19 (University of Warwick).

Price, R. and Bain, G. S. (1983) 'Union Growth in Britain: Retrospect or Prospect', *British Journal of Industrial Relations*, Vol. XIX, March.

Prices and Incomes Policy (1965) Cmd 2639 (London: HMSO).

Prices and Incomes Policy After 30 June 1967 (1967) Cmd 3235 (London: HMSO).

Prices and Incomes Policy: An Early Warning System (1965) Cmd 2808 (London: HMSO).

Prices and Incomes Standstill (1966) Cmd 3073 (London: HMSO).

Priestley (1955) *See Royal Commission*.

Prior, J. (1986) *A Balance of Power* (London: Hamish Hamilton).

Productivity, Prices and Incomes in 1968 and 1969 (1968) Cmd 3590 (London: HMSO).

Productivity, Prices and Incomes Policy After 1969 (1969) Cmd 4237 (London: HMSO).

Purcell, J. and Sisson, K. (1983) 'Strategies and Practice in the Management of Industrial Relations', in Bain, G. (ed.), *Industrial Relations in Britain* (Oxford: Blackwell).

Purcell, J. (1987) 'Mapping Management Styles in Employee Relations' *Journal of Management Studies*, Vol. 24, No. 5, September.

Removing Barriers to Employment (1989) Cmd 655 (London: HMSO).

Report of an Inquiry into Civil Service Pay (Megaw) (1982) Cmd 8590 (London: HMSO).

Roberts, B. C. (1987) *Mr Hammond's Cherry Tree: The Morphology of Union Survival* (London: Institute of Economic Affairs).

Robinson, D. (1986) *Monetarism and the Labour Market* (Oxford: Clarendon).

Rose, R. and McAllister, I. (1986) *Voters Begin to Choose: from Closed-class to Open Elections in Britain* (London: Sage Publications).

Ross, A. M. and Hartman, P. T. (1960) *Changing Patterns of Industrial Conflict* (New York: Wiley).

Royal Commission on Trade Unions and Employers' Associations Report (Donovan) (1968) Cmd 3623 (London: HMSO).

Royal Commission on the Civil Service 1953–1955: Report (Priestley) (1955), Cmd 9613 (London: HMSO).

Scamp, A. J. (1968) *Report on the Activities of the Motor Industry Joint Labour Council* (London: HMSO).

Scott, B. (1981) *Committee into the Value of Pensions*, Cmd 8147 (London: HMSO).

Seifert, R. V. (1989) 'Industrial Relations in the School Sector', in Mailly, R. *et al.*, *op cit.*

Standing Commission on Pay Comparability (1980) Report No. 9, *General Report*, Cmd 7995 (London: HMSO).

Stevens, M. and Wareing, A. (1990) 'Union Density and Workforce Composition: Preliminary Results from the 1989 Labour Force Survey', *Employment Gazette*, August.

Tebbit, N. (1988) *Upwardly Mobile: An Autobiography* (London: Weidenfeld & Nicolson).

TUC (1980) *The Organisation, Structure and Services of the TUC* (London: TUC).

TUC (1984) *TUC Strategy: a TUC Consultative Document* (London: TUC).

TUC (1988a) *Europe 1992: Maximising the Benefits, Minimising the Costs* (London: TUC).

TUC (1988b, 1989, 1990) *Special Review Body Reports* (London: TUC).

TUC (1988c) Annual Report (London: TUC).

TUC (1991a) *Unions in Europe in the 1990s* (London: TUC).

TUC (1991b) *Collective Bargaining Strategy for the 1990s* (London: TUC).

TUC (1991c) *Towards 2000* (London: TUC).

Turner, H. A. (1968) 'The Royal Commission's Research Papers', *British Journal of Industrial Relations*, Vol. VI, No. 3, November.

Undy, R. and Martin, R. (1984) *Ballots and Trade Union Democracy* (Oxford: Blackwell).

Waddington, J. (1991) *Trade Union Membership in Britain 1980–1987: Unemployment and Restructuring*, British Journal of Industrial Relations, Vol. 29, No. 4, December.

Weekes, B., Mellish, M., Dickens, L. and Lloyd, J. (1975) *Industrial Relations and the Limits of the Law* (Oxford: Blackwell).

Wilberforce Report (1972) *See* Court of Inquiry.

Willman, P. (1984) 'The Reform of Collective Bargaining and Strike Activity in BL Cars 1976–82', *Industrial Relations Journal,* Vol. 15, No. 2.

Willman, P. and Morris, T. (1988) *The Finances of British Trade Unions 1975–85,* Department of Employment Research Paper, No. 62 (London: Department of Employment).

Willman, P. (1989) 'The Logic of Market-Share Unionism' *Industrial Relations Journal,* Vol. 20, No. 4.

Willman, P. (1990) 'The Financial Status and Performance of British Trade Unions 1950–88', *British Journal of Industrial Relations,* Vol. 28, No. 3, November.

Index